Collins

BTEC FIRST

Sport
Level 2

Kirk Bizley
Simon Chalk
Carl Halliday
Mark Walsh

Published by Collins Education
An imprint of HarperCollins Publishers
77–85 Fulham Palace Road
Hammersmith
London
W6 8JB

Browse the complete Collins Education catalogue at
www.collinseducation.com

© HarperCollins Publishers Limited 2010
10 9 8 7 6 5 4 3 2 1

ISBN 978 0 00 734264 8

British Library Cataloguing in Publication Data.
A Catalogue record for this publication is available from the British Library.

Commissioned by Emma Woolf
Project managed and edited by Jo Kemp
Design and typesetting by Thomson Digital
Text design by Nigel Jordan
Cover design by Angela English
Artwork by Jerry Fowler and Stella Macdonald
Index by Christine Boylan
Picture research by Geoff Holdsworth/Pictureresearch.co.uk
Printed and bound by L.E.G.O. S.p.A.

Every effort has been made to contact copyright holders, but if any have been
inadvertently overlooked, the publishers will be pleased to make the necessary
arrangements at the first opportunity.
All Crown Copyright Material is reproduced with permission of the Controller,
Office of Public Sector Information (OPSI).

Contents

Dedication

Dedicated to my darling Louise. Not only a wife but my inspiration, my constant, my best friend and continual source of encouragement and support. None of this would be possible without you!

Acknowledgements

Special thanks to Simon Chalk and Carl Halliday at Northumberland College and Paul Lazarus at Hackney Community College.

Photographic acknowledgements

iStockphoto (1/technotr); iStockphoto (3t/mikedabell); Alamy (3b/Juice Images); iStockphoto (4/barsik); iStockphoto (5/Galina Barskaya); iStockphoto (6/oleg filipchuk); iStockphoto (9/Christopher Pattberg); iStockphoto (11/Yvonne Chamberlain); iStockphoto (12/Juanmonino); iStockphoto (13/Don Bayley); Alamy (18/Design Pics Inc.); iStockphoto (21/Jonathan Downey); iStockphoto (22/Libby Chapman); Rex Features (25/Sipa Press); iStockphoto (27/Daniel Laflor); iStockphoto (29/Bill Grove); Alamy (31/Action Plus Sports Images); iStockphoto (33/Bill Grove); Rex Features (34/KPA/Zuma); iStockphoto (35/c-vino); iStockphoto (39t/eril nisbett); iStockphoto (39cl/Neil Merchant); iStockphoto (39b/redmal); iStockphoto (39cr/luxxtek); Alamy (41/ialbert); Rex Features (42/MC Films); Alamy (45/David Edsam); iStockphoto (47/martin garnham); Alamy (49/Jim Powell); iStockphoto (50/rudi wambach); iStockphoto (52/Judy Allan); Alamy (54/Greenshoots Communications); Alamy (57/Marc Hill); Dan Wilson (58); Rex Features (59/Andy Hooper/Daily Mail); Ken Hughes (60); Plas Menai (62); Andy Spinks (63); Emma Garbett (64t); Carl Halliday (64b); Ben Graham (69); iStockphoto (72/craftvision); iStockphoto (74l/pamspix); iStockphoto (74r/David Safanda); Alex Patrick (76); Carl Halliday (77); Emma Garbett (78); iStockphoto (81/graham heywood); iStockphoto (85/Max Delson Martins Santos); iStockphoto (97/james steidl); iStockphoto (105/technotr); iStockphoto (106/David H. Lewis); iStockphoto (109/vm); iStockphoto (110/Nicholas Rjabow); iStockphoto (111/Nicole S. Young); Rex Features (112/Peter Brooker); Rex Features (113/Andy Hooper/Associated Newspapers); iStockphoto (114/freddie vargas); Alamy (117/Jack Sullivan); iStockphoto (118/daniel sainthorant); iStockphoto (120/Marjan Laznik); iStockphoto (123t/amygdalaimagery); Alamy (123b/Alex Folkes); iStockphoto (124t/technotr); iStockphoto (124b/Kevin Russ); iStockphoto (125/Cindy Singleton); Carl Halliday (126); Alamy (129/ukscapes); iStockphoto (133/Majoros Laszlo); iStockphoto (135/Guillermo Lobo); Alamy (137/Ted Pink); Alamy (139/moodboard); iStockphoto (140/YouraPechkin); iStockphoto (143/Renee Lee); iStockphoto (144/arturbo); iStockphoto (147/Ana Abejon); iStockphoto (149/Chris Schmidt); Alamy (153/Sally and Richard Greenhill); Alamy (155/Jim Lane); Alamy (157/Image Source); iStockphoto (158/Rich Legg); iStockphoto (161/Michael Krinke); iStockphoto (162/technotr); iStockphoto (164/Chris Schmidt); Alamy (166/Aflo Foto Agency); iStockphoto (168/Nicholas Rjabow); Rex Features (170/Newspix); iStockphoto (172/james boulette); iStockphoto (174/Edward Bock); Alamy (175/image100); Rex Features (177/Back Page Images); Alamy (178/Image Source); Alamy (181/Fancy); Alamy (182/Photo Network); Alamy (183/Emilio Ereza); Food Standards Agency (185/Food Standards Agency: Crown copyright material is reproduced with the permission of the Controller of HMSO and Queen's Printer for Scotland); iStockphoto (186/Jiang Dao Hua); iStockphoto (187/Ljupco); iStockphoto (189/Alex Bramwell); iStockphoto (190/Sean Nel); iStockphoto (193/Arjan de Jager); Alamy (195/Science Photo Library); Alamy (196/MBI); iStockphoto (199/Xavi Arnau); Alamy (200/UpperCut Images); iStockphoto (203/Allie van Niekerk); iStockphoto (205/technotr); iStockphoto (206/David Lewis); iStockphoto (210/Steve Debenport); iStockphoto (211t/robert lerich); iStockphoto (211b/kzenon); Rex Features (212); Rex Features (215/Sipa); iStockphoto (216/Andresr); Alamy (218/Image Source); iStockphoto (223/Bob Ingelhart); iStockphoto (225/Catherine Yeulet); iStockphoto (227t/Dan Wilton); Alamy (227b/Associated Sports Photography); Alamy (231/Carl Skepper); iStockphoto (232/Winston Davidian); iStockphoto (235/Michael DeLeon); iStockphoto (239t/meadowmouse); Alamy (239b/Seren Digital); iStockphoto (241/Peter Garbet); iStockphoto (242/Silke Heyer); iStockphoto (244/Zsolt Nyulaszi); iStockphoto (247/kristian sekulic); iStockphoto (249/Hshen Lim); iStockphoto (250/Catherine Lane); iStockphoto (251t/Sebastian Kopp); Alamy (251b/Simon Rawles); iStockphoto (252t/Pete Saloutos); iStockphoto (252b/FreezeFrameStudio); iStockphoto (253/Alberto L. Pomares G.); iStockphoto (254/Damir Spanic); iStockphoto (255t/Reniw-Imagery); iStockphoto (255b/ gaspr13); iStockphoto (259t/Steve Mcsweeny); iStockphoto (259b/han3617); http://www.nsca-lift.org (261t/http://www.nsca-lift.org); Alamy (261b/allOver photography); iStockphoto (262/Peter Kirillov); iStockphoto (265/Joe Norman); Getty Ed (266/AFP); Alamy (268/PhotoAlto); iStockphoto (271/Hans F. Meier); iStockphoto (273/PeskyMonkey); iStockphoto (275/filipe varela); iStockphoto (276/Jim Kolaczko); Alamy (278/Jim Lane); Alamy (280/PhotoEdit); Alamy (283/Paul Doyle); Alamy (284/Anna Yu); iStockphoto (287/Chris Schmidt).

Introduction

This aim of this book is to help you to develop the knowledge and understanding you will need to complete your BTEC Firsts in Sport course. The BTEC First award you achieve at the end of your course will have one of the following titles, depending on how many credits you obtain overall:

▶ Edexcel BTEC Level 2 Certificate in Sport (15 credits)

▶ Edexcel BTEC Level 2 Extended Certificate in Sport (30 credits)

▶ Edexcel BTEC Level 2 Diploma in Sport (60 credits).

Your tutor will create a learning programme that gives you opportunities to explore a wide range of sport and sporting topics and obtain the credits you need for the qualification you wish to obtain. It is helpful to find out at the start of your course which BTEC Firsts qualification you are aiming to achieve and which units you will be studying.

Each chapter in this book covers one BTEC Firsts in Sport unit. The chapters provide you with opportunities to develop the knowledge and understanding that will be needed to successfully complete assignments and cover the assessment criteria that are part of your BTEC Sport award.

Features of the book

The book closely follows the specification (syllabus) of your BTEC Firsts in Sport award. This means that all of the topics and issues referred to in these units of the specification are fully covered. You will find the following features in the book:

▶ **Chapter introduction** – this is a short, introductory section at the start of each chapter that tells you what the chapter is going to focus on.

▶ **Key terms** – the main ideas (concepts) and the language of sport and physical education are briefly explained in this feature.

▶ **Over to you!** – these are activities that aim to get you thinking about an issue or topic. These short activities can usually be completed on the spot without doing any more research.

▶ **Activities** – these are designed to extend your knowledge and understanding by encouraging you to find out a bit more about a topic or issue you have been learning about. Some of these will be 'active' topics for you to actually take part in, either individually or in a group.

▶ **Case studies** – these are scenarios that encourage you to apply your knowledge and understanding to realistic situations in a sporting environment.

▶ **Topic check** – this is a list of questions about the topic you have been studying. You should try to answer as many of these as you can.

▶ **Chapter checklist** – you will find this feature at the end of each chapter in the assessment summary. It provides you with an opportunity to think about what you have been studying and to check that you have covered everything you need to. The chapter checklist also provides you with brief information on how the topics you have been studying are assessed.

Assessment

BTEC First Level 2 awards are assessed through coursework assignments. You are required to demonstrate that you have met assessment and grading criteria for each unit. The Pass, Merit and Distinction grade criteria for each unit are outlined at the end of each chapter in the book. They are then listed again at the end in Appendix 1, so that you can check that you have covered all of the criteria you need to.

I've tried to write a book that helps you to gain a good, clear understanding of a range of topics related to sport in a way which makes it as practically based as possible, with plenty of guidance to help you plan your own route through the various tasks which are set. Taking a BTEC Firsts in Sport course enables you to think about both the theory and practice of sport and link the two components together to enable maximum levels of attainment and success. It is hoped that you'll think about taking your interest in sport further when you've worked through the book and completed your BTEC First award.

Good luck with your course!

Kirk Bizley

1 Fitness testing and training (Unit 1)

Unit outline

Sports training involves a cycle of testing levels of fitness and then training to increase these. This is a vital stage of preparation for any sports performer. In this unit you will participate in a series of fitness tests and investigate your own personal fitness levels. It is important to be aware of the factors affecting fitness, so that you understand what can be tested and improved and consider some of the training methods available. In addition to physical factors, it is also important to take psychological factors into account.

Learning outcomes

1 **Know the fitness and training requirements necessary to achieve excellence in a selected sport.**
2 **Know the lifestyle factors that affect sports training and performance.**
3 **Be able to assess your own level of fitness.**
4 **Know the effects of psychological factors on sports training and performance.**

Fitness and training requirements necessary to achieve excellence in sport

▶ Getting started

This topic looks at different types of fitness and fitness training methods. When you have completed this topic, you should know:

- what the components of physical and skill-related fitness are
- about different fitness training methods
- how different training methods can improve each component of fitness.

🔑 Key terms

Aerobic endurance: is also known as cardiorespiratory or aerobic fitness. It indicates how much oxygen can be transported around the body for the muscles to use

Agility: a combination of flexibility and speed, and the ability to change the position of the body quickly without losing balance

Balance: the ability to retain the body's centre of gravity (mass) over a base of support in order not to fall over

Body composition: the ratio of body fat to lean body weight

Coordination: the ability to use two or more body parts together; the most common is hand–eye coordination

Flexibility: the range of movement around a joint

Muscular endurance: the ability of muscles, or groups of muscles, to lift a weight repeatedly

Power: the combination of the maximum amount of speed with the maximum amount of strength

Reaction time: how quickly a performer can respond to something

Speed: the ability to move all or parts of the body as quickly as possible

Strength: the ability to withstand or exert great force or pressure

The components of fitness

The components of fitness can be divided into physical fitness and skill-related fitness.

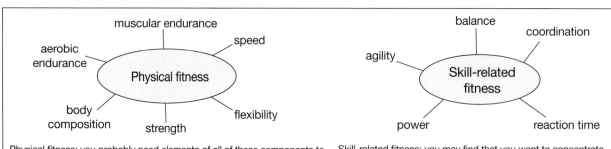

Physical fitness: you probably need elements of all of these components to be sucessful in sport, although some may be more important than others.

Skill-related fitness: you may find that you want to concentrate on particular components for particular sports or activities.

Figure 1.1 The components of fitness

Physical fitness

Physical fitness consists of the following components:

- aerobic endurance
- speed
- muscular endurance
- strength
- flexibility
- body composition.

A person's physical fitness is made up of a combination of these components, which affect different parts of the body and different body systems. For example, **strength** is most closely linked to your muscular system, whereas **aerobic endurance** is linked to your respiratory and cardiovascular systems. Aerobic endurance depends on the ability of the cardiorespiratory system to supply nutrients and oxygen to muscles during periods of physical activity.

Sport-specific physical fitness

Different sports require different levels and types of physical fitness. Knowing about the different components of physical fitness can help a performer improve both their training and their sports performance. For example:

- Rugby players usually possess strength (e.g. pushing in the scrum) and need to have good aerobic endurance (to last the whole of an 80-minute game).

- Gymnasts usually possess **flexibility** (to perform some of the complex moves, such as a cartwheel) and have good **muscular endurance** (to carry out a difficult routine, such as one on the pommel horse).

- A sprinter clearly requires **speed**, but there are also activities such as hockey where being fast could enable you to beat an opponent more easily, or get into position more quickly.

- A performer's **body composition** can also benefit them, e.g. being small and light is a real advantage for a long-distance or marathon runner.

Rugby players need strength.

Gymnasts need muscular endurance.

There are different types of strength:

- *Dynamic strength* is the strength needed to support your own body weight over a prolonged period of time, or to be able to apply force against some type of object, e.g. in a marathon race.

- *Explosive strength* is used in one short sharp burst or movement, e.g. a sprinter leaving the blocks.

- *Static strength* is the greatest amount of strength that can be applied to an immovable object, e.g. pushing in a rugby scrum.

Activity

Can you think of any examples where a particular factor could be an advantage to a player in one playing position in a sport but a disadvantage in another playing position?

Do you think all of the components contribute equally, or are some more important than others?

Are there any sports where a high ratio of body fat might be an advantage to a performer?

It is important that you are aware of the different components of physical fitness and that you know how each one can be tested and improved through training. It is also important to remember that an individual's physical fitness levels can decrease if they are not maintained – this is known as the process of reversibility.

Activity

Levels of muscular endurance are required in most sports. In a small group, make a list of sports that you each regularly take part in. Discuss when muscular endurance is important in each of the sports listed. When you have discussed each sport, put them in order, with the one demanding most muscular endurance first and the one demanding least muscular endurance last.

Over to you!

Consider one of the main sports which you regularly participate in. Which of the components of physical fitness do you think are the most important in that sport? Which would be the main two, in order of importance, to allow you to achieve excellence?

Skill-related fitness

Skill-related fitness consists of the following components:

▶ agility

▶ balance

▶ coordination

▶ power

▶ reaction time.

There are different types of **balance**:

• *Dynamic balance* is maintaining balance when you are moving your body or changing position, e.g. on the pommel horse.

• *Static balance* is where your centre of gravity remains the same, so you are staying still rather than moving, e.g. in a handstand.

Everybody requires a certain level of skill-related fitness in order to carry out everyday activities such as getting dressed and undressed, eating and drinking and catching the bus. People who participate in sport need higher levels of skill-related fitness to cope with the demands of their chosen sport and compete against others. Also, the level of each component varies between individuals. For example, a skilled footballer, skier or tennis player is likely to have greater **agility** than a skilled weightlifter or sprinter, who will require greater levels of **power**. Similarly, an international-standard 100-metre sprinter is likely to have a faster **reaction time** to the starting pistol than a local club runner.

Over to you!

How would you describe your own agility levels? How do you think you could improve your agility?

Handstands require static strength and balance.

For rackets players (e.g. playing badminton and tennis), both balance and **coordination** are important. Because of the speed of the ball or shuttle heading towards you, it is important to be well balanced in order to be able to move quickly in any direction. You have to have good levels of coordination in order to get into position and make an effective shot or return. All sportspeople need to keep up their basic skill-related fitness levels. Knowing about the different components of skill-related fitness can help an individual to prioritise aspects of their training and work out ways to improve their sports performance.

It is quite simple to test an individual's levels of each skill-related component of fitness. It is useful to do this as it can help an individual to set targets for improvement and development. Methods of testing fitness levels are covered in more detail in Topic 1.3.

Over to you!

Think about two of the sports you regularly take part in. Which components of skill-related fitness are most important in these sports? List the components in order of most to least important.

Case study

Susie is now in Year 10 at school. She has been a keen and active gymnast from a very young age. Susie is a member of the school gymnastics club and also attends a gym club out of school two evenings a week. Over the last 6 months, Susie has become involved in helping to train some of the younger members of the club. She understands that the young gymnasts need to work on their agility, balance, coordination and power during training sessions.

Susie still competes quite regularly in competitions herself, and considers her best apparatus to be the balance beam. She has very good balance but has had to work at improving other aspects of her skill-related fitness to raise her performance levels on this apparatus. She has found it harder to maintain her levels of flexibility as she has become older.

1. Which of the physical fitness and skill-related components of fitness are likely to be most important to Susie?

2. Are there any skill-related components of fitness that Susie is less likely to have to concentrate upon?

3. Why do you think that levels of flexibility are causing Susie the most concern?

Fitness training methods

People taking part in sport can use a variety of fitness training methods to prepare themselves for, and improve their performance in, a chosen game or sports activity. The fitness training methods a person chooses need to match their training goals, which should be relevant to the demands of their chosen sport, as shown in Figure 1.2. Training methods are covered in more detail in Chapter 9.

Figure 1.2 Sport-specific fitness requirements and training methods

Sports training	Fitness requirements	Suggested training methods
Marathon running	Endurance and dynamic strength	Endurance training and continuous training
Basketball	Endurance, flexibility, speed, coordination, reaction time	Continuous/endurance, circuit training (sport specific) and speed (acceleration sprints)
Rugby	Endurance, flexibility, speed, coordination, power	Continuous/endurance, circuit training (sport specific), weight training
Long jump	Speed, flexibility, power	Weight training (resistance machines), speed (acceleration sprints), plyometrics
Football	Endurance, flexibility, speed, coordination, power	Continuous/endurance, circuit training (sport specific), weight training
Golf	Flexibility, strength, power, balance, coordination	Endurance, weight training (resistance machines), flexibility

However, no one sport has one particular training method – performers are likely to use a variety of different methods to work on aspects of fitness that will help to improve their performance. Even within a sport there may be positional differences that the individual has to take into account. For example:

▶ A football goalkeeper is likely to have different priorities from an outfield player. The goalkeeper is likely to concentrate on flexibility, agility, reaction time and coordination training in preparation for saving shots on goal. The outfield player will be moving constantly for 90 minutes, so endurance training would be a high priority.

▶ A sprinter would need to concentrate primarily on speed training. They might also want to increase their strength and power to help with their speed, and their reaction times to react to the starting gun.

▶ A gymnast primarily needs a high level of flexibility to be able to perform well, but they also need strength to perform moves and hold movements using balance and agility.

This gymnast is displaying very high levels of flexibility and strength.

Performers in all sports will carry out some degree of general fitness training and then add specific training to this. Together with their coaches they will prioritise these and work on the most important aspects required for their sport and the ones they most need to improve on as an individual.

Activity

Find out what the ten different events are in the decathlon. Then, choose three events and match the specific fitness training method that would be most suited to each.

Activity

Each of the following people wants to improve their sports performance. You have been asked to advise them on:

- the fitness requirements of their chosen sport
- a suggested training method for improving their performance.

1. Michael Isles is an 18-year-old long jumper. He has represented his school and has now joined the local athletics club where he is aiming to get into the senior squad team.

2. Michelle Joseph is 35 years of age. She has completed a 5 km fun run but is now keen to complete a half-marathon.

3. Jasvinder Kaur is a 14-year-old swimmer. She has competed in 400-metre races in school galas, but would now like to improve her times to get into the county team.

Assessment activity 1.1 (P1, M1, P2)

You have gained a sports coaching work experience placement at a local university. You have been asked by the Head of Sport to prepare a presentation to give to one of the university teams. Your presentation should focus on the fitness and training methods that the team members will need to use to achieve excellence in their sport. You will need to:

- Select a sport to focus on.
- Describe and explain the fitness requirements needed to achieve excellence in the chosen sport.
- Describe three different fitness training methods that members of the team could use to achieve excellence in their chosen sport.

You should produce appropriate written or ICT-based materials for your presentation that can be used as evidence to show you have completed grading criteria P1, M1 and P2.

Topic check

1. Identify the six components of physical fitness.
2. What is the difference between muscular endurance and aerobic endurance?
3. Describe the three different types of strength.
4. Identify the five different components of skill-related fitness.
5. What is the combination of speed and flexibility known as?
6. What are the two types of balance that are possible?
7. Explain the difference between power and explosive strength.
8. Describe three training methods and how they can be used in a selected sport.

Lifestyle factors affecting sports training and performance

▶ Getting started

Your lifestyle reflects your attitudes and values. There are a great number of factors that can affect this, and you do not necessarily have control over all of them. These factors will also affect your ability to train and perform, so you need to be aware of them.

The information in this topic should enable you to think and make informed choices about your lifestyle. When you have completed this topic, you should know:

- which lifestyle factors you have some control over
- the problems that can be caused by alcohol, smoking and drugs
- that different jobs have different demands
- some of the physical differences between males and females
- how the culture you live in can influence you.

⚷ Key terms

Anabolic steroids: compounds based on testosterone or produced synthetically that are used to stimulate muscle growth

Anorexia nervosa: an eating disorder characterised by extremely low body weight and distorted body image

Eustress: a healthy form of stress that helps a person to achieve their maximum performance

Obesity: a condition characterised by excess body fat and a body mass index of 30 or more

Sedentary: describes a job that requires a lot of sitting down and includes little or no exercise

Lifestyle factors

Some of these factors are likely to be more relevant to you than others. Some you have a degree of control over and can choose how much they will affect you.

Stress

Stress is something that most people would try to avoid, but which everyone feels at some time. It is a state of mental strain closely linked to anxiety and tension. High levels of stress can improve or decrease levels of performance, so sometimes it can be a positive and at other times a negative factor. **Eustress** is a positive form of stress that can occur when a sports performer is pushing themselves, in an enjoyable way, to reach their potential. For some activities stress is beneficial (e.g. sprinting); for others stress can decrease performance (e.g. archery and golf). There is an optimum level of stress for each sport. For some sports insufficient stress can lead to a decreased performance (insufficient motivation or arousal), but too much can also have a negative effect (a player losing control).

Stress in everyday life is a different matter. It can be dangerous and even lead to illness. One of the good things about taking part in sport is that it reduces everyday stress levels.

Alcohol

Drinking alcohol is a lifestyle choice people are able to control. You need to consider the effect of the levels of alcohol you might drink, and the overall quantities.

▶ Alcohol prevents muscle growth and can lead to muscles shrinking. Competing with alcohol could also be dangerous and lead to an increased risk of injury.

▶ Alcohol contains calories which can affect your long-term training plan if you drink a lot.

▶ In the long term it can damage vital body organs such as the liver, muscles and heart, and it can even cause mental illness.

▶ The immune system can also be affected.

Alcohol is actually a banned substance in some sports (e.g. shooting, archery and fencing) and it is against the law to drive a car with excess levels in the bloodstream. All of these potential problems should indicate to you that drinking too much alcohol is a poor lifestyle choice!

Smoking and drinking excessive amounts of alcohol are poor lifestyle choices.

Over to you!

Can you think of any sporting situations you have been in when you were suffering from stress? Do you think it helped or hindered your performance?

Smoking

This is again a matter of personal choice. The difference between smoking and consuming alcohol is that even small amounts of smoking are harmful to your health. Each packet of cigarettes carries a government health warning for a reason! There are a great number of dangers caused by smoking, such as greater risk of serious diseases (e.g. lung cancer and heart disease) and other health problems (e.g. 'smoker's cough', sore throats and shortness of breath, headaches, dizziness and nausea). It is fairly obvious that none of these are going to help you to train and perform well. Smoking also reduces your aerobic fitness levels and therefore your ability to train properly.

Activity

In small groups, discuss the factors of smoking and alcohol and consider which is likely to be most influential in affecting sports training and performance.

Over to you!

If you know any smokers, ask them if they would mind talking to you about it. Try to find out if they are aware of the effects smoking is having on them in both the short term and long term. Ask them if they think smoking is a good lifestyle choice and, if so, why.

Drugs

These fall into three main categories.

Prescription drugs

These are drugs you can obtain from chemists if you have a doctor's prescription (e.g. asthma inhalers). A prescription drug is controlled by regulations and should only be used with medical advice. Taking someone else's prescription drug can be very harmful.

Some drugs can affect the level at which you can train safely, particularly your aerobic fitness training. It is fairly common for performers who have minor injuries to be given pain relief treatment to help them carry on training and competing or when they are returning from injury. This often involves cortisone injection into the soft tissue or joints as this can reduce inflammation. However, there is then the danger that these mask the injury symptoms so well that the performer 'plays through it', resulting in even greater, or long-term, damage.

Illegal drugs

These include all 'recreational' drugs (e.g. marijuana and the more serious drugs like heroin and cocaine), which have many harmful effects, including decreasing your motivation to train. Being found to have taken illegal drugs can result in a permanent ban from certain sports. Taking any illegal drugs is a poor lifestyle choice.

Performance-enhancing drugs

These can be divided into many categories, with different drugs having different effects. Their use in sport is banned as it is considered to be cheating. Professional sportspeople are regularly tested to make sure they are not using them. The most common of these drugs are **anabolic steroids**, of which there over 100 different types that can be taken as tablets or injections. They can increase muscle mass, which increases strength so that performers can train harder. They are commonly known as 'training drugs' because of this. There are many dangerous side effects to these drugs, which can result in serious health issues. In extreme cases they can even cause death.

Activity

Unfortunately, drug taking in sport is very common. Using the internet or other sources, investigate a recent example of a sportsperson who has been caught 'cheating' by taking performance-enhancing drugs. Find out about the drugs they took, the effects they had and the consequences for the sportsperson.

Sleep

This is probably not something you would automatically think of as a lifestyle factor, but it is one. You need a certain amount of sleep to give your body time to recover from exercise and the everyday demands you make upon it. Being tired can cause problems, especially if you are training or performing. A lack of sleep will cause tiredness, and if you are tired you will not function as well. Different people need different amounts of sleep, and you are responsible for ensuring that you get enough sleep to be able to train and perform at your best.

Demands of work

This will vary depending on the type of work you do. If someone has a **sedentary** job, their activity levels are likely to be low. However, others, such as construction workers, have very active jobs and often end their work day feeling physically tired. While you are at school or college it is likely that the only really active parts of your day are when you are involved in some sort of PE lesson.

Construction workers often have very active working days.

Activity

In pairs or a small group, discuss the different ways a person's work life can have an impact on their sports training and performance. Start by identifying as many work-related factors as you can (e.g. physically demanding work, having to commute to work, having a sedentary job, having a high-pressure job). When you have done this, identify the impact that each factor could have on a person's sports training and performance (e.g. lack of energy, lack of time, increased stress). Produce a diagram to summarise the ideas you come up with.

Medical history

This includes any medical condition you currently have and anything you have already experienced. Any medical condition needs to be taken into account when you are training or performing. When taking this unit you are likely to be asked to increase your levels of training and performance, so it is very important to seek medical advice regarding any medical conditions you have. For example, a medical condition such as asthma (see Chapter 5) can affect the respiratory system and can often reduce your ability to train and compete. If you have recently had any form of muscle injury this will also take time to heal properly before you are able to train to your full capacity.

Level of activity

Most people who are interested in sport participate in sporting activities in their leisure time. Being very active during your leisure time is likely to help to increase your fitness levels. However, if your leisure activities are too demanding they may leave you with little energy for your educational or work commitments. A very low level of activity is bound to have the opposite effect and will inevitably lead to low levels of general fitness.

Diet

Your diet is extremely important for your health and fitness. You need to make sure that it is both balanced and suitable to supply you with enough energy for the physical demands you make on your body. Too many calories will lead to excess fat and limit your ability to train. Too few calories will also limit your ability to train, as you will run out of energy.

A balanced, healthy diet will include:

▶ Carbohydrates, which are essential for quick release of energy and to ensure that you have enough energy to train.

▶ Protein, which is needed for muscle growth.

▶ Vitamins and minerals, which are essential for growth and repair, to achieve good aerobic fitness levels and to develop strong bones.

Diet and physical activity are dealt with in more detail in Chapter 8 (Unit 10).

Weight

Your body weight is linked to other lifestyle factors, mainly your diet, levels of activity and the demands of work. In Chapter 8 (Unit 10) you will learn that the amount of energy you require for physical activity needs to be balanced against the amount you take in through your normal diet. Being extremely overweight (**obese**) can be medically dangerous. It is important to keep your weight at a normal level for your size. Being underweight can also be a health risk and, in extreme cases, can result in a medical condition known as **anorexia nervosa.**

Gender

Some physical differences exist between males and females. These include the facts that women's bodies have 30% higher fat content than men's and only two-thirds the strength. In general, women have a flatter, broader pelvis with a smaller heart and lungs, but they do tend to be far more flexible. Obviously, your gender is not something you have control over, but it is important to know about and understand the physical differences between men and women.

Activity

Find out if there are any organised sporting events where males and females compete against each other head to head as they are considered to be on equal terms with regard to gender. Equestrian events (e.g. show jumping) are one example, but see if you can find any others.

Culture

Different cultures have different values, beliefs and traditions, many of which are linked to lifestyle. For example, in many western countries the growth of fast-food outlets and the decreasing levels of physical activity have led to higher levels of obesity. Some of the blame is placed on the culture in these countries, where the pace of life is fast and people tend to lead more sedentary daily lives than they used to.

Over to you!

What illnesses and injuries have you had which have affected, or might now affect, your participation in sport? Summarise all of the conditions or injuries that may affect your future sports training or performance.

Over to you!

How do you think culture influences your participation in sport and the sports you participate in?

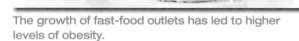

The growth of fast-food outlets has led to higher levels of obesity.

Sports participation

Levels of sports participation are very much a lifestyle choice. There is a great number sporting activities available to the public, but it is the choice of the individual whether or not to take part in these. It is possible to both train and compete almost as often as you like, but there is also the option of not doing either. However, participation can be affected by a range of factors including: cost, distance, availability, quality and access.

Activity

Some cultures have religion-based laws which prevent females from wearing 'revealing' clothing in public. This can reduce levels of sports participation. Investigate particular examples of this or any other cultural influences on the levels of sports participation. Using your findings, produce a short profile or case study outlining the link between culture and sports participation.

Case study

Darren is in Year 11 and is studying Unit 1 of his BTEC First Sport course. Darren says he has a fairly stressful home life, living with his mother, brother and two sisters. His father does not live with the family. Darren has asthma and uses a ventilator when he takes part in sports activities. Despite this, Darren has smoked cigarettes for the last 2 years. He also binge drinks alcohol at the weekends. Darren has started to stay out late at night because his younger brother and sisters are noisy and irritate him. He spends most of his leisure time with his friends, sometimes at a youth club, but he does not do any sport outside of school. Darren considers himself to be a bit overweight and blames this on the amount of fast food he eats.

1. Which aspects of Darren's lifestyle are likely to affect his ability to train and perform in sport?

2. Which of the lifestyle issues Darren has to deal with are within his control?

3. If you were advising Darren to improve his lifestyle, what are the three main points you would deal with first?

Assessment activity 1.2 (P3)

Choose four different lifestyle factors and describe how they could affect both sports training and performance. Use examples from your own experiences of sports training and performance or from research into the experiences of professional sportspeople to support your descriptions. Produce a short report or case study identifying and describing the four factors. Make sure that you support your work with appropriate examples.

Topic check

1 Identify five lifestyle factors that can have an impact on an individual's sports training and performance.

2 What can the term 'stress' refer to?

3 Describe two possible effects of stress on sports performance.

4 Explain why drinking too much alcohol can affect sports performance.

5 How can smoking cigarettes damage a person's ability to take part in sport?

6 Name three different categories of drugs.

7 What category of drugs is also known as 'training drugs'?

8 What basic problem does a lack of sleep cause for sports performers?

9 Explain how over-eating and under-eating are both related to health problems.

10 What impact can a person's culture have on their participation in sport?

Topic 1.3

Assessing your own level of fitness

Getting started

This topic focuses on ways of assessing your own fitness levels. When you have completed this topic, you should know:

- about a range of tests and the fitness components they measure
- the correct way to administer and take the various tests
- how to interpret and use fitness test results.

Key terms

Calibrated: checked for accuracy and set to measure in the correct units
Hamstrings: the group of muscles at the top rear (back) of the leg
Normative data: the average results of fitness tests that have been carried out

Carrying out fitness tests

It is very important that any physical fitness tests you carry out are completed correctly and accurately.

Pre-test procedures

A person's informed consent must be obtained before they take part in a fitness test. Some fitness tests involve some quite personal measurements being taken, while others may require strenuous exercise. The informed consent form should provide full details of the test methods, and should ask participants to confirm:

- their ability to follow the test method
- that they understand what the test involves
- their full, informed consent to participate in the fitness test
- that they understand that they can withdraw their consent and stop the test at any time.

A participant should be asked to sign and date the consent form. If the participant is under 18 years of age, the form must be signed by a parent or guardian before the test can be carried out.

It is also important to make sure that all of the equipment to be used in the fitness test is properly set up, **calibrated** and adjusted if necessary before the test begins. For example, if an exercise bike is being used, its resistance will need to be set. Similarly, if weighing scales are to be used, they must be checked and re-set before use.

22

INFORMED CONSENT FORM
Please read the questions carefully and answer each one honestly, ticking the appropriate box or adding information if necessary. Your responses will, of course, be kept in the strictest confidence.

Name: _____ Postcode: _____

Telephone number: _____ email: _____

Has your doctor ever said that you have had a heart problem?
No ☐ Yes ☐

In the past month have you had any chest pain when…
You were doing any activity No ☐ Yes ☐   You were resting No ☐ Yes ☐

Are you currently taking medication for…
A heart condition No ☐ Yes ☐   Any other problems No ☐ Yes ☐

Do you suffer from any bone or joint problems?
No ☐ Yes ☐

In the past year have you had any major illness or major surgery?
No ☐ Yes ☐

Have you ever been diagnosed with…

Diabetes No ☐ Yes ☐	Asthma No ☐ Yes ☐
Epilepsy No ☐ Yes ☐	Other problems No ☐ Yes ☐
Are you pregnant? No ☐ Yes ☐	Have you recently had a baby? No ☐ Yes ☐ How long ago?

Do you ever…
lose your balance because of dizziness or lose consciousness?   No ☐ Yes ☐

Are you feeling unwell at present due to a cold, etc?
No ☐ Yes ☐

If you have answered YES to one or more questions we may need you to contact your doctor before participating in this test. If your health changes so that you may then answer YES to any of these questions, tell a member of staff as soon as possible.

I understand what the test involves and that I can withdraw at any time.
I have read, understood and completed this questionnaire.
Any questions that I had were answered to my full satisfaction.

Signature: _____	Date: _____

Signature of Parent/Guardian (if aged under 18) _____

Figure 1.3 Example of an informed consent form

Test protocols

Test protocols are the ways in which tests are actually carried out. There are a number of issues to consider, including:

▶ *Reliability* – use a recognised test, which has set equipment, guidelines and procedures. Don't make up your own tests! Fitness tests should be repeated on the same day, or after a longer recovery period if necessary, to ensure the results are reliable.

▶ *Validity* – in order for a test to be valid it has to actually measure what it set out to measure. For example, if you reduced the distance run in the multi-stage fitness test from 20 metres to 15 metres it would lose its validity.

▶ *Practicality* – you have to be able to actually carry out these tests. For example, if you do not have calipers then you cannot use this method to measure body composition.

It is also advisable to:

▶ practise carrying out each fitness test before you begin collecting data

▶ record test results on an appropriate form as soon as you get them

▶ use the correct units of measurement for the test you are carrying out.

Recording test results

You must make sure that you record all of your test results accurately. You should do this straight away after taking them. You will have the opportunity to make graphs, charts and tables, and you can use computer programmes to compile these. Be sure to label all of your results data clearly so that you do not get them muddled up.

Over to you!

What computer programmes do you have in school, college or at home that will enable you to record your fitness test results and create graphs, charts and tables to summarise them?

Fitness tests

Flexibility

As mentioned in Topic 1.1, flexibility is the range of movement around a joint. There are various ways to measure this. The most common is by using the *sit and reach test* (as shown in the diagram) which measures the levels of flexibility in the **hamstrings** and lower back. This is a very easy test to take:

▶ Sit with both of your legs flat against the floor, facing the sit and reach box.

▶ Push forward against the marker as far as possible.

▶ Hold your stretch for 2 seconds.

▶ Measure how far you have been able to stretch.

▶ The best of three trials should be recorded.

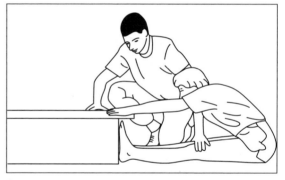
Sit and reach test

Compare your results with those shown in Appendix 2, Figure 1 to see how flexible you are. Another method you can use to measure flexibility is a *goniometer*. This is a device like a protractor with extending arms, which measures the joint angles formed by different movements. You will have to work with a partner and follow precise instructions if you use a goniometer, but it will give you some very accurate measurements.

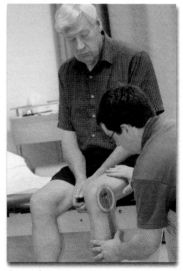
A goniometer

Strength

This can be very difficult to test as there are different types of strength (see Topic 1.1), so you might need to use both of the tests outlined here.

The first test is known as the *one-repetition maximum* (1RM). This involves you lifting the maximum weight possible for one repetition. You can use different techniques for this, such as a bench press or straight lift, to involve different muscle groups. You can use this with gym-based equipment as well as free weights.

The second test involves using a *grip dynamometer*, a handheld device that measures grip. You can compare your scores with those in Appendix 2, Figure 2.

Over to you!

Look at the table for the sit and reach test and the one for the dynamometer and compare the results for males and females for each. Then look at the text about gender in Topic 1.2. What do you learn from this?

Aerobic endurance

Remember that aerobic endurance refers to how well the lungs take in oxygen to be transported around the body for the muscles to use.

The multi-stage fitness test

The first test for this is the multi-stage fitness test. This is also commonly known as the 'progressive shuttle run' and the 'bleep test', and it is often carried out in schools and colleges. It involves playing a series of pre-recorded bleeps that are spaced apart at various time intervals.

▶ An area measuring 20 metres in length is marked out.
▶ Participants line up at the start point.
▶ On the starter's orders, they run to the 20-metre mark and then run back to the start point.
▶ They continue to run back and forth, but each run must be in time with the electronic bleeps of the recording, so they have to run at the pace the bleeps are dictating.

At the start this is quite easy (not much more than brisk walking), but every minute the time between the bleeps decreases and you have to speed up. You have to keep going for as long as you can (there are 25 levels in total), and the higher your score the higher your level of aerobic endurance. You can compare your score against those in Figure 3 in Appendix 2.

The Chester step test

The second test is the Chester step test. This is used by the fire service as part of its recruitment process. It involves stepping up onto and then down from a step. The step can be set at different heights. Like the multi-stage fitness test, this has an accompanying recording of timed bleeps that dictate the pace at which you must carry out the steps. The speed of the bleeps changes every 2 minutes.

When you exercise, your heart rate increases. The aim of this test is to see how quickly your heart is able to recover back to its normal, resting rate after exertion, as this is an indicator of your level of fitness (the more quickly it returns to normal, the fitter you are). So, you need to measure your resting heart rate and then work out your maximum heart rate (MHR).

To work out your MHR, take your age away from 220, then work out 80% of this. Your heart rate has to be monitored throughout the test so that the changes can be noted. You can use your results from the Chester step test to give you an indication of your fitness levels (see Figures 4 and 5 in Appendix 2). The lower your heart rate is the fitter you are.

> **Over to you!**
>
> Work out your maximum heart rate (MHR) by subtracting your age from 220 and then working out what 80% of this is.

Speed

The 40-metre sprint measures your ability to accelerate and run at maximum speed. To carry out the test, mark out a 40-metre running track and run down it at full speed. Record how long it takes you to do the run.

You should carry out this run six times, with a 30-second break between each sprint, timing each run. You then multiply your fastest time by six to get your 'optional sprint time'. The difference between your total times (all six of your times added together) and your optional sprint time indicates the level of fatigue (tiredness) you have experienced. If you re-take the test regularly it will give you an indication of your improvement (the lower your level of fatigue, the fitter you are becoming).

Power

There are two recommended tests for this. The first is the *vertical jump* (also known as the Sarjent jump – see page 261). You will need a measuring tape, or a marked wall, and chalk for marking.

▶ Stretch up to your full height and make a mark against the wall.

▶ Then leap up as high as you can and make another mark against the same wall.

▶ Record the distance between the two measurements and check this against the scores in Figure 6 in Appendix 2.

The second test for power is the *Wingate test*, which tests the power in the lower body. You need some specialist equipment for this – a modified, or Monark, cycle ergometer. You have to pedal as fast as you can for 30 seconds against a pre-determined resistance level which is related to your body weight.

Muscular endurance

The two tests for this are very similar and involve performing press-ups or sit-ups for one minute. For both of these tests you need to make sure that you perform the exercise correctly and complete the whole movement. You can then compare your results against Figures 7 and 8 in Appendix 2, and chart your own improvement.

Body composition

This is the percentage of your body weight that is fat, muscle and bone. It is divided into two categories:

▶ body fat – the percentage of your body that is fat

▶ lean body mass – the total mass of your bones, muscles, connective tissue and body organs.

There are three ways you can measure this.

1. You can use skinfold callipers as shown in the photograph. These are used to take seven measurements of skinfolds: at the biceps and triceps, just below your shoulder blade, just above your hip bone, your thigh, calf and lower back. These calipers must be used correctly, so make sure that someone who knows how to use them helps you with these measurements. Add all of the readings you have taken from the seven areas to give you a total. You can then compare these totals against those for a normal male and female and those for an elite performer, as shown in Appendix 2, Figure 9.

2. A second method is using bioelectrical impedance analysis, which passes a small safe electrical signal through the body. This has to be carried out by an expert with the correct equipment.

3. The final method is to work out your body mass index (BMI). This is quite easy to do – you just need to know your weight and height, and the same method applies to males and females.

Multiply your weight in pounds by 703, then divide it by your height in inches twice. The example that follows is for a typical teenager of 68 inches tall and 140 pounds in weight:

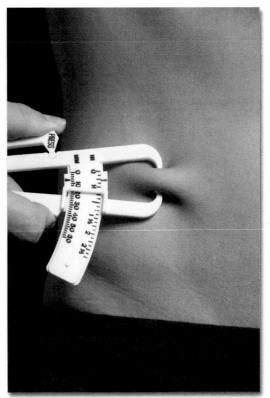

Taking a skinfold measurement using callipers.

140 × 703 = 98,420

98420 ÷ 68 = 1447.35

1447.35 ÷ 68 = 21.28

This result is rounded down to 21.

If you compare this with Figure 10 in Appendix 2 you will see that this teenager would be considered to have a normal weight.

Activity

Go to http://www.linear-software.com/malesites.html to see exactly how the other measurements are taken. What are the more scientific terms for the measurement under the shoulder blade, and the one above the hip?

Interpretation of results

Once you have all your results, it is important that you interpret them correctly. You should do this by considering the following two procedures in particular.

The first procedure is to compare your results against what is known as **normative data**. This involves comparing your data with tables of data that have already been produced, such as the sit and reach test scores for the flexibility test. This will then give you an indication of how you compare to a 'normal' (average) person of the same gender and age. Remember that gender is very important as there are distinct differences between males and females.

The second procedure is to compare your results with those required for levels of excellence. This involves comparing your results with those of someone such as an elite performer. For instance, how would your flexibility levels compare with those of an Olympic gymnast?

Activity

Investigate some of the results that an elite performer would be expected to record for some of the tests which you have taken.

Case study

Cassie has managed to complete at least one test for each of the categories apart from the body composition one, as she could not get hold of any specialist equipment. When she took the multi-stage fitness test she did it with one of her friends and had to estimate the distance run by measuring it out with strides. She was a bit disappointed with her 40-metre sprint results, so waited half an hour and then had another attempt. She is a bit disorganised about collecting her results and recording the data. She keeps it all in a folder which she updates when she remembers.

1. Do you think it matters if Cassie misses out one of the tests completely?

2. Do you think all of Cassie's results are totally reliable?

3. What comments would you give Cassie regarding the correct protocol for carrying out tests?

4. Was her decision to re-take her sprint test a wise one?

5. What advice would you give Cassie regarding recording and interpreting her test results?

Assessment activity 1.3 (P4, P5, M2, D1)

You have recently joined a local sports club, and the coach wants to assess your fitness levels in order to design a training programme. You have been asked to:

- Identify four different tests for different components of fitness that you are willing to undertake by giving your informed consent.

- Participate in these four different tests, recording the results accurately.

- Explain your test results in terms of your personal level of fitness, identifying your strengths and areas for improvement.

- Evaluate your test results and personal levels of fitness, considering the level required to achieve excellence in your chosen sport.

Present your results, explanation and evaluation in the form of a Personal Fitness Profile.

Topic check

1 Identify two ways of testing a sportsperson's flexibility.
2 Explain what 1RM stands for in relation to strength testing.
3 What does a dynamometer measure?
4 Describe how the multi-stage fitness test works.
5 What does the vertical jump test measure?
6 How can muscular endurance be measured?
7 What does BMI (Body Mass Index) provide a measure of?
8 What is meant by 'validity' when carrying out fitness testing?

The effects of psychological factors on training and performance

Getting started

This topic focuses on the effects of psychological factors on sports performance or activity. Psychological factors can affect the mental preparation and state of mind of sports performers. When you have completed this topic, you should know:

- about psychological factors that can influence sports performance
- how different psychological factors can impact on sports performance
- about ways of dealing with the psychological aspects of sports performance.

Key terms

Extrinsic motivation: motivation based on external rewards such as winning medals or titles

Extrovert: a person who is outgoing, sociable and concerned with what is outside the self

Intrinsic motivation: motivation based on self-satisfaction and a personal sense of achievement

Introvert: a person who is inward-looking, shy and more concerned with their own thoughts and feelings

Psychological factors

The mental preparation and state of mind of a sports performer is widely recognised as an important element in their overall performance. Sports performers need to know about and understand the effects of a number of different psychological factors. Knowledge of psychological factors helps during training and in actual performance situations.

Motivation

This is the desire and determination a person has to do well. Highly motivated performers are more likely to cope with anxiety, stress, tension, boredom and pressure because they are positive about what they are doing and they want to succeed.

Some people can be motivated just by the desire to win. This is known as **intrinsic motivation**. For others, it is the rewards that go with winning, such as money and fame or even a trophy, which motivate them. This is known as **extrinsic motivation**.

If someone is used to winning, and being the best, it can become more difficult for them to motivate themselves. This is why top sports performers often employ a coach or trainer to help with their mental preparation as well as their physical condition.

You might find that there are times when you lack motivation. This is more likely to occur during your training, as there may not be a clear goal at the end of it. If you are performing competitively then you will have an opponent, or opponents, and beating them may be motivation in itself.

Spectators can motivate performers to be highly competitive.

Over to you!

Reflect on the reasons why you train and take part in sport. What are you motivated by? Divide your ideas into extrinsic and intrinsic reasons.

Arousal

In sports terms, arousal means that your physical state has been stimulated or made more responsive. This is obviously important because if you are not aroused you are likely to be lacking motivation and rather slow and sluggish in your movements. Your levels of arousal can be raised in different circumstances, especially when you are performing or competing. If you have a crowd of people watching you in a match, you are more likely to be aroused than if you are just playing on your own. For some sports though arousal can be positive (sprinting) or negative (archery).

Anxiety

Someone who is anxious is uneasy or troubled. All performers experience some level of anxiety before or during a performance, and this is normal. It can even help some people, who need to be slightly anxious in order to become aroused. However, if you become over-anxious, this can lead to you making mistakes and your performance can get worse. For example, a footballer who makes a bad pass and is then criticised by teammates may become very anxious and then make another mistake.

Over to you!

Try to gauge your own levels of arousal when you are taking part in a sporting activity. You might be able to do this by thinking back to some of your sporting performances and comparing those where you were on your own with others where you performed in front of a group of people.

Personality

Your own personality will have a bearing on how you perform and on your choice of sports activities. For example, **introverts** often prefer to take part in individual activities, whereas people with more **extrovert** personalities generally prefer team sports and more active situations. Also, your personality may determine whether you are likely to continue training or drop out when your training starts to become difficult and your motivation suffers.

Over to you!

Do you think you fit into the category of introvert or extrovert? Which type of activities do you prefer taking part in?

Concentration

When you are either training or performing it is important that you are able to concentrate on what you are doing. If you lack concentration you can make mistakes and this could be dangerous. If, for example, you do not concentrate on tackling properly in rugby, you could badly injure yourself; if you are not concentrating when a teammate passes the ball to you in hockey, you are unlikely to receive it. Coaches often talk about 'concentration levels' when they are referring to focusing on what you are doing. This can be very difficult when you are trying to carry out a number of skills, such as checking where other players are, listening to instructions from various people and deciding what to do next! Elite sports performers are usually very good at processing information and maintaining focus during their sports performances.

Effects

All of the psychological factors discussed so far will have an effect on your training and performance. It is important that you know what these effects are likely to be, so that you can plan for them and take them into account. Effects will generally fall into two categories, short term and long term.

Short term

In the short term, motivation can be increased by setting targets that are attainable and achievable. You can set specific targets and goals which can be challenging, but which you are capable of achieving. This could be as simple as improving your one-minute press-up and sit-up score by one in the first week of training. This is likely to be realistic and would motivate you to improve further during the next week's session. In the short term, your levels of motivation, arousal, anxiety and concentration, and the way they affect your performance, may vary from situation to situation. However, it is possible to set targets aimed at preventing them from adversely affecting your performances. In the short term, you can start to work on aspects of these factors that may help you deal with them more effectively in the longer term.

Long term

It can be harder to maintain motivation long term, so long-term targets tend to be more challenging. Many people performing at excellence levels will work with a sports psychologist to ensure that, in the long term, they find ways of keeping themselves motivated. They will also try to ensure that their levels of arousal, anxiety and concentration are optimal and have a positive effect on their performance.

Longer-term targets are more likely to be linked to your actual sports performance than your training. Top-level athletes plan to 'peak' at certain times, and all of their short-term goals are aimed towards their long-term target of performing well. A world-class athlete may, for example, set targets that are four years ahead – when the next Olympic games take place!

Case study

Sanjeev prefers to take part in individual activities and does not like participating in contact sports such as rugby. He is not really worried about whether or not he wins; he just enjoys taking part, particularly in golf, which is his favourite activity. Sanjeev does not like people watching him when he performs – he finds that this puts him off and makes him anxious. He has set himself some short-term targets and finds these quite easy to come up with, but has more trouble deciding on long-term targets.

1. What sort of personality do you think Sanjeev has?

2. Does Sanjeev have intrinsic or extrinsic motivation?

3. How does anxiety appear to be affecting Sanjeev in his performances?

4. Why do you think Sanjeev might be experiencing problems setting some long-term goals?

Assessment activity 1.4 (P6, M3, D2)

Imagine that you have been asked to take on the role of 'sports psychologist' to investigate the impact of psychological factors on the sports training and performance of a group of young people. To carry out this investigation you will need to conduct interviews or group discussions with young people (15–19 years old) to find out about their experiences.

The data and information you obtain should be used to produce a report that describes, explains and analyses the effects that motivation, personality, concentration, anxiety and arousal have on sports training and performance.

You should present your investigation, including the questions you ask and the findings, in the form of a written report.

Topic check

1 Identify four different psychological factors that affect sports performance.
2 Explain the difference between intrinsic and extrinsic motivation.
3 What is meant by 'arousal' in sporting terms?
4 Why is arousal important for a sports performer?
5 How can a person's personality affect their involvement in sport?
6 Why is it easier to set short-term rather than long-term training and performance targets?

Assessment summary

The overall grade you achieve for this unit depends on how well you meet the grading criteria set out in Appendix 1 (see page 291). You must complete:
- all of the P criteria to achieve a **pass** grade
- all of the P and the M criteria to achieve a **merit** grade
- all of the P, M and D criteria to achieve a **distinction** grade.

Your tutor will assess the assessment activities that you complete for this unit. The work you produce should provide evidence which demonstrates that you have achieved each of the assessment criteria. The table below identifies what you need to demonstrate to meet each of the pass, merit and distinction criteria for this unit. You should always check and self-assess your work before you submit your assignments for marking.

Remember that you MUST provide evidence for all of the P criteria to pass the unit.

Grading criteria	You need to demonstrate that you can:	Have you got the evidence?
P1	Describe the fitness requirements for achieving excellence in a selected sport	
M1	Explain the fitness requirements for achieving excellence in a selected sport	
P2	Describe three different fitness training methods used to achieve excellence in a selected sport	
P3	Describe four different lifestyle factors that can affect sports training and performance	
P4	Carry out four different fitness tests for different components of fitness, recording the results accurately	
P5	Interpret your test results and personal level of fitness	
P6	Describe the effects of psychological factors on sports training and performance	
M2	Explain your test results and personal level of fitness, identifying strengths and areas for improvement	
M3	Explain the effects of psychological factors on sports training and performance	
D1	Evaluate your test results and personal level, considering the level required to achieve excellence in a selected sport	
D2	Analyse the effects of psychological factors on sports training and performance	

Always ask your tutor to explain any assignment tasks or assessment criteria that you don't understand fully. Being clear about the task before you begin gives you the best chance of succeeding. Good luck with your Unit 1 assessment work!

2 Practical sport (Unit 2)

Unit outline

Taking part in sport is extremely popular and is one of the main ways in which people participate in physical activity. However, there are many factors that contribute to a person being able to participate fully, safely and successfully in sport.

This unit is primarily aimed at developing your knowledge of the rules, skills and techniques for one team and one individual sport through taking part in them. You are likely to experience a variety of team and individual sports during the course, but for this unit you should concentrate on the two on which you will be assessed.

Learning outcomes

1 **Be able to demonstrate a range of skills, techniques and tactics in selected sports.**
2 **Know the rules, regulations and scoring systems of selected sports.**
3 **Know the roles and responsibilities of officials in selected sports.**
4 **Be able to review sports performance.**

Demonstrate skills, techniques and tactics

This topic looks at the ways in which you can become a better player or participant by making full use of all of the skills, techniques and tactics available to you in two chosen sports. When you have completed this topic, you should know:

- the basic and more advanced skills needed in your chosen sports
- the connection between a skill and a technique, and how improving your technique can improve your performance
- about tactics in general and those specifically related to your chosen sports
- how to choose the sports you are going to be assessed on
- how to record evidence for your assessment.

🔑 Key terms

Offensively: when attacking

Skills: an athlete's ability to choose and perform the right techniques at the right time, successfully, regularly and with a minimum of effort

Tactics: pre-arranged and rehearsed strategies or methods of play

Techniques: the basic movements of any sport or event

Skills and techniques

These will be specific to the sport you are performing, and will be the main factors that enable you to perform the sport effectively. For many games activities, the basic **skills** and **techniques** required include passing, receiving, shooting, dribbling, tackling and creating space. For other sports, such as athletics, other skills and techniques will be required (e.g. a pole vaulter has to be able to sprint while holding the pole upright and then jump, take off, rotate over the bar and land successfully on the landing area – an extremely complex series of skills and techniques). It is the use you make of these skills and techniques, and the ways in which you are able to develop and improve them, that is important.

Skills

Figure 2.1 gives an idea of how skills can vary between different sports. It does not list of all of the basic and specific skills in badminton and basketball, but it is interesting to note that there are five basic skills that are common to both but no specific skills that are common to both. However, if you recreate the action of the overhead pass in basketball and the overhead clear in badminton, you will find that the technique you use and the movements you make are virtually the same.

Figure 2.1 The skills required in two sports

Sport	Basic skill	Specific skill
Basketball	Good footwork, dodging, creating space, speed, agility, endurance, passing/throwing, receiving, shooting	Dribbling, bounce pass, overhead pass, chest pass, lay-ups, set shots, free shots, 3-point shots
Badminton	Good footwork, creating space, speed, endurance, agility	Low and high serves, overhead clear, drop shot, smash, forehand and backhand drives, net shots

Techniques

Technique can also be broken down into basic and specific levels. Using basketball as an example, the basic technique for a free shot is much the same as for the 3-point shot, but the distance is far greater. So, you would have to practise and develop the specific technique required to get the ball to travel further with full power and accuracy for the free shot.

Even basic skills and techniques that are common to different activities will vary, as you can see from the following comparison of good footwork for basketball and badminton:

▶ In badminton singles you will be the only player on your side of the court. You will be covering a fairly small area, which will be decided by where your opponent sends the shuttle, which you have to reach to play shots.

▶ When playing basketball, you have a much larger playing area. There will be nine other players who you have to avoid. You will have to decide where to go when you are attacking and, when you are dribbling the ball, you will have to adapt your footwork to abide by the rules of the game.

A badminton singles player is on their own.

So, you can see that something that is common to two activities can be very different when you are actually taking part.

One key point to remember at all times is that your skill and technique levels will only develop if you practise! There is no short cut to achieving this – studying the theory of skills and techniques will not help you to improve if you do not allow enough time to practise.

Activity

Identify the skills and techniques for two sports that you are interested in. Rate your initial performance for each one on a scale from 1 to 10, with 1 being the lower level and 10 being the highest.

Tactics

The **tactics** you choose to use in any sports performance will almost certainly contribute to how successful that performance is. In most activities it is possible to use tactics defensively, **offensively**, in set plays and for marking. In team sports good communication is also very important to ensure that the chosen tactics are understood and used by everyone. Many sports have tactics specifically linked to their rules (e.g. the 'offside trap' in football), which are only possible because of the specific rules of the game.

As with skills and techniques, tactics vary greatly between different sports (see Figure 2.2 contrasting basketball and badminton).

Figure 2.2 The tactics required in two sports

Sport	Offensive/defensive tactic	Sport-specific tactic
Basketball	Zone defence when the opponents are in possession. Staying in a particular area around the defended basket to cut down any shooting opportunities.	The fast break, which is where one player stands close to the half-way line and is quickly passed the ball by a defender. This enables them to dribble up to the opponents' basket to shoot before the defence has a chance to get set up.
Badminton	Keeping the shuttlecock in play by playing defensive long shots to the rear of the court in order to overpower a player and force them into making mistakes; or lifting the shuttle as little as possible and playing flat with drives and net shots.	Playing alternative deep and short shots, to the back of the court and close to the net, until the opponent plays a weak or loose shot which enables the rally to be finished off with a simple smash into the vacant area of the court.

You will see in Figure 2.2 that some tactics are linked to very basic skills and others are linked to more advanced skills and techniques. In basketball, for example, just being able to move to a specific area to carry out your zone defence could be quite straightforward and simple. However, being able to play consecutive short and deep shots to the back of the court and close to the net at badminton is going to require quite a high skill level. This raises the question of which tactics are most suitable for you, as well as which are required in any particular sport. It also establishes the link between skills, techniques and tactics — you will have to be realistic in deciding whether you are sufficiently skilful to employ a certain tactic. It is best to have a variety of tactics 'up your sleeve'. You must be prepared to counter your opponents' tactics, but you must also have alternatives in case 'Plan A' is not working!

Over to you!

Can you think of examples of sport-specific tactics that are linked to the rules of a particular sport?

Tactics should be planned for any 're-start' situation.

Activity

Imagine that you are the team captain in one or more of the following scenarios. Suggest some tactics that could be used to achieve each aim:

- Your cricket team is bowling at the opposition team's last two batsmen. They need to score 12 runs off the final two overs. You need to use tactics that stop them doing this.

- Your football team has had one player sent off. The score is 0–0 but the opposing team is attacking strongly with five minutes left to play. You need to choose some tactics that will ensure that you don't concede a goal.

- Your tennis opponent has a very strong forehand and is excellent at playing from the baseline. However, they struggle to return backhand shots at times and are a little slow to react to play that varies in depth. What tactical changes can you make that may help you win the match?

Choosing your sports for assessment

Remember that you have to choose one team sport and one individual sport, and you have quite a wide variety of sports to choose from. However, your choice of team games in particular is likely to be restricted to those on offer at your centre. You will be asked to concentrate on specific skills, techniques and tactical drills in these sessions.

Team sports

There are factors common in team sports, which you might need to consider:

▶ Any team sport will involve you with both teammates and opponents, and you must work closely with your teammates to be fully effective. You will have to take into consideration their levels of skill, technique and tactical ability. You might find that you are one of the strongest players in a team, in which case you may be able to take on extra responsibility and a leading role (e.g. captain). However, if you are one of the weaker players in the team you may have less responsibility.

▶ Team sports tend to have specific positions for each player, and for each of these positions there may also be specific responsibilities. For example, goalkeepers in hockey and football have a specific role and are expected to stay within a fairly limited section of the playing area. They also have specific rules which apply only to them, such as football goalkeepers being the only ones allowed to handle the ball.

▶ Playing areas tend to be larger, and therefore more complex, in team sports due to the number of players taking part. For example, there will be 30 players on a rugby pitch and ten players on a basketball court, and in both of these sports there is a great number of playing zones/areas and line markings.

Basketball has a restricted court size and number of players.

Individual sports

The factors that relate to individual sports will be similar to each other in some ways, but significantly different in others.

▶ Most individual sports have a specific opponent, but in some (e.g. golf), there may be a number of individual opponents, depending on the format of play being used.

▶ An activity such as cross-country running will have a great number of opponents, up to as many as 100 in a large race.

▶ In any individual sport you have to rely on your own abilities, skills and judgement, rather than looking to others for support. You must be able to cope with every aspect of the sport, not just one specific aspect.

Activity

Make a list of the individual and team sports that you could choose to focus on for the purpose of your unit assessment. Discuss your options with your tutor, taking into account the issues raised in the text and what your centre can offer. Choose one individual sport and one team sport to focus on.

Over to you!

Think about your chosen team sport, and consider what position and responsibilities you are likely to take on. What skills and techniques will you need to be most effective in this position?

▶ If you have only one opponent (e.g. in singles tennis or judo) you have to deal with their strengths and weaknesses – you do not have the option of choosing a weaker player to focus on, which you might have in a team sport.

Martial arts are clearly individual sports.

Recording evidence

Recording evidence of your participation in your two chosen sports is an important part of this unit. The simplest and most effective way of doing this is to keep a diary or logbook. You can also put together a portfolio (a collection of documents and evidence) and include video and audio recordings. You could also use observation feedback sheets and witness testimony.

The way you record your evidence will depend on the sports you have selected, as one method may be more suitable than another for your sports. However, there are some general points you might like to consider:

▶ Using video in a large team sport can be difficult due to the large playing area. As it is not possible to keep the whole area in view, the camera cannot be set up and left running in one place, so you will need someone else to do the filming for you.

▶ For an individual sport it might be possible to set the camera up to cover your designated playing area (e.g. your side of a tennis court) and record the whole performance without any help.

▶ A diary or logbook gives you the option of writing something down straight after your performance, while it is fresh in your memory.

▶ There will be others involved in your performance as either teammates or opponents, and you can collect feedback from them at the end of a performance.

▶ You could produce some specific feedback sheets relating to particular aspects of your performance. For instance, you could identify some specific skills and record how often and successfully they were used (e.g. the number of successful passes made in hockey, football or netball).

Activity

Find out what evidence recording options are available to you and whether you will have the option of using video recording. If so, familiarise yourself with the equipment and learn how to use it, and find out if anyone will be able to help you with the recording.

Over to you!

For your chosen team sport, think about the skills you would be able to include in a specific observation record sheet. Also consider what you want to have observed, e.g. simply the number of passes you make, or also the distance passed and the accuracy of the shot?

Case study

Jerzy, a BTEC First Sport student, has chosen basketball as his team sport to be assessed on. He considers himself to be a relative beginner in basketball, although he has a basic knowledge of the game, having played in ordinary PE lessons since he was 11 years old. Jerzy has chosen basketball because this unit is designed to enable him to develop and improve his practical skills and techniques. He has decided not to base this unit on his major team game (rugby), at which he is already competent. Jerzy thinks he can take some of the general and specific skills he has developed playing rugby and use them in basketball.

1. Jerzy may have developed some basic skills (e.g. passing, receiving and creating space) through playing rugby. Can you think of any others he may already have?

2. Do you think Jerzy has made a wise decision in choosing a sport he does not play at a particularly high level?

3. Are there any differences Jerzy should consider between the skills and techniques required for rugby and basketball (e.g. differences in technique related to the shape of the ball)?

Assessment activity 2.1 (P1, P2, M1, D1)

You have been invited to participate in a performance development programme for young sportspeople. The aim of the programme is to give participants opportunities to improve their skills, techniques and tactics in practical sport. You will need to:

- Select one team and one individual sport to participate in.
- Produce evidence demonstrating, describing and justifying your use of practical skills, techniques and tactics appropriate to the *team* sport.

- Produce evidence demonstrating, describing and justifying your use of practical skills, techniques and tactics for one *individual* sport.

Your evidence should include a diary or logbook commenting on your own development and describing skills, techniques and tactics covered in each performance or session.

Topic check

1 What is a tactic?

2 Using a named sport as an example, explain what 'skills' are.

3 Describe the relationship between a skill and technique.

4 What is the difference between a basic skill and a specific skill?

5 How can a sports performer improve their skill levels?

6 Who could you ask to provide feedback on any of your sports performances?

Rules, regulations and scoring systems

▶ Getting started

All sporting activities have rules, or laws, which are applied by the **National Governing Body (NGB)** for that sport. These are sets of principles, policies, descriptions and conducts which have been agreed upon. The **rules** (laws in the case of cricket) govern the general 'playing' or 'performing' of the sport; the **regulations** go into greater detail about such things as age groups, competition rules and equipment guidelines. It is important that you concentrate specifically upon the team and individual sports you will be involved with.

When you have completed this topic, you should know:

- how many players/performers are allowed in the sports you are involved with, and how many substitutes can be used
- what equipment *must* be worn, what is recommended and what is acceptable
- the referee/umpire/judge and scorer signals you will see in a contest in your sports
- the points/scoring/goals/points systems in your chosen activities.

Key terms

National Governing Bodies (NGBs): these come in various forms, and have a variety of functions, but essentially they are the organisations which make sure that a particular activity is performed properly and safely (e.g. the English Basketball Association)

Regulations: often describe or relate to equipment, playing surfaces, referees or umpires

Rules: regulations or laws relating to the conduct of a game or sporting activity

Rules in sport

All sports have a variety of different rules and regulations. These have often been developed gradually as the sport has changed with time. An example of this is the 100m sprint, where sprinters were disqualified if they were individually responsible for two false starts. This rule allowed races to be restarted so many times that the sprinters often lost focus. It also often delayed the timing of other events. This was changed in 2003 to one false start. Anyone causing a second false start is immediately disqualified. The rules that govern a sport or activity can cover issues of safety, sportsmanship, equipment or facility design, and competition. Although the terms 'rules' and 'regulations' mean slightly different things, they are often used interchangeably in sport. In some sports they are also referred to as the 'laws'.

Regulations

All sporting activities have specific and detailed regulations relating to different aspects of the activity.

Players and participants

Regulations about this can include:

▶ the number of players allowed to play

▶ the number of replacements/substitutes

▶ other participants, such as managers and coaches (e.g. in professional football matches they have designated areas)

▶ physiotherapists (e.g. in rugby union matches these are allowed on the pitch during play to treat injured players, but in football they are not allowed on unless play is stopped)

▶ the crowd or spectators.

In an American football match, for instance, there are seven officials who all have specific areas and responsibilities on and around the pitch. There are also 11 players from each team on the pitch – a total of 29 people! In addition to this, the teams are subdivided into an offensive unit (on the pitch when their team has the ball), a defensive unit (on the pitch when the opposition has the ball) and a special unit for defending and taking kicks at goal.

> ### 💡 Over to you!
>
> For both of your chosen sports, find out about any specific regulations there are about players and participants. Produce a short information sheet summarising the key points.

Equipment

The regulations regarding equipment are wide and varied. There may be regulations regarding:

▶ different sizes of equipment (e.g. ball in football and rugby, rackets in tennis and bats in cricket)

▶ what must be worn with regard to safety (e.g. shin pads in football, helmets for batters in cricket)

▶ the materials used for the equipment (a professional cricketer once used a metal bat until it was outlawed!)

▶ any apparatus used in the activity (e.g. vaulting boxes in gymnastics or protective padding around rugby posts).

This is a very large area that requires a lot of background knowledge. It is vital that anyone taking part in sport is fully up to date with equipment regulations for that sport.

Cricket requires a variety of equipment.

Playing surface

Regulations about this can relate to the normal surface that is used (e.g. whether it needs to be grass or artificial), the effects of the weather on the surface (e.g. if it is frozen, waterlogged, too dry/hard) and the condition it is in (e.g. whether the grass is too long or if there are any sharp or dangerous objects on it). There may be specific regulations relating to indoor and outdoor surfaces, which could then affect the size of the playing surface (e.g. indoor hockey and cricket are played in a far smaller area than the outdoor games, as is five-a-side football).

Facilities

The regulations regarding facilities will also vary greatly between activities. For example, the regulations for gymnastic facilities would be far more detailed and complex than those for badminton. At higher levels of sport there are set regulations regarding first aid and emergency facilities, and changing/showering facilities – there are even regulations regarding the size of changing rooms.

Health and safety

This is linked to legal requirements. All sporting activities are governed by general and specific regulations which safeguard the people involved in the activity. These include general rules that apply to most activities (e.g. those regarding the removal of jewellery) and specific activity rules (e.g. netball players keeping their nails short – this is checked by the officials before players are allowed on court). Health and safety regulations may even state the number of people allowed to watch an event.

Time

This, again, varies with each activity. For example, a tennis match is played for as long as it takes for a winner to emerge – there is no time limit. However, in other sports the timings allowed for each activity can be crucial, e.g. in netball and basketball there are very specific time allocations for each period of the game. Even a cricket test match, played over 5 days, can come to a very dramatic conclusion during the final minutes. It is very important to know of all time, and timing, regulations for your sports.

Over to you!

For your two chosen sports, find out if there are any specific regulations about the equipment you must use or wear.

Over to you!

Investigate the regulations that relate to the playing surface in football. A useful starting point would be to examine the FA website at www.theFA.com and look at the FIFA laws of the game.

Activity

Investigate the regulations concerning timing for five different sports and clearly identify how each of the timings differ. For example, is the game played in quarters or halves? How long is each period? You can also include regulations for extra time.

Officials

The titles and types of sporting officials varies. They might be a referee, an umpire, a judge, a starter or a timekeeper. Some sports also have referee's assistants and linesmen who help the main official. In some sports it is possible to play games with just one official, but as competition levels increase the number of officials increases too. For example, in some tennis matches there is only an umpire, but in tournaments there will be a net cord judge, service line judges, sideline judges and baseline judges, so there could be an extra seven officials around the court.

The officials in this tennis match can clearly be seen.

Activity

Find out about the main signals the officials are likely to use in the two sports you have chosen to be assessed on. Produce a table summarising your findings, which explains the meaning of each signal.

Case study

John has recently qualified as a football referee. He is approaching his first competitive match and needs to remind himself of the basic rules and regulations he must follow. Although he can referee effectively, he often forgets some key rules and regulations and is worried that he will not follow the current FA guidelines.

1. John has recently qualified, but his role requires lots of practice. With practice his memory of rules and regulations will improve. Can you think of anything that he could do to assist him in remembering key points before he goes onto the pitch?

2. Would you expect a new referee to know all of the rules and regulations?

3. What advice could you give to a new referee? Think about their role in the game.

Scoring systems

Each activity has regulations relating to its particular scoring system, some of which are discussed below.

The method of scoring goals or points

This can vary greatly. For example:

▷ in hockey goals can only be scored from shots within a certain area

▷ the counting system in tennis is unlike any other sport

▷ in some sports goals can be disallowed if a player made the shot from an incorrect position (e.g. offside in football).

In a sport such as rugby union there are four different ways in which points can be scored, with different numbers of points awarded: five points for a try, two points for a successful conversion kick and three points for a successful penalty conversion or drop kick.

The method and requirements for victory

Again, these vary greatly. Golf is won by the player with the lowest score, while a netball match is won by the team with the highest score. It is acceptable for some games to finish in a draw, but in another format there may have to be an outright winner, so extra time may be added on, or a penalty shootout or a 'bowl off' (in cricket) may be played. The nature of the competition may determine the regulations, for example in a league format draws might be allowed, but in a knockout format there has to be a winner. There is no set format for competitions and most sports make use of a variety of formats. For example, in the football World Cup, the first stage of qualifying matches is played in leagues, as are the initial stages of the main competition. The tournament then moves to a knockout stage for the semi-finals and the final. The final may have to go to extra time and even penalties to make sure that there is an outright winner.

The football World Cup uses a league and then a knockout format.

Assessment activity 2.2 (P3, P4, M2)

Research the rules, regulations and scoring systems of both the team and individual sport you have chosen to be assessed on. Produce a written report that:

- describes and assesses the rules, regulations and scoring system of your chosen *team* sport
- describes and assesses the rules, regulations and scoring system of your chosen *individual* sport.

Topic check

1. Is there a difference between rules and regulations? If so, what is it?
2. Name one sport which has laws and another which has rules.
3. Name three different types of officials who are likely to be in charge of a sport.
4. Name at least three different categories of assistant officials who help the main official in charge.
5. What is the link between rules and safety?
6. What is meant by a 'legal requirement'?
7. When might you need a greater number of officials for a particular sport?
8. List at least four different reasons why a playing surface might be considered to be unsuitable for play.
9. Why is it a general rule that jewellery has to be removed when taking part in sport?
10. Name one sport where the lowest score wins and one where the highest score wins.

The roles and responsibilities of officials

Getting started

The roles and responsibilities of officials have to be based on the rules and regulations of the sport, so this topic is closely linked to Topic 2.2. You are not expected to become an 'expert' in all sporting activities, but you will be required to have sufficient knowledge to be able to officiate effectively in your chosen sports. You may find that you are able to take a Level 1 officiating course to help you with this. You need to be able to summarise the main rules and be aware of the basic rules needed to participate successfully.

When you have completed this topic, you should know:

- the particular role each of the officials in your sports has, and the responsibilities placed upon them to carry out these roles successfully
- any qualifications officials need, or whether they can take on the role successfully without qualifications
- the rules which exist to help you deal with controlling players
- how important other people, such as spectators and assistant officials, might be and the responsibilities the main official has to them.

Key terms

Etiquette: the unwritten rules or conventions of any activity

General fitness: a person's level of general good health and ability to carry out activities at a relatively low level

Specific fitness: a level beyond general fitness where a person is able to meet the higher, more specific, demands of an activity or sport

Roles

An official's role will depend entirely upon the type of official they are and the level they are at. A referee is likely to be in sole charge, whereas a referee's assistant will have an advisory role regarding particular areas of the pitch or specific infringements. In some activities there are officials (e.g. the 3rd umpire in cricket and the 4th official in rugby and football) who are placed away from the field of play. They are responsible for communicating decisions to the official in charge after reviewing video evidence or replays.

Officials who do not have sole charge of a sporting activity are referred to as 'minor officials' or 'assistants'. It is a good idea to take on one of these lesser roles first, before progressing to the role of main official. In rugby, for instance, taking on the role of a touch judge would involve you in the following:

▶ letting the referee know when the ball has gone out of play, and who put it out

▶ showing where line-outs should be taken from

▶ looking out for foul play on your side of the pitch

▶ going behind the posts for any conversion attempts to judge if the ball went over the bar and between the uprights.

In this role you would be mainly an adviser as it is always left up to the referee to make the final decision. The referee even has the authority to overrule the touch judge if they do not think you have made a correct decision.

Over to you!

For both of your chosen sports, find out how many minor officials' or assistants' roles there might be for a match. You could develop this by trying out one of these roles.

Responsibilities

Many of the responsibilities of officials are fairly general, but there are others that are specific to certain sports. For instance, a referee in football and rugby has to be very fit to keep up with play, but an umpire in tennis sits still and controls the match from the umpire's chair. Some other considerations are discussed below.

Appearance

Many officials have to wear a uniform which distinguishes them from the players/performers. They have to be appropriately dressed and need the correct footwear for the surface they are appearing on – rugby and football officials could fall over if they did not wear studded boots.

Over to you!

For both of your chosen sports, make a list of the specific uniform, footwear and equipment the officials require.

Equipment

Something as basic as a whistle is likely to be required, but most officials also need a notebook, or something similar, with which to record scores, names etc. For example, cricket umpires use 'counting stones' to keep check of the number of deliveries in an over, and red and yellow cards are now common in many sports for disciplinary offences. An accurate watch, or stopwatch, is likely to be another essential piece of equipment.

Tennis umpires have specific roles.

Fitness

This could include **general fitness** as well as **specific fitness**. Certain aspects of fitness might be more important in some activities, e.g. a football referee might need good speed to keep up with play, as well as high levels of endurance to last a whole match.

Qualifications

These will depend on the level at which you are officiating. To officiate a match in a normal PE lesson or an inter-school match, you will need to have experience and to have your ability checked by a qualified member of staff, or you will need to have a formal qualification at Level 2. As competitions/matches move up to higher levels, so does the level of qualification required. This is why attaining a Level 1 qualification is recommended. Level 1 allows you to assist and, with experience, possibly take charge in certain circumstances. Governing bodies usually require you to take Level 1 before you can progress to Level 2.

> ### Activity
>
> Find out if there any specific guidelines regarding the age of officials for the two sports you have chosen. You should consider both the minimum and maximum ages that are recommended.

The interpretation and application of rules

Just knowing the rules is not enough as, once any form of competition is underway, you have to be able to apply them and make quick decisions based on them. The way in which you interpret a rule or regulation needs to be consistent and correct in order for the performers to have respect for and belief in you.

Control of players

This can be a very challenging responsibility – it is likely that you will be in situations where you know the players involved, who may even be former teammates or older people. Controlling the players is one of the main responsibilities of an official, and each sport has some discipline methods you can use to maintain this control, such as red and yellow cards.

Accountability to spectators

The spectators will expect the official in charge to do a good job, but they will also support one particular player, performer or team, so it is unlikely that they are all going to be happy all of the time. In order to avoid any accusations by spectators of bias by the official, decisions must be correct and consistent at all times.

Health and safety

This applies specifically to any regulations referring to equipment, facilities and players. The officials are ultimately responsible for making sure that all health and safety regulations are in place and enforced. They have to check they are in place before any activity starts and they can even call events off if they are not satisfied with the situation. For example, many sports matches are called off after pitch inspections when the officials consider it unfit to play due to health and safety considerations.

If a player is not complying, such as not wearing the correct safety equipment, then the officials can stop them from taking part.

Fair play

This should be encouraged at all times. Officials should encourage players to use good **etiquette**, such as stopping a game by kicking the ball out of play if a player is injured in football. All sports have expectations of fair play and good etiquette, such as:

▶ shaking hands with opponents at the end of a game of football, hockey, rugby, basketball, tennis etc.

▶ 'clapping a batter in' at cricket as a batter makes their way out to the wicket at the start of their innings

▶ batters 'walking' when they know they are out in cricket

▶ shaking the officials' hands and thanking them at the end of a match

▶ calling 'not up' and 'double hit' during squash games (these are foul shots that are often only noticed by the player who is playing a shot – it is accepted fair play to admit to these)

▶ correctly calling if a ball is in or out in tennis.

None of the above are rules that you *have* to observe, but in the spirit of fair play you would be expected to abide by them.

> 💡 **Over to you!**
>
> Find at least one example of good etiquette for each of the two sports you will be participating in.

When players are injured in football, opponents should kick the ball out to stop play.

Use of technology

Technology is being used increasingly to aid officials. For example, many football and rugby officials use microphones and headsets to keep in touch with each other, and football referees have sensor pads attached to their arms, which are activated by controls in their assistants' flags.

If there is any specific technology used in an activity, it is the officials' responsibility to know and understand how it works and to make full use of it. A common piece of technology used in professional sport is Hawkeye, which is able to detect the path of a travelling ball. It is used in the following sports:

▶ tennis – to check if the ball is in or out of court on the service line, sidelines and baselines

▶ cricket – to clarify LBW decisions, to show if the ball was predicted to hit the wickets

▶ snooker – for commentary and playback assistance

▶ basketball – currently being developed to check when the ball may be out of play.

Due to the success of this system, there is quite a lot of pressure to allow it to be used in other sports, especially football where it could be used to show if the ball crossed the line for a goal to be scored.

Effective communication

This can include the use of your voice (a loud voice is necessary in an outdoor environment), as well as effective use of a whistle (if one is used), but the most important form of communication is the use of the correct signals for a particular sport. In basketball, for example, the officials use a great number of signals (e.g. for a double dribble, travelling etc.), and cricket umpires have to give signals from the batting area to the scorers who are a long distance away. Officials in many sports now use electronic communication systems to communicate with each other, and it is quite common to see officials wearing an earpiece and microphone.

Assessment activity 2.3 (P5, P6)

Research the roles and responsibilities of the officials who participate in both the team and individual sport you have chosen to be assessed on. Produce a written report that:

• describes the main roles and responsibilities of officials in your chosen *team* sport

• describes the main roles and responsibilities of officials in your chosen *individual* sport.

Case study

Aisha has chosen tennis as her individual activity, mainly because she considers it to be one of her strongest sports and one she plays quite regularly. Aisha does not play at a particularly high level, but she has played in a club since she was a junior and would consider herself to have a good knowledge of the rules, regulations and scoring systems. In order to prepare herself for this unit, Aisha volunteered to be a line judge at her tennis club annual tournament, and she has also decided to take a Level 1 tennis umpire's course in her own time.

1. Do you think it is a good idea for Aisha to choose a sport she is already competent at and familiar with?

2. Is the knowledge Aisha has as a player likely to be enough to enable her to be a successful line judge?

3. How much more difficult is it likely to be for Aisha to move up from being an advisory official, such as the line judge, to being the official in overall charge when she is an umpire?

4. What particular roles and responsibilities of an official should Aisha consider as the most important ones?

5. Can you think of any particular technology which Aisha might have the opportunity to use?

Topic check

1. Identify at least two roles and responsibilities of officials in one of your chosen sports.
2. What is the difference between a main official and a minor official?
3. Why is it a good idea to be an assistant before being a main official?
4. Why do some officials have to wear specific clothing?
5. For one of your chosen sports, name a piece of equipment the main official would need to have.
6. Give a reason why an official might need a high level of specific fitness.
7. Why is it important for an official to be consistent?
8. In what ways is an official accountable to spectators?
9. What is meant by 'etiquette'?
10. Give an example of good etiquette in a sporting situation.

Topic 2.4

Being able to review sports performance

Getting started

This topic focuses on observing and reviewing sports performance. When you have completed this topic, you should know:

- which form of assessment will be the most useful and suitable for the two sports you have chosen
- the most important factors to look out for and comment on in a performance
- what is meant by an analysis, and how to carry one out successfully
- how to write up a review of a sports performance, which includes feedback and clear identification of your strengths and areas for improvement.

Key terms

Data: information that can be used to analyse sport

Feedback: information a performer receives about their performance

Objective evidence: factual evidence which is not just based on an opinion or prejudice

Statistics: figures obtained during a performance

Statistical evidence: facts and figures obtained during a performance

Subjective evidence: evidence which is the personal opinion of an individual

Performance

You should consider the following factors in relation to a performance in each of your two chosen sports.

Specific sport factors

These will vary between activities. For example, a golfer will need to be able to play a range of strokes (e.g. drive, chip, putt); a badminton player will need to be able to perform a range of skills (e.g. low and high serves, forehand and backhand drives, net shots).

Statistics and data

You will need to gather and record **statistics** and **data** as you go along, to use later as evidence in your review. It is important to make sure that you keep up to date with these as it will be very difficult to catch up if you do not make a record immediately after a performance.

Scoring and conceding

These will be two of the main indicators of how successful a performance has been. However, they must be considered in relation to the standards of the opposition and the environment. Scoring a lot of goals in a football match against very weak opposition does not necessarily mean that the performance was good. On the other hand, if you are competing against particularly strong opposition, you may play well and still concede goals. The environment can also affect your performance (e.g. strong winds in tennis and golf). In order to help you put your statistics and data into perspective it will be useful for you to get some **feedback** from a teacher or coach.

> ### Over to you!
>
> Design a form to record statistics and data you gather from your two chosen sports. This will depend on your particular sport, but in an invasion game (any game where teams have to get into their opponent's area in order to score) it could record the number of successful passes made or the number of times you were actively involved in the play.

Other factors

Other factors you could review, specific to particular sports, might include:

- time (e.g. in athletics running events)
- distance (e.g. in long jump, triple jump, discus etc.)
- height (e.g. in high jump, pole vault)
- the number of passes and interceptions made (in all invasion games)
- levels of discipline displayed throughout the performance – picking up red and yellow cards when performing would indicate poor performance levels!

Analysis

To carry out a successful analysis of your performance, you will have to put together an observation checklist which matches the particular sport you are taking part in. This can be completed while a performance is underway (in which case you may need to get someone else to fill this in for you), or by using a video recording to analyse the performance after it has been completed.

The checklist should consider the following:

- *Strengths and areas for improvement* – these could be shown through your demonstration of particular skills, techniques and tactics used, and link back to the basic and specific skills considered in Topic 2.1.
- *Knowledge* – making a lot of technical mistakes that infringe the rules of the activity would indicate a lack of knowledge.
- *Application of and respect for the rules and regulations* – you will demonstrate this by participating fairly and being fully aware of the correct rules and regulations at all times.
- *Communication* – in the team event, in particular, it is vital that you communicate well with teammates. This can be done through the use of gestures or signals, or can be verbal if appropriate. Depending on your role (e.g. if you are team captain), you may have extra responsibility for communication.

▶ *Teamwork* – this will be vital in the team activity, but even in an individual event you could be a member of a team overall (e.g. you might be a member of the tennis squad in a tennis fixture).

▶ *Preparation* – you can also analyse your preparation for a performance (e.g. levels of training, pre-match team talks, strategies etc.).

▶ *Health and safety* – this is an important aspect to consider in your final analysis. For example, in some trampoline performances the final skill in a series of ten is often the hardest and can result in a poor landing. The routine may be performed successfully, but would you regard it as safe when it's analysed? In rugby, you could consider whether a player put themselves at risk from inappropriate and overly aggressive behaviour. If they lost focus, did they miss-time any tackles, potentially causing injury?

⚙ **Activity**

Find out if there are any specific health and safety rules or guidelines in place for your two chosen sports.

Review

You can review your performance using feedback (some of which will be **subjective evidence**) from other participants (these could be teammates or opponents), supervisors, your peers and any other observers who were present at any sessions. Depending on the type of feedback you receive, you may be able to use this as **subjective evidence** or **statistical evidence**.

Your review should also help you to identify strengths and areas for improvement. As part of your assessment you will be asked to justify any recommendations you make for improvement.

💡 **Over to you!**

Design a basic feedback form which teammates, supervisors or observers can use to help you with your review. Make sure that you identify the particular areas which you would like feedback on, and that the form is easy to follow and fill in. It is a good idea to try it out yourself first, on someone else.

Improvements

Identifying particular areas for improvement is clearly very important, and the following will give you some guidance regarding the areas you might like to consider:

▶ *Short- and long-term goals* – for some of the individual skills, you might be able to identify changes that can be made quite quickly (e.g. learning a particular rule or regulation). However, you may also need to consider others changes that will take longer to develop (e.g. improving a particular aspect of fitness, such as endurance).

▶ *Tactics and teamwork* – in this area there will probably be several different options for you to choose from. You might not always be able to choose the tactics you use, especially in the team activity, but you can review the success of those that you were asked to use. In the individual activity you should have more choices available and you should be able to make your own decisions about which to use. You can review the tactical decisions you made and whether these need to be improved.

▶ *Fitness* – this could be in the category of either general or specific fitness. It may also vary between the individual and team activities, which may have different physical demands. You might want to consider concentrating on one specific aspect of fitness which could lead to an improvement in both of your chosen activities.

▶ *Training programme* – you will have to do some level of training to bring about changes and improvements, so reviewing this will be important. This is something you will be able to log quite accurately, and for which you should be able to gather quite a large amount of statistics and data to create statistical evidence and **objective evidence**.

▶ *Use of technology* – this is not necessarily going to be available for all activities, but if it is available then you should consider it. If some appropriate technology is available in your school (e.g. video recording equipment) then it is a good idea to make full use of it. Any visual analysis programmes, such as Dartfish, will help you to record performances and then review them in more detail.

▶ *Courses* – some additional courses may have been available to you (e.g. to qualify you to become an official), but you may like to suggest others which would have been useful.

▶ *Where to seek help and advice* – you are likely to have received quite a large amount of help and advice from different people, so you can comment on this and suggest other areas of help and guidance which might have been useful.

> ## Over to you!
>
> Identify two short- and two long-term goals that you particularly intend to focus on improving.

> ## Activity
>
> Find a partner in one of your practical sporting sessions and practise observing them and giving feedback. This should help you with ideas for what to include on your feedback form.

Case study

Paul has chosen rugby as his team sport and badminton as his individual sport. Paul plays in the school rugby team and, as a result, he attends a lot of practice and training sessions, and also plays an inter-school match at least once a week. Paul's level of activity and experience in badminton is not as high, and he is intending to play badminton in his scheduled PE lessons while he is taking the course. Three of Paul's classmates have also opted to play badminton, so he is sure of having some people to train with and play against. One of Paul's friends, Aaron, is a club- and county-standard badminton player and Paul is not sure how he is going to cope with playing against him, as the difference in standard might be a problem.

1. What specific sports factors might Paul need to consider when he is playing in his chosen team sport, where he will be one of a team of 15?

2. In which of the two sports he has chosen is Paul likely to be able to gather statistics and data more easily?

3. Which of the two sports Paul is playing in would be more suited to making use of any visual analysis programmes, such as Dartfish?

4. Paul could obtain feedback from all three of the other pupils who are playing badminton with

him, but what advice would you give him regarding who should feed back in rugby sessions?

5. Are there likely to be any aspects of fitness or a training programme which would be common to both of Paul's chosen sports?

Assessment activity 2.1 (P7, M3, P8, M4, P9, M5, D2)

This assessment activity focuses on your ability to review and assess practical sports performance. You are required to:

• Produce an observation checklist to assess the sports performance of an individual or team.

• Use the observation checklist to review the performance of an individual or team, identifying strengths and areas for improvement.

• Use the observation checklist to review your own

sports performance in an individual or team sport, identifying strengths and areas for improvement.

• Explain and analyse your own strengths and areas for improvement in an individual or team sport, providing and justifying recommendations for improvement.

Your evidence for this assessment activity should include completed observation checklists and a written report relating to your practical sports performance, strengths and areas for improvement.

Topic check

1 What is meant by 'statistical evidence'?

2 What is meant by 'objective evidence'?

3 What is meant by 'subjective evidence'?

4 Explain how it might not always be totally reliable to use scoring and conceding as evidence in performances.

5 How might the environment affect the level of performance?

6 Give two examples from a sporting situation where effective communication is important.

7 State two factors which could be considered in regard to preparation for a performance.

8 What is meant by the term 'feedback'?

9 What is the difference between short- and long-term goals?

10 What is a 'visual analysis programme'?

Assessment summary

The overall grade you achieve for this unit depends on how well you meet the grading criteria set out in Appendix 1 (see page 292). You must complete:

- all of the P criteria to achieve a **pass** grade
- all of the P and the M criteria to achieve a **merit** grade
- all of the P, M and D criteria to achieve a **distinction** grade.

Your tutor will assess the assessment activities that you complete for this unit. The work you produce should provide evidence which demonstrates that you have achieved each of the assessment criteria. Remember that you MUST provide evidence for all of the P criteria to pass the unit.

Grading criteria	You need to demonstrate that you can:	Have you got the evidence?
P1	Demonstrate use of practical skills, techniques and tactics appropriate for one team sport	
P2	Demonstrate use of practical skills, techniques and tactics appropriate for one individual sport	
M1	Describe use of tactics appropriate for one team and one individual sport	
D1	Justify use of tactics appropriate for one team and one individual sport identifying areas for improvement	
P3	Describe the rules, regulations and scoring systems for one team sport	
P4	Describe the rules, regulations and scoring systems for one individual sport	
M2	Assess, using appropriate examples, the rules, regulations and scoring systems for one team and one individual sport	
P5	Describe the main roles and responsibilities of officials in one team sport	
P6	Describe the main roles and responsibilities of officials in one individual sport	
P7	Produce, with tutor support, an observation checklist that could be used to review the sports performance of an individual or a team	
M3	Independently produce an observation checklist that could be used to review the sports performance of an individual or a team	
P8	Use the observation checklist to review the sports performance of an individual or a team identifying the strengths and areas for improvement	
M4	Explain the strengths and areas for improvement of an individual or a team, in one individual sport or one team sport, justifying recommendations for improvement	
P9	Use the observation checklist to review own sports performance in an individual sport or team sport, identifying strengths and areas for improvement	
M5	Explain own strengths and areas for improvement in an individual sport or team sport, providing recommendations for improvement	
D2	Analyse own strengths and areas for improvement in an individual sport or team sport, justifying recommendations for improvement	

Always ask your tutor to explain any assignment tasks or assessment criteria that you don't understand fully. Being clear about the task before you begin gives you the best chance of succeeding. Good luck with your Unit 2 assessment work!

3 Outdoor and adventurous activities (Unit 3)

Unit outline

This is a very practical unit in which you will be expected to take part in outdoor and adventurous activities. You must take part in at least two activities, which can be ones you already take part in or ones that are new to you. The 'taking part' element is vital in this unit. At the end of the unit you will be expected to review your own and someone else's performance. You should bear this in mind and ensure that, throughout, you keep records as you go along and look at basic target setting.

This unit will give you a greater understanding of outdoor and adventurous activities and for some, may be the first step towards a career in the outdoor industry.

Learning outcomes

1 Know the organisation and provision of outdoor and adventurous activities.
2 Know health and safety considerations and environmental impacts associated with participation in outdoor and adventurous activities.
3 Be able to demonstrate techniques and skills associated with selected outdoor and adventurous activities.
4 Be able to review performance in outdoor and adventurous activities.

The organisation and provision of outdoor and adventurous activities

▶ Getting started

In this unit you have to find out about two outdoor and adventurous activities in particular. This topic will cover some generic factors (common to all) by mainly focusing on two activities as examples: rock climbing and canoeing. You can use these two as the basis of your work, or you can choose different activities.

When you have completed this topic, you should know:

■ about the organisation of the two activities you have chosen, e.g. national governing bodies, coaching schemes and awards

■ about the provision of the two activities, e.g. locally and nationally.

🔑 Key terms

Bouldering: a type of rock climbing without the use of ropes, close to the ground, on boulders or very small crags

Canoeing: a generic term for paddle sports that use a range of craft, e.g. kayaks, canoes, sit-on-tops

Canoe: a type of boat in which you usually kneel and use a paddle with one blade

Consolidation: a period of practice to improve skills

Crag: a steep, rugged rock or peak

Empathy: the ability to understand another person's feelings

Kayak: a type of boat in which you sit and use a paddle with two blades

National Governing Bodies (NGBs): organisations that represent the interests of their members and the general public involved in the activity, e.g. the British Canoe Union is the NGB for paddle sports (e.g. canoeing and kayaking)

Providers: organisations and outdoor businesses providing outdoor and adventurous activity opportunities

Remit: the area of authority or responsibility that an award covers (or of an individual)

Residential: a course run with at least one overnight stay, e.g. at an outdoor centre

Sport-climbing: a style of climbing where the climber clips the rope to fixed metal bolts to protect them from a fall

Your choice of activities may be restricted by various factors, but below is a list of the most likely options you will be able to choose from. It includes the main outdoor and adventurous activities and the most popular options available:

▶ orienteering
▶ rock climbing
▶ skiing
▶ snowboarding
▶ canoeing

▶ kayaking
▶ hill walking
▶ mountaineering
▶ sailing
▶ windsurfing

▶ mountain biking
▶ surf and body boarding
▶ caving
▶ white water rafting
▶ coasteering.

Organisation

Every recognised outdoor and adventurous activity (O and AA) has what is known as a **National Governing Body (NGB)**. NGBs promote their O and AA and represent the interests of their members and the general public involved in those activities. They are also involved in access and conservation issues, and are responsible for recommending health and safety guidelines. In addition, NGBs are responsible for overseeing training and assessment in relation to their own personal performance, coaching and leadership awards. These are offered through a large number of course **providers** around the UK.

> 💡 **Over to you!**
>
> Find out what the National Governing Body is for the two activities you are intending to participate in. Find their website addresses and make a note of them.

Coaching schemes

Some governing bodies prioritise coaching in their organisation. This helps them to ensure that people are performing the activity safely, and that the standards in their sport are kept high.

For many people, their participation in outdoor and adventurous activities is for recreational purposes, or the activity is used for personal development. Coaching is still vitally important in these areas to ensure that participants develop the correct techniques, to maximise their performance and enjoyment, and to minimise the risk of injury.

Coaching awards in most O and AAs are organised into different levels. Each level usually revolves around specific conditions and environments in which the coaching can take place, e.g. size of surf for surfing, grade of rapids for **canoeing**. It is therefore important that coaches know the **remit** of their award and work within it. In most O and AAs, the majority of coaching takes place at recreational level and most employment opportunities are within this area.

> ⚙️ **Activity**
>
> Using the two national governing body sites that you previously identified, describe the coaching schemes available through each NGB.

For some activities, it is possible to participate competitively, and performers may compete at local, national or even international level. For example, some types of rock climbing (e.g. **bouldering** and **sport-climbing**) can be competitive, although these competitions are often held indoors. Some areas of canoeing can also be participated in competitively (e.g. slalom, wild-water racing, sprint and distance racing, surfing). Some O and AAs are recognised Olympic sports, e.g. some areas of canoeing, sailing, skiing and snowboarding. It is possible to become a competition coach and coach individuals, teams and squads from local level through to international level.

David Florence, British silver medalist in **canoe** slalom at the 2008 Olympics.

Leadership awards

For some non-competitive activities (e.g. hill walking, caving) the governing bodies provide leadership awards, which train and assess people to lead groups effectively in the activity. Leaders in these types of activities require a combination of 'hard' technical skills (e.g. navigation, rope work, first aid) and 'soft' people skills (e.g. the ability to understand and motivate a group, good communication, **empathy**).

Leaders must also have a good level of background knowledge about their activity and the environment. A large part of leadership in O and AAs involves judgement and decision-making. NGB leadership awards aim to help people develop these skills and knowledge through a process of training, **consolidation** and assessment.

A group of students training for a walking leader award.

There are no legal requirements for leaders of activities to be NGB qualified, and some organisations use in-house training through an appropriately qualified technical adviser. However, NGB awards are commonly recognised and used as benchmarks in the outdoor industry and most organisations employ people in relation to their NGB awards. Because there is a range of different leadership awards at different levels, it is important that leaders know the remit of their award and work within it.

Activity

Describe the leadership awards you can gain from NGBs for each of the two activities you are interested in. Identify the level of award you might like to progress to and explain why.

Clubs

NGBs are involved in supporting clubs for their activities. Clubs are often a good and relatively inexpensive way for people to gain experience in an activity and can be found locally, regionally and nationally. O and AA clubs tend to be run by community, college or university groups. Many of these clubs will be 'affiliated', which means they are official members of the NGB and have met a set of standards set out by the NGB. Because clubs are voluntary organisations, they don't have the same obligations as other outdoor activity providers in terms of qualified coaches and leaders, but should still have appropriate safety management systems in place to ensure safe participation.

Activity

Using the internet or other available resources, try to find local clubs in the two activities that you are interested in. Identify the nearest and most accessible club and contact it to find out how easy it is to join and how old you need to be to participate.

Training opportunities

Continuing professional development (CPD) is important for people working in the outdoor industry. CPD is a common approach, and most outdoor staff are working towards the next level of qualification for their activity, to enable them to work within a wider remit (e.g. to coach at a higher level, or to lead groups in more challenging environments). Alternatively, they may want to gain additional qualifications at the same level but in a different discipline. For example, you could become a canoeing coach at the same level in a range of disciplines (e.g. sea, surf, inland river). Others may want to gain an award in a completely different activity, so they have more to offer and have more employment opportunities.

Employment

There is a wide range of employment opportunities within the outdoor industry, and it is possible to develop a career working as a coach and/or leader in O and AAs. Although it is possible to specialise in one activity, it is common to gain qualifications in a range of activities to increase employment opportunities. Many outdoor centres will request a minimum of two NGB qualifications when recruiting staff, and will often look for land- and water-based activity qualifications. Some outdoor centres will offer work experience to unqualified people and offer NGB training as part of the work placement. Many jobs in O and AAs require applicants to be a minimum of 18 years old. People under 18 who wish to pursue a career in the outdoor industry could use SMART targets (see Topic 3.4) to help identify what they can do in preparation for future employment.

Provision

Provision refers to how and where each particular activity takes place in relation to levels of participation. The nature of outdoor and adventurous activities means that they can have unique requirements. For example, only certain locations can offer surfing opportunities or natural features such as caves, and to participate in mountaineering, you need mountains! However, some activities, such as orienteering, can take place almost anywhere, and activities such as canoeing can use basic facilities such as swimming pools for some training, and different types of water such as canals, rivers, lakes and the sea. Most counties have a range of recognised crags or boulders that can be used for climbing, and most major cities and towns now have indoor climbing walls.

Other influences on levels of participation, and hence provision, may include factors such as transport, financial implications, media portrayal and publicity of the activity.

Activity

Using the information you have been able to gather from the NGBs and websites, write a description/comparison considering what the activities you chose involve, the roles of their NGBs and the provision made for them.

Local provision

Local provision will depend on population size and, possibly, demand. In major towns and cities, local provision may include outdoor centres, climbing walls, colleges, freelance providers, clubs, scout groups and so on. In addition, there are many outdoor centres in more remote rural locations around the UK that offer **residential** courses. Some local provision is helped by council funding and grants to enable cheaper participation at grassroots level.

Over to you!

Find out where the nearest local provision is for the two activities you have decided to participate in.

National provision

Most activities have a base for their national provision. Often these are based in a high-profile provision area. For example, the national base for sailing provision is at Weymouth on the south coast of England, at the National Sailing Academy. There are three national mountain centres in the UK (Plas y Brenin in North Wales, Glenmore Lodge in the Scottish Highlands and Tollymore in Northern Ireland), which offer a range of provision relating to mountaineering and climbing, as well as other activities.

Plas Menai, the National Watersports Centre for Wales

Activity

For the two activities you have chosen, find out about what national provision is available and whether there is a specific base for their national provision. Compare what is available for the two activities.

Access

Access is a factor that varies greatly in relation to the activity. If it is an activity that relies on a natural feature, then access is obviously restricted to where these exist. There are other barriers to some activities, however, such as land access issues (e.g. rivers that go through private land), and seasonal restrictions such as issues relating to nesting, hunting and fishing. Weather can also affect access in relation to some O and AAs (e.g. dry weather can make river levels too low for canoeing).

Providers of O and AAs work around these factors and make the most of whatever resources they have access to in their area. This means, however, that providers in certain parts of the UK can offer provision that others can't (e.g. only providers close to the coast can provide surfing opportunities).

Range

This usually refers to the range of options available within a particular activity. For example, if you are involved in rock climbing, you might have the option of indoor climbing walls, local **crags** or boulders, gorges or far more challenging areas such as mountain crags and sea cliffs. Mountain biking would offer a similar range of options in terms of the terrain you could use and the level of challenge they would offer.

Geographical differences

These are closely linked to the range factors discussed above. In addition to the different types of climbing venue available, where you are in the UK will also determine what type of rock is climbed. Sandstone, limestone, grit-stone and granite, for example, are all climbed on, and often have very different characteristics and offer different challenges for the climber.

Surf kayaking

Canoeing activities can also be affected by geographical factors. For example, the possibility of surf kayaking and wave skiing is not only determined by access to the sea, but also by the type of waves generated (e.g. regularity, size and quality of the surf). Some beaches and coastal areas of the British Isles will only ever get very small or poor-quality waves for surfing.

Sites and centres

Sites and centres offering O and AAs are varied and wide-ranging. They make the most of any natural resources available in their area, and provision is offered accordingly. Sites and centres may include outdoor centres, some schools, colleges, universities, clubs, scout groups, ski centres, water-sports centres, mountain centres and so on. Provision through artificial structures such as climbing walls, ski slopes and white-water courses in urban areas has become more available in recent times. These may be purpose-built sites or part of leisure centres. The location of all sites and centres will be determined by all of the factors discussed above (access, range and geography).

Comparing organisation and provision

As part of Unit 3, you will have to describe and compare the organisation and provision for two outdoor and adventurous activities. Figures 3.1 and 3.2 provide examples for the activities of rock climbing and canoeing, which should help you with this task.

Figure 3.1 Rock climbing – organisation and provision

Organisation	
Aspect	**Details**
National Governing Body	The Mountain Leader Training England (MLTE) was established in 1964 to develop training and assessment courses in mountaineering. The range of courses it offers has developed over the years and include rock climbing, as well as walking and mountaineering. The MLTE is based in North Wales and, as a training body, works closely with the British Mountaineering Council (BMC), which represents the interests of climbers, hill walkers and mountaineers in England and Wales. (www.mlte.org) (www.thebmc.co.uk)
Coaching schemes	The MLTE offers a Climbing Wall Award (CWA). This award is primarily concerned with ensuring good practice as an instructor and covers the supervision and management of activities such as bouldering, roped climbing on climbing walls and abseiling on artificial towers. There is a coaching element to this award, however, and the teaching and coaching of basic movement skills is part of the syllabus.
Leadership awards	The MLTE's climbing awards (such as the CWA and the Single Pitch Award (SPA) – an award for instructors working with groups climbing and abseiling on non-mountainous outdoor crags) are primarily instructor or supervisor, awards. However, these instructors are also often in leadership situations with regard to decision-making. The MLTE does offer leadership awards in hill walking and mountaineering. There are also options to progress in climbing leadership qualifications beyond SPA level with MLTUK (Mountain Leader Training UK).
Clubs	There are many clubs around the UK. These include community, college and university clubs. Some are affiliated with the BMC, which offers support and advice. Information on clubs locally and nationally can be acquired from the BMC or from www.climbingclub.co.uk.
Training opportunities	Training is provided for instructors through MLTE courses. Additional skill development courses are also offered by some outdoor providers, e.g. outdoor centres and colleges. In addition, training and coaching opportunities for participants climbing recreationally or in competition are often offered through climbing walls or clubs.
Employment	There is a range of employment opportunities for qualified climbers, both in the UK and abroad. This could include working at climbing walls, outdoor centres and colleges, doing freelance work or youth work, instructing, coaching, competition climbing and so on. Various websites, climbing magazines and the NGBs all advertise jobs.

Rock climbing using a 'bottom-rope' system.

Traditional (trad) lead climbing.

Figure 3.1 Rock climbing – organisation and provision *continued*

Provision	
Aspect	**Details**
Local provision	This will depend on where you live. Due to the nature of the activity, provision tends to be in areas close to crags and mountains. There are, however, climbing walls in most major cities and towns.
National provision	There is a network of providers throughout the UK who offer courses and climbing opportunities. These include clubs, outdoor centres, freelance instructors, some schools, colleges and universities. The most common and often most practical introduction to rock climbing is through a climbing wall. This can be used as a stepping-stone to outdoor rock climbing.
Access	Access to crags in the UK is generally very good. As a result of good work by the BMC with landowners, and recent changes in access laws, people have free access to most crags across the UK. It should be remembered, however, that many of these crags are on private land and climbers have a responsibility to look after them and act appropriately. There can occasionally be access restrictions because of bird nesting, but this is relatively uncommon. Some crags are very popular at certain times of the year, and some routes can become crowded. The weather obviously has an impact on when crags can be used for climbing, as can the time of year. O and AA providers will have a good understanding of which crags to use in certain weather conditions and at different times of the year.
Range	The range of climbing opportunities and venues is vast. These include: indoor and outdoor artificial bouldering walls, indoor roped climbing walls, crags of different rock types and sizes, boulders, gorges, mountain crags and sea cliffs. There is also a range of different climbing types or disciplines that can be explored.
Geographical differences	Rock climbing takes place on a wide range of rock types (e.g. sandstone, granite, grit-stone, limestone), and where you are in the country will determine the rock type and characteristic of the climbing. The larger crags tend to be in mountainous areas and offer long, adventurous routes. Some sea cliffs offer a similar experience. Bouldering has become a popular form of climbing and involves working out problems and linking moves together close to the ground to successfully complete short routes on boulders or very small crags. These can be found around the UK and again the geographical area will determine the rock type.
Sites and centres	There are many sites and centres throughout the UK. Virtually every county has crags of some sort that can be used for rock climbing. Climbing walls are also becoming increasingly popular and now exist in most major towns and cities.

Activity

Using the internet and/or outdoor magazines, research and locate one employment opportunity that will involve each or both of your chosen activities. Describe how close you are to meeting the job description and clearly identify any areas that you need to improve on and develop.

Over to you!

Using Figures 3.1 and 3.2 (overleaf) as examples, complete your own tables for the two activities you have chosen.

Figure 3.2 Canoeing – organisation and provision

Organisation	
Aspect	**Details**
National Governing Body	The British Canoe Union (BCU) was formed in 1936 specifically to prepare a team for the Berlin Olympics. Since then, the organisation has grown considerably, as has the range of canoeing opportunities. The BCU is the UK's lead body for canoeing, which encompasses a range of paddle-sports. (www.bcu.org.uk).
Coaching schemes	The BCU offers a number of BCU Coaching Qualification Courses from Level 1 to Level 5, with various other options also available. Some of these are UKCC (UK Coaching Certificates). Each region in the UK has a Regional Coaching Organiser (RCO) and a number of Local Coaching Organisers (LCOs). These people can be contacted for advice on coaching issues, and can help put people in touch with course providers around their region. They also organise update days for coaches in their region. BCU coaches must update within a 3-year period to keep their level of qualification valid.
Leadership awards	Four- and five-star leader awards are also available from the BCU and can be taken in a range of disciplines. Prior to these, candidates complete 1–3-star personal performance awards or the Paddle-Power youth awards.
Clubs	There are many clubs in each of the home nations of the UK. England, for example, is divided into 12 regions, and there are clubs in all of them. There are 28 registered clubs in the London area alone, and 34 in the East Midlands area. Details of affiliated clubs in your part of the UK can be found at www.bcu.org.uk.
Training opportunities	Canoeing is an Olympic sport, so training is available at all levels from beginners up to the elite performers in the national squads and teams. Canoeing offers many different options relating to different types of boat (e.g. **kayaks**, canoes and sit-on-tops) and different water types (e.g. sea, surf, white water, placid or open inland water). Specialised and/or general-purpose boats are available and used for each of these water types. General coaching, skills training and BCU courses are offered widely throughout the UK through various providers and clubs.
Employment	There is a range of employment opportunities for qualified canoeists, both at home and abroad. This could include working at outdoor centres and colleges, doing freelance work or youth work, coaching, leading, guiding, competition paddling, white-water rafting safety boater (providing safety cover for white-water rafters). Various websites, canoeing magazines and the BCU all advertise jobs.

Case study

Kerry has been chosen by her tutor to give a presentation as part of her assessment on this topic. She has decided to use the activities of rock climbing and canoeing, as she found both activities interesting. Kerry has used all the options available to her – she has produced a booklet, a poster and a written report to describe and compare the two activities.

Kerry has not had any actual experience of either of the two activities and is not sure if this will count against her. When preparing this presentation, Kerry, was not sure if she should consider organisation and provision equally or talk about one in more detail.

1. When comparing the two activities, which aspect of coaching and leadership is Kerry most likely to focus on?

2. What is Kerry likely to point out as the most significant difference between the two activities?

3. Are there any generic factors that Kerry might identify?

4. When comparing the two activities, what geographical differences is Kerry most likely to focus on?

5. As Kerry does not take part in either activity, where do you suggest Kerry gets her information from?

Figure 3.2 Canoeing – organisation and provision *continued*

Provision	
Aspect	**Details**
Local provision	Provision is available throughout the country. Due to the range of different types of water that can be used, there will always be local options available within a fairly short distance.
National provision	The BCU's 'affiliated club' and 'approved centre' network in the UK ensures that there is a wide range of national provision. This also offers the options of the different water conditions for the different types of canoes and kayaks. You can visit your home nation's website and find affiliated clubs and approved centres in your region at www.bcu.org.uk.
Access	The legal access situation in relation to inland waterways in England and Wales is a problem for canoeists. Compared with the rest of the world, canoeists in the UK have very poor legal rights of access and the BCU is strongly lobbying the government for this to be changed. Currently, access agreements with some landowners exist for certain stretches of water to be open for canoeing at agreed times of the year. Information on access agreements can be obtained from the BCU and their access officers. Coastal access isn't so much of a problem. People normally require a vehicle to transport their craft to the water, but there are many clubs and outdoor centres that already have the canoes and kayaks in place for use. Many clubs and centres also have facilities in place for disabled access.
Range	There is a wide range of options available. It is possible to canoe in a swimming pool and use this to master the basic skills and techniques. Other options are rivers, lakes, large ponds, canals and the sea. Artificial white-water courses also exist around the country. Access agreements in relation to inland water, as mentioned above, should be considered.
Geographical differences	These can be a significant factor. A steep landscape will result in fast-flowing rivers, which can produce rapids used for recreational white-water paddling, wild water racing and slalom events. Some regions have more geographical features than others (e.g. natural lakes, rivers, sea and surf).
Sites and centres	There are many sites and centres throughout the country. Virtually every water feature offers the opportunity for canoeing to take place.

Topic check

1 What does NGB stand for?

2 Explain the purpose of NGBs.

3 Identify the two types of skill required by leaders.

4 What does CPD stand for?

5 Identify two main factors that affect the levels of local provision.

6 Identify two geographical factors that may affect the provision of two named activities.

7 Name three types of organisation that might provide opportunities to participate in O and AAs.

8 What is the range of opportunities available in the two activities you have chosen?

Health and safety considerations and environmental impacts

▶ Getting started

For the majority of O and AAs the environment is what offers the opportunity in the first place. Many of the environments are beautiful, yet challenging and potentially dangerous. Although O and AAs vary greatly and can take place in totally different environments, there are some general health and safety and environmental issues that should be taken into account. It is your responsibility to make sure you are aware of these in relation to your two chosen activities.

When you have completed this topic, you should know:

- about the health and safety aspects of your chosen activities
- why risk assessments are important and how to carry one out
- the possible environmental impacts of O and AAs.

🔑 Key terms

Abrasion: damage caused by friction

Experiential learning: learning through experience, practice and reflection

Legislation: written laws, also known as statutes and Acts of Parliament

Health and safety

This has to be of primary importance in all types of outdoor and adventurous activity. You need to know where you can obtain relevant information and guidelines for individual activities.

National Governing Body (NGB) guidelines

All NGBs provide information and recommended guidelines in relation to health and safety. These will identify specific information relating to the particular activity. It is important to keep up to date with this, as there are often changes and updates in relation to health and safety. The NGBs have to respond to any **legislation**, any incidents which might have occurred and any changes in ideas of best practice, adapting their guidelines accordingly.

⚙ Activity

Research the bodies that regulate your two chosen activities. Describe the main health and safety considerations for each one and ways in which they can be managed.

The Adventurous Activities Licensing Authority (AALA)

The AALA was introduced in April 1996 as a government-sponsored scheme under the Adventure Activities Licensing Regulations. The aim of AALA has been to ensure that providers offering O and AAs on a commercial basis to young people (under 18s) have the appropriate safety management systems in place. If these are all correctly in place and a successful inspection has taken place, then a licence can be issued to the provider.

In April 2007, the Health and Safety Executive (HSE) was designated as the AALA. This now means that the organisation that carries out the inspections and issues licences on behalf of the HSE and AALA is the Adventure Activities Licensing Service (AALS). The AALA covers 25 different identified activities, which it places in the following four broad categories:

1. climbing   **2.** watersports   **3.** trekking   **4.** caving.

The Health and Safety Executive (HSE)

This is the government body in charge of guidance and legislation in matters of health and safety. It states: 'our job is to prevent death, injury and ill health to those at work and those affected by work activities'. One of the industries identified by the HSE is the entertainment and leisure industry. This combined with their designation of AALA in April 2007 highlights the relevance of HSE in relation to outdoor and adventurous activities.

Risk assessment

One of the appeals of O and AAs to some people is the element of risk taking. The excitement or 'adrenalin buzz' that may come from participation in such activities, and the sense of achievement from overcoming or managing a fear, can be viewed by some as life enhancing. By definition, adventurous activities must have an element of risk or uncertainty. The risk may be only 'perceived risk' or could be 'actual risk'. For example, a beginner climbing a roped route at a climbing wall may perceive the activity to be 'high risk' because of the height involved and their increased anxiety levels, but so long as the equipment is being used correctly, the 'actual risk' of harm is very low. In contrast to this, an inexperienced hill walker might try to cross a seemingly shallow but fast-moving river while walking in the mountains. They could easily perceive crossing the river as 'low risk', but in reality the 'actual risk' of harm in relation to slipping and falling in the water could be 'very high'.

O and AA coaches and leaders need to be able to manage and balance both perceived and real risk to ensure that their groups have a positive and worthwhile experience. Climbing at a crag outdoors would inevitably involve more 'actual risk' than a climbing wall, as it is a less controlled environment (e.g. weather conditions may change and affect the climbing). However, because of this it could be argued that climbing outdoors is more adventurous than climbing indoors and, as a result, more rewarding for some. This level of adventure in an impressive natural environment can often be a powerful vehicle for personal development and **experiential learning**.

> ### Over to you!
>
> Find out which AALA category the following come under:
> - ghyll scrambling
> - improvised rafting
> - off-road cycling
> - mine exploration
> - dragon boating.

Whatever the activity, it is important that O and AA coaches and leaders have a 'dynamic risk assessment' approach. A dynamic risk assessment is an ongoing, on-the-spot risk assessment performed mentally throughout the activity. Dynamic risk assessment in O and AAs is important because the environments in which many activities take place are constantly changing (e.g. river levels can rise, surf size can increase, weather conditions on a crag can suddenly change).

It is important that participants are also encouraged to develop an understanding of risk taking and adopt their own risk assessment approach.

By law, O and AA providers are required to carry out a risk assessment for all their activities. This is usually done as a formal (written) risk assessment. This needs to be completed by someone who has the relevant experience for a given activity and should be reviewed and updated regularly. A formal risk assessment focuses on 'actual risk'.

Hazards

The start of a risk assessment involves identifying the hazards. A 'hazard' is anything that has the potential (however great or small) to cause harm.

Who might be affected?

In many of these activities it is not just the participants who might be affected. For example, in mountain biking it would be possible to injure walkers who might be in the area. When surf kayaking, a canoeist's actions could put surfboarders at risk. A risk assessment should identify all the people who may be affected.

Measures to minimise and manage risk

It is not possible to make any activity 100% free of risk. However, appropriate efforts to minimise the risk of harm where possible should be made. Part of the risk assessment process is to identify, and put in place, measures to ensure that the risk is minimised and managed. As many realistic safeguards as possible should be put in place to minimise the risk.

Likelihood of occurrence, severity and risk ratings

In risk assessment it is necessary to work out how likely it is that the identified hazard may cause harm, and identify the severity of the hazard. These should take into consideration the 'measures' that are already in place. These factors combined give you a risk rating, which in turn indicates whether the level of risk is low, medium or high. A table (see Figure 3.3) is often used.

If something is given a 'high' risk rating even after control measures are in place, then it must be looked at closely to see if further measures are possible, or if the activity can be justified. All coaches and leaders involved in delivering the activities need to see the risk assessments.

Figure 3.4 considers the whole risk assessment process, using kayak surfing as an example.

Severity			
3	MEDIUM	MEDIUM	LOW
2	HIGH	MEDIUM	MEDIUM
1	HIGH	HIGH	MEDIUM
	A	B	C
Likelihood			

Key
Severity: 1 = death or major injury; 2 = injury lasting more than 3 days; 3 = minor injury, damage to equipment, etc.
Likelihood: A = extremely likely; B = may happen occasionally; C = extremely unlikely

Figure 3.3 Example of a risk rating table

Activity: Introduction to surf kayaking for intermediate paddlers						
Venue: Sunny Sands Beach						
Risk assessment carried out by: _____						
Date of risk assessment:_____ Date for review:_____						
Hazard	Who is affected?	Potential outcome/injury	Control measures	Severity of hazard	Likelihood of occurrence	Risk rating
Surf/water (beach wave)	Kayakers, other surfers	Loss of control over kayak Loss of consciousness Drowning	Check forecast and conditions. Surf in appropriate and relevant conditions/location. Set boundaries/identify a surf zone. Ensure safety cover is in place, e.g. surf as a group and look out for each other or use a buddy system. Wear wetsuit and buoyancy aid. Avoid other surfers.	1	C	Medium
Reef/rocks	Kayakers	Head injury Cuts and bruises Drowning Damage to equipment	As above, plus: Avoid reef and rocks through use of a surf zone. Wear helmets.	1	C	Medium
Jellyfish	Kayakers	Sting	Avoid if possible. Cover up if jellyfish seen, e.g. wear gloves. Carry vinegar as part of first aid kit.	3	C	Low
Poor technique	Kayakers	Damage to muscles Dislocated shoulder	Ensure surfers have been coached on correct technique. Don't push off bottom with paddle. Provide feedback.	2	B	Medium

Figure 3.4 Example of part of a risk assessment showing some possible hazards

It must be stressed that risk assessments also relate directly to the participants and their level of experience and ability. For example, in Figure 3.4 the measure of avoiding reef/rocks is relevant for a group of intermediate canoeists. If they were more advanced surfers, they may actually use the reef/rocks if the feature was generating surf. The risk assessment for this group would then be different. The same can be said of conditions. With a group of beginners, the risk assessment is likely to indicate that conditions should involve small surf and on-shore winds. For advanced surfers, the opposite conditions would be more favourable and the risk assessment would have to reflect this.

It should also be understood that the above risk ratings are only deemed as 'medium' if the control measures are in place. In all O and AAs, a low- or medium-risk activity can easily change to a high-risk activity if the control measure is taken away.

Over to you!

Using Figure 3.4 as an example, carry out a basic risk assessment for one of your two chosen activities.

Environmental impacts

Minimising the impact (effect) of an activity on the environment must be a priority in all O and AA participation. A balance must be struck between using the environment for the pleasure and enjoyment of your chosen activity, and the possibility of causing damage or disruption. All of the following have to be considered.

Erosion

Erosion is when something (usually earth or rocks) is worn away by wear and tear. This could apply, for example, to a track through woods that is constantly being used by mountain bikes, or to footpaths in areas that are very popular with walkers. Crags can also be damaged through overuse. Rock erosion can occur as a result of ropes running over the top of a crag or simply through **abrasion** caused by feet. Once the initial process of erosion has started, it is often speeded up by natural processes (e.g. rainfall leading to water running down footpaths).

It is important that we all take some responsibility for this, first by being conscious of the problem and then by trying to minimise the potential of erosion. For example, the impact of rock climbing can be minimised simply by making sure that footwear is free from dirt (this will reduce the effects of abrasion) or using rope-protectors when running a rope over the edge of a crag.

Wildlife disturbance

As many activities take place in remote and rural areas, the wildlife in them may not be used to human presence. This could scare the wildlife away from its natural habitat and may also damage the habitat itself. It is important that we minimise our impact as much as possible when in these environments. We should respect and enjoy the wildlife (flora (plants) and fauna (animals)) around us without disturbing it unnecessarily.

Pollution

This can take many forms. Litter is a common form of pollution that causes many problems, and the soil, water and atmosphere can all be contaminated if care is not taken. When you are doing activities or camping in the countryside it is important to take care not to pollute it. Toilet areas must be away from any natural water supplies and, if using stream water to cook and wash with, then this should be taken away from the stream rather than washing in the stream. Special care should be taken if carrying or using any chemical products. All food and litter should be carried out and you should strive to leave the countryside as you found it, if not improved by taking other people's litter home as well! You should also consider your transport options in relation to all activities. Noise and light pollution can also cause problems.

Construction of facilities

There are many rules and regulations relating to the construction of facilities to make sure that they do not impact on the environment. Unsightly buildings, storage sheds or accommodation blocks have to be considered very carefully. This area is regulated (with laws in place and enforced) to minimise the effects. Temporary structures often have fewer restrictions in terms of building regulations than permanent structures, and this may have relevance to some outdoor providers (e.g. climbing/abseil towers, changing/storage areas etc.).

Activity

Using the internet (www.countrysideaccess.gov.uk), find out about 'the countryside code'.

List the five main sections of 'the countryside code' aimed at the public.

List the three key words found in 'the countryside code' logo.

Over to you!

Explain the environmental impacts associated with the two O and AAs you have chosen. Describe precautions and actions that could be taken to reduce these impacts.

Case study

Tyrone is friends with Kerry and has also decided to use rock climbing as one of his activities. His only real experience so far is through using the indoor climbing wall at the local leisure centre. Because he has no actual experience of outdoor climbing, he is unsure how to go about considering environmental aspects under the four categories his tutor is covering.

1. What particular erosion factors do you think Tyrone is going to have to consider?

2. What level of wildlife disturbance is Tyrone most likely to encounter? Is there any specific form of wildlife which is most likely to be disturbed?

3. Are there any specific pollution factors which Tyrone might need to be aware of when climbing?

4. Would the 'construction of facilities' factor be particularly relevant to Tyrone? If not, why not?

Assessment activity 3.1 (P1, P2, M1, M2, D1)

You are working at an outdoor pursuits centre and have been asked to assist the instructors with an induction of a group of students who are on a residential visit. You have been asked to prepare written materials that provide:

1. a description and comparison of two outdoor and adventurous activities, the roles of their NGBs and the provision of these activities

2. a description and explanation of the health and safety considerations associated with participation in your chosen outdoor and adventurous activities.

Your material should identify and explain precautions and actions that can be taken, or used, in relation to each activity.

Assessment activity 3.2 (P3, P4, M3, D2)

The second part of your induction materials for a group of students visiting an outdoor pursuits centre has to focus on safety issues. You have been asked to produce:

1. a risk assessment for a selected outdoor and adventurous activity that demonstrates the application of risk assessment principles

2. a description and explanation of environmental considerations associated with participation in outdoor and adventurous activities.

Your materials should identify and explain precautions that can be taken, or used, to reduce the environmental impacts of participation in two outdoor and adventurous activities.

Topic check

1 What is legislation?
2 Explain the role of the AALA in O and AAs.
3 Under how many categories does the AALA group O and AAs?
4 What is the HSE?
5 Identify the two factors that, combined, give the risk rating for a hazard.
6 What is erosion?
7 Name three of the main forms of pollution.
8 How can you ensure that you do not cause pollution when camping?

You are required to take part in two activities and show evidence of skill acquisition in both of them, demonstrating techniques and skills you have mastered. You will be given challenges that will require you to select and use these techniques skilfully.

While you are participating in the activities you should also be managing a process of reviewing another performer for final review in Topic 3.4.

When you have completed this topic, you should know:

- the techniques and skills required for your activities
- about the variety of O and AAs available and that they all require specific skills and techniques
- how to record evidence of your participation and development in your chosen O and AAs.

Techniques and skills

As in other sports, the techniques and skills will vary greatly between different activities, but there are some general areas to consider.

Movement

All O and AAs require some form of movement. It is up to you to identify what these are for your chosen activities and to start to master them. Movements required of windsurfers are different from those of climbers, but both will be equally challenging. With good technique, climbing should look smooth and effortless. Efficient movement skills take time to develop.

Tactics

Not all activities are competitive, so they do not all require the use of tactics. If you were in a sailing race you might have a specific tactic for your starting position, or a tactic to 'take the wind' from another competitor. If you were caving you would mainly be doing it for your own personal satisfaction, sense of adventure and enjoyment and would not necessarily use specific tactics. However, there are some non-competitive situations where tactics might be used. For example, a climber's tactic may be to plan a particular route for their climb; canoeists may discuss tactics on how they plan to tackle a set of rapids.

Use of equipment

Most O and AAs require the use of specialist equipment. For example, a range of different boats and types of paddles are used in canoeing. Different designs are used for different purposes and disciplines within the activity. In climbing, it is important to develop the correct techniques involved with safe rope work, and this requires understanding the equipment used. You will have to learn about the equipment you need for your activities and develop the skills to use it effectively.

Decision-making

When and where to go and what to do when you get there are decisions that need to be made for many O and AAs. Even when the activity is underway you have to decide which skills and techniques to use at certain times. For example, if you were going climbing you would have to decide where to go. Once there, you would have to choose a route and attempt to work out the moves to successfully climb it. There is a lot of problem-solving involved with rock climbing, so once climbing you would have to decide on every move for your hands and feet, which techniques to use, and whether to go up, move across in either direction (traverse) or even go back down again. Most O and AAs require this level of individual decision-making, so you will need to develop your decision-making skills.

Communication

Effective communication is vital in most O and AAs. For example, if more than one person is sailing, they must constantly communicate with other members of the crew about where to sit or how to control the sails. Canoeists use techniques such as hand and paddle signals to communicate on rivers, because verbal communication is often hampered by the noise of the water or by distance. Climbers use a universal set of clear and precise 'climbing calls' to minimise the chances of confusion when on a crag. Some O and AAs can be solo activities, but even in these situations, communication skills might be necessary. For example:

▶ You should never go walking (or do any other O and AAs) alone without informing someone else of your plans.

▶ Surfers often communicate with other surfers using hand signals and calls.

Activity

Make a list of the equipment you will need for your two chosen activities and consider the factors of size (some equipment can be dependant upon the size of the individual), availability (whether you would be able to get hold of it or not) and cost.

Interaction

Most O and AAs involve working with others. For example, the majority of rock climbing involves working with a partner whose job it is to support the climber, control the rope and offer advice and encouragement. In canoeing, it is often important to work as a team and provide safety cover for each other on challenging sections of water. O and AAs are therefore good for developing friendships and bonds, teamwork and trust. People participating in O and AAs also often interact with members of the public or other people using the same natural resource, e.g. surfboarders and surf kayakers. It is therefore important that they conduct themselves well and represent their sport in a positive light. There is also interaction within competition in some O and AAs, which may involve tactics and strategies. Most NGBs have codes of good practice available on their websites.

Techniques and skills specific to activities

Due to the variety of activities available, it is not possible to list all of the techniques and skills you may require. Many are specific to certain activities. For example, in rock climbing there is a wide range of different techniques used in relation to hands, feet, body position and movement. Flexibility, strength and endurance may all play a part in how these techniques and skills are performed, as will your ability to manage your anxiety levels. All of these factors will be improved and developed with practice, training and time spent out of your comfort zone. There are also techniques and skills that need to be learnt to ensure safe rope work. In canoeing, there are many different 'strokes' that can be used to control and move your boat in different ways.

Over to you!

What specific skills and techniques can you identify for your two chosen activities? Are all of the categories discussed here relevant to them?

Outdoor and adventurous activities

As you have seen from the list at the beginning of this unit (page 59), there is a variety of outdoor and adventurous activities for you to choose from, ranging from orienteering to surfing and skiing to sailing. All of the activities will require you to use the range of skills and techniques discussed in the previous section to a greater or lesser degree, depending on the activities you have chosen.

Open canoe and kayaks: skill development session.

Recording evidence

Your tutor is going to observe and assess you demonstrating two skills you have acquired. You need to keep a diary or logbook of all the training sessions you take part in for your activities, to keep track of the skills and techniques that you are learning. You will also carry out a self-review based on the evidence you have recorded. Bear the following in mind when deciding how to keep your records.

▶ A diary will record everything you do. It will include all of the skills and techniques you used and the 'challenge' of the activity or event.

▶ A logbook may link in with your diary or may be an alternative way of recording all the information.

▶ A portfolio is another form of record of what you have been doing. You could include photographs or even short video clips in this as part of your evidence.

▶ Video is another recording method you can use. However, it does rely on someone else working with you to make the recording.

Videoing a kayak session.

▶ A sound (audio) record of what you do can also be used. This has the advantage that you can record it yourself.

▶ An observation record is something you can ask someone else to fill in for you while they observe you. You will have to produce it and make it specific to what you are doing.

▶ Feedback sheets can be used by anyone else you might be working with, e.g. a teammate in a team event such as orienteering.

You might find that the best way of recording evidence is to use a combination of the above. You should choose the methods that record the information in the most accurate and easiest way for your activities.

Over to you!

Look at the list of evidence recording options. Decide which one, or ones, you are going to use.

Case study

Sport-climbing on an indoor wall.

Kerry is still in the process of deciding which two activities to choose. Her school is in the centre of a large city and she feels that her options are rather limited. She has narrowed down her choices to mountain biking (she does own a mountain bike),

orienteering (there is a course marked out around the school campus) and climbing (there is a climbing wall at the local leisure centre).

Kerry's tutor has told the group that they may be able to go on a limited number of trips away to suitable locations. The tutor needs to know as soon as possible which activities the students want to do so that she can decide which trips to organise.

1. What do you think are the main points in favour and against the three options Kerry's has come up with?

2. Which two activities do you think she should choose and why?

3. What specific skills, techniques and tactics might Kerry's have to learn for these two activities?

4. What forms of evidence recording would you recommend Kerry's to use?

Assessment activity 3.3 (P5, M4)

This assessment activity requires you to demonstrate the use of safe and appropriate techniques and skills in two outdoor and adventurous activities. To complete the assessment you need to:

1. Select two outdoor and adventurous activities and identify examples of techniques and skills that you intend to demonstrate.

2. Demonstrate in safe, practical ways the techniques and skills you have selected for the two outdoor

and adventurous activities you have chosen. Your tutor will need to observe your performance of this task. You should also keep a record of when and how you demonstrated the skills and techniques you wish to be assessed on.

3. Review and justify your choice and use of the techniques and skills demonstrated in your chosen outdoor and adventurous activities. You should produce written evidence for this task.

Topic check

1 Name at least two O and AAs in which you might be able to use tactics.

2 Choose two activities and, for each one, describe two pieces of specialist equipment which would be needed.

3 Name at least two O and AAs in which communication skills are important.

4 What sort of interaction with others will your chosen activities involve?

5 Name two skills and techniques that you will need to master in order to be successful in each of your chosen activities.

Review performance in outdoor and adventurous activities

> ▶ **Getting started**
>
> The final part of this unit requires you to review your own performance and the performance of another individual participating in these activities. This topic considers how this review should be carried out. When you have completed this topic, you should know:
> - how to review your own performance
> - how to review other people's performance.

Review

Reviewing is the process of reflecting back over a performance with the intention of learning and improving from it. A review should identify what went well and what could be improved. The ability to review personal performance is an important part of skill development for sportspeople of every level, from novice through to elite athlete.

You should have been planning for this review from the beginning of this unit. You will not have sufficient information and evidence to complete this topic if you have not prepared for it by recording your evidence as discussed in Topic 3.3. You need to consider all of the areas discussed in this topic in order to satisfy the requirements for this part of your assessment.

Performance

In Assessment activity 3.3 you demonstrated techniques and skills that you had learnt in your two chosen activities. You now need to reflect on how well these demonstrations went. You can do this by getting feedback from a variety of sources and considering your strengths and areas for development.

Feedback

Feedback can come from a number of sources (e.g. yourself, your peers, your instructor, coach or tutor). Remember that other performers also have to carry out a review on someone else, so you should be able to get feedback from the person who is reviewing you.

Feedback is an essential part of the learning process and can be given and received in verbal, written or visual forms. It should be positive and constructive. Feedback is most effective when the performer is in a safe, comfortable environment, which often requires some thought in an adventurous environment. Feedback should be given as close to the end of a performance or session as possible, while the information is still fresh in the mind of the performer. The performer should however, be given time to digest their own internal feedback first.

A 'praise burger' approach works well as a method for giving feedback: start with a positive point, then give constructive criticism, before ending on another positive point. It is hoped that this will send the performer away knowing what they need to improve, and with an idea of how they can achieve this, yet feeling positive and motivated enough to act on it.

Your strengths and areas for development

There will be parts of your performance you will consider to have been your strong points. There may be other aspects of your performance which you do not feel went so well. These should be identified as your areas for development. These are also the areas you need to consider when you are reviewing another person on your course.

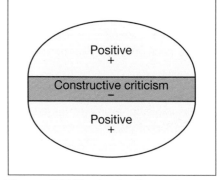

Figure 3.5 The 'praise burger' approach

You need to consider strengths and areas for development in terms of:

▶ Your plan – what you planned to carry out in both of your chosen activities. You will have decided in advance what skills and techniques you will be using. Your tutor will have set appropriate challenges to test your ability to select and use your techniques skilfully.

▶ The National Governing Body guidelines for your activities. Depending on which two activities you have chosen, these may have been your starting point to identify what is required. This will link to the work you will have done in Topics 3.1 and 3.2.

Over to you!

Check that you have a system in place for obtaining feedback on your performance from someone else.

Whatever your chosen activity, feedback is required to improve performance.

Setting SMART targets

These are clearly identified targets for progression that you should set yourself once you have reviewed your performances. These should be:

▶ **S**pecific to your chosen activities, for example ascending a particular climbing route would be specific for climbing.

▶ **M**easurable, for example measuring the improvement (e.g. faster, further, smoother) of your ascent of a set climb.

▶ **A**chievable within the time you have available.

▶ **R**ealistic, both in terms of your ability and the time you have available (e.g. choose a climb that is challenging, yet achievable).

▶ **T**ime-bound, in other words you need to give yourself a time limit by which you will achieve your target.

Development plans

Part of your assessment is based on how you plan to develop your skills and progress in this area. You should do this using the SMART targets discussed above.

You should be looking particularly at development opportunities. These will include any specific training that could be undertaken and any relevant courses that are available. If you are considering a possible career in this area then this development plan would be very useful and relevant for you, as discussed above.

Assessment activity 3.4 (P6, P7, M5, D3)

The final assessment activity of this unit requires you to review your own and another person's performance in two outdoor and adventurous activities. You are required to:

1. Review the performance of another person participating in two outdoor and adventurous activities. You should identify the strengths and areas for improvement observed in each performance. Produce and complete a detailed review form or feedback report as evidence for this task.

2. Using the review form or report structure from task 1, reflect on your own performance in outdoor and adventurous activities, identifying and explaining strengths and areas for improvement.

3. Make and justify some recommendations relating to the areas for improvement that you have identified in task 2.

Topic check

1 How many reviews in total will you be required to carry out?

2 Why is reviewing an important part of your skill development?

3 Who should you go to in order to obtain feedback?

4 In what forms might you give or receive feedback?

5 Why will your tutor be setting you appropriate challenges during your practical performance?

6 Explain the 'praise burger' approach.

7 What are SMART targets? Say what each of the letters stands for.

8 What two particular development opportunities are possibilities for you?

Assessment summary

The overall grade you achieve for this unit depends on how well you meet the grading criteria set out In Appendix 1 (see page 293). You must complete:

- all of the P criteria to achieve a **pass** grade
- all of the P and the M criteria to achieve a **merit** grade
- all of the P, M and D criteria to achieve a **distinction** grade.

Your tutor will assess your work, which should provide evidence to demonstrate that you have achieved each of the assessment criteria. Remember that you MUST provide evidence for all of the P criteria to pass the unit. Always ask your tutor to explain any assignment tasks or assessment criteria you don't understand. Good luck with Unit 3!

Grading criteria	You need to demonstrate that you can:	Have you got the evidence?
P1	Describe the organisation and provision of two outdoor and adventurous activities	
M1	Compare the organisation and provision of two outdoor and adventurous activities	
P2	Describe the health and safety considerations associated with participation in two outdoor and adventurous activities	
M2	Explain health and safety considerations associated with participation in two outdoor and adventurous activities, identifying precautions and actions than can be taken, or used, in relation to them	
D1	Explain precautions and actions that can be taken, or used, in relation to health and safety considerations associated with participation in two outdoor and adventurous activities	
P3	Produce a risk assessment for a selected outdoor and adventurous activity	
P4	Describe environmental impacts associated with participation in two outdoor and adventurous activities	
M3	Explain the environmental impacts associated with participation in two outdoor and adventurous activities, identifying precautions and actions that can be taken, or used, to reduce them	
D2	Explain precautions and actions that can be taken, or used, to reduce the environmental impacts associated with participation in two outdoor and adventurous activities	
P5	Demonstrate techniques and skills appropriate to two outdoor and adventurous activities	
M4	Review and justify choice of techniques demonstrated in outdoor and adventurous activities	
P6	Review the performance of another individual participating in two outdoor and adventurous activities, identifying strengths and areas of improvement	
P7	Carry out a review of own performance in outdoor and adventurous activities, identifying strengths and areas for improvement	
M5	Explain identified strengths and areas for improvement in own performance in outdoor and adventurous activities, making recommendations for further development of identified areas for improvement	
D3	Justify recommendations relating to identified areas for improvement in own performance in outdoor and adventurous activities	

4 Anatomy and physiology for sport (Unit 4)

Unit outline

Our bodies are the tools that allow us to perform physical activities. A healthy body enables us to lead an active life, and to train and participate in sports. It is therefore important that we understand how our bodies work and which body systems are being used at different times. This unit looks at the four main body systems that enable us to be active and successful performers.

This is a basic introduction to anatomy and physiology. Some of the terms may seem quite complex, so it is important to relate them to practical situations to help your understanding.

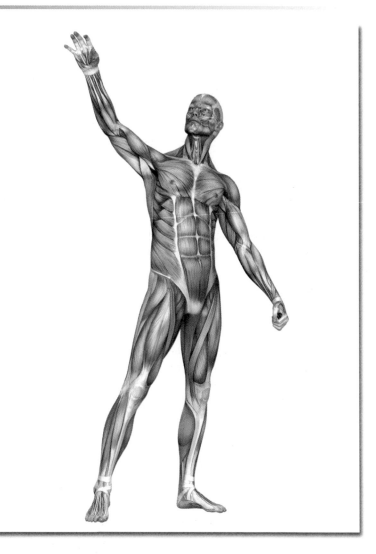

Learning outcomes

1 **Know the structure and function of the skeletal system.**
2 **Know the structure and function of the muscular system.**
3 **Know the structure and function of the cardiovascular system.**
4 **Know the structure and function of the respiratory system.**

The structure and function of the skeletal system

▶ Getting started

Your skeleton is the basic frame of your body and it is important that you know its structure and the different functions it performs. It is made up of over 200 bones, the main ones of which are shown in the diagram below.

When you have completed this topic, you should know:

- the structure of the human skeletal system
- the functions of the skeletal system
- about the different joints
- how the bones and joints move.

Structure of the skeletal system

The diagram of the skeletal system gives you an idea of its overall structure and you can see the location of the major bones. Although there are many other bones in the body (more than half of them – 106 to be precise – are in your hands and feet!) you do not need to know about them specifically.

You can clearly see from the diagram that there are different types of bones. These can be divided into four categories:

1. *long bones* – such as the femur, which is your longest bone

2. *short bones* – such as those in your hands and feet

3. *flat, or plate, bones* – such as those in the pelvis and the ribcage

4. *irregular bones* – such as those in the spine (vertebrae).

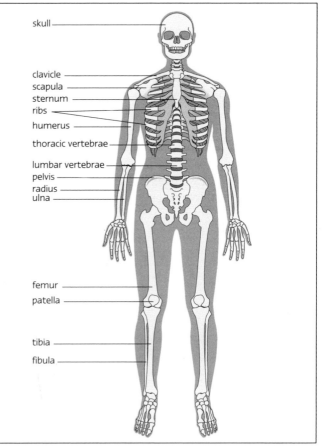

Figure 4.1 The main bones in the human body

Function of the skeletal system

It is very important to know the five functions of the skeletal system. You will need to be aware of how they are actively involved when you are performing movements.

Protection

All of the vital organs in your body are protected by bones. Your brain is encased within your skull, and your heart and lungs are behind your ribs. Without this basic protection any blows to the body would cause very serious injuries.

Movement

This is achieved through the joints. However, you must remember that the bones do not move on their own – movement only occurs through the combined action of bones with muscles. The role of the muscles is discussed in Topic 4.2.

Shape

As the framework of your body, your skeleton also gives you your basic shape. It determines your height and contributes to other aspects of your size and shape. Muscles and body fat are other factors that contribute to your shape and size.

Activity

Examine three different sports and consider the physical characteristics required for an athlete to be a successful performer in these. Clearly identify which sports an athlete will be suitable for because of their skeletal structure. Think about size, height and the forces that are exerted.

Support

The skeleton keeps everything in place and provides support for muscles and some of the other more delicate vital organs. It is the framework around which our bodies are constructed and without it our bodies would collapse.

Blood production

Red blood cells (which carry oxygen) and white blood cells (which protect against infection) are produced in the bone marrow of some bones.

Activity

Using the internet or available books, try to find out how many blood cells are produced each day and how many are destroyed. Also try to find out how much blood an average person has in their body.

Joints

A joint is where two or more bones meet. There are over 100 joints in the body but, like the bones, you do not have to learn them all! Joints are classified into three main groups:

1. *Fixed joints* – these are also sometimes referred to as immovable joints. The main examples are those in the pelvis and the skull.

2. *Slightly moveable joints* – as the name suggests, some movement occurs at these joints. The main examples are the vertebrae in the spine.

3. *Freely moveable or synovial joints* – these are the most common joints in the body. This group can be divided further into the following types of joint:

 ▶ gliding joints – such as those in the hands and feet (Figure 4.2)

 ▶ hinge joints – such as the elbow and the knee (Figure 4.3)

 ▶ pivot joints – such as the top of the neck and the bottom end of the arm (Figure 4.4)

 ▶ ball and socket joints – such as the hip and the shoulder (Figure 4.5)

 ▶ condyloid joints – such as the wrist (Figure 4.6).

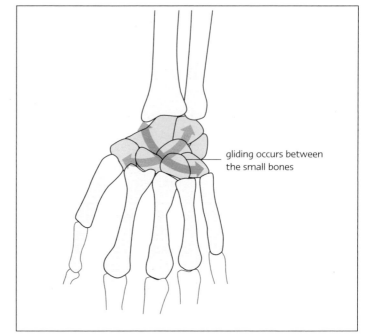

gliding occurs between the small bones

Figure 4.2 Gliding joints in the hand

> ## Activity
>
> Work with a partner to name and identify as many joints as you can on each other's bodies. While you are doing this, see what types of basic movements are possible at these joints.

The knee is the largest and most complex of all the joints (see Figure 4.3). As most of our movements involve the legs in some way, particularly in sporting activities, the knee is subject to a lot of 'wear and tear' and it is a common place for injuries to occur.

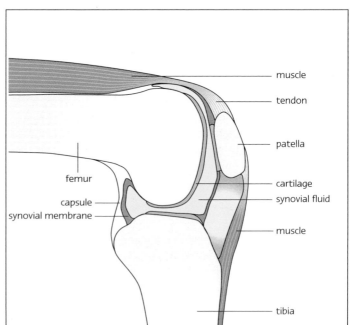

muscle
tendon
patella
femur
cartilage
synovial fluid
capsule
synovial membrane
muscle
tibia

Figure 4.3 The knee is a hinge joint.

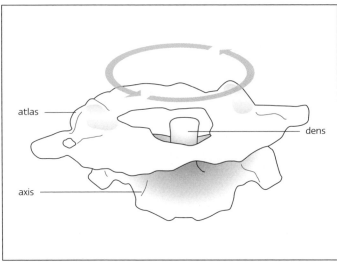

Figure 4.4 The pivot joint in your neck allows you to turn your head.

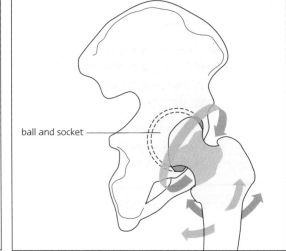

Figure 4.5 The hip is a ball and socket joint.

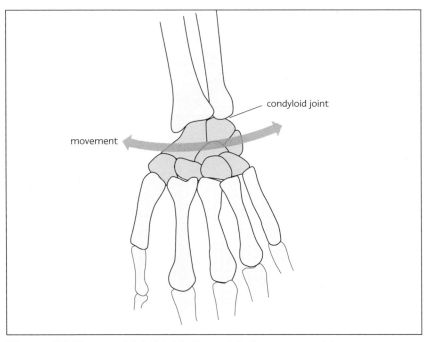

Figure 4.6 The condyloid joint in the wrist allows some sideways movement.

 **Activity**

Using examples from football, clearly identify the joints that are involved in the following actions: crossing the ball, a throw in, a penalty, heading the ball from a corner.

Movement

Just about every movement the body makes has a specific technical name, especially the major ones involved in sporting movements. However, you only need to know the basic movements explained below. You will need to be able to identify these movements and explain which movements occur during physical activity.

The main movements are:

▶ *Flexion* is where the angle between the two bones is decreased, such as when you bend your arm at the elbow.

▶ *Extension* is where the angle between the two bones is increased, such as when you straighten your arm at the elbow.

> Flexion and extension are opposite movements. Kicking a football involves flexion and extension: preparing by swinging the leg back is flexion, and straightening the leg to kick the ball is extension.

▶ *Abduction* is the movement of a bone or limb away from the body, such as raising your arm away from the side of your body.

▶ *Adduction* is the movement of a bone or limb towards the body, such as bringing your raised arm back in towards the side of your body.

> A useful way to remember the difference between *adduction* and *abduction* is that if you *add* something you are putting it in and if you *abduct* someone you would be taking them away. Figure 4.7 is a good illustration of both adduction and abduction. The movement shown by the arrows aiming inwards is adduction and the arrows pointing away show abduction.

Figure 4.7 Adduction and abduction

▶ *Rotation* is where the bone is able to move around in an arc, such as at the shoulder when you rotate your arm, e.g. when performing a tennis serve.

▶ *Circumduction* is a combination of flexion, extension, adduction and abduction in a circular movement, e.g. when a pitcher winds up to deliver a ball in softball.

Activity

Try to identify the six different movements as they occur. You can do this when you are watching sports performers on television, or you can do it with teammates when you are training.

Set yourself the target of finding one example of each of the movements, and record them so that you can include them as examples in your notes file.

Topic check

1 Name the four different types of bones in your body.
2 Give an example of the skeleton providing protection.
3 Give an example of the skeleton allowing movement.
4 What are the other three functions the skeleton performs?
5 Identify the three different groups of joints.
6 Give one example of a ball and socket joint.
7 Give one example of a hinge joint.
8 What type of joint is the knee?
9 Which two movements occur when the arm is bent and straightened?
10 Identify the two movements that would occur if you were doing star jumps.

The structure and function of the muscular system

▶ Getting started

Remember that the muscular system has to work together with the skeletal system, as outlined in Topic 4.1. Movement can only take place when the two body systems work together, when they are known as the **musculoskeletal system**. The main muscles in the body are shown in Figure 4.8.

When you have completed this topic, you should know:

- the major muscles in the human body
- the different types of muscles
- how the muscles move.

🗝 Key terms

Cardiac muscles: the muscles in the heart

Involuntary muscles: muscles that work automatically, e.g. those in the walls of the intestines

Musculoskeletal system: the muscles and skeleton when they work together to cause movement

Skeletal muscles: muscles that are under voluntary control (you choose to move them) and attached to the skeleton, e.g. biceps

Major muscles

There are approximately 639 **skeletal muscles** on the body, but you will be pleased to know that you do not have to know them all! You only need to be able to identify the ones shown in the diagram and know where they are located on the body.

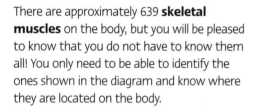

💡 Over to you!

Write the name of each of the muscles identified in the diagram on a sticky note. With a partner, practise putting these on the correct muscle.

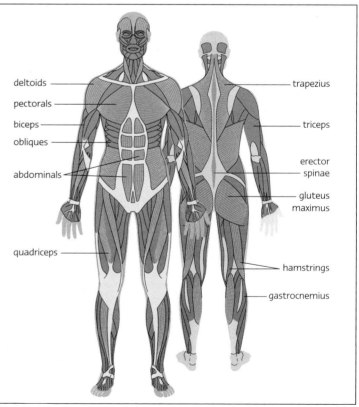

deltoids
pectorals
biceps
obliques
abdominals
quadriceps

trapezius
triceps
erector spinae
gluteus maximus
hamstrings
gastrocnemius

Figure 4.8 The skeletal muscles in the human body

Types of muscles

There are three different types of muscle.

1. *Voluntary* or *skeletal muscles* are attached to the skeleton and make up the majority of the muscles. They are under your conscious control through the nervous system and you can move them at will. These are the muscles shown in Figure 4.8.

2. Involuntary muscles or *smooth muscles* are the muscles that you cannot control and that contract and relax automatically. They are found in the digestive and circulatory systems.

3. *Heart* or **cardiac muscles** are a specific type of muscle that is found only in the wall of the heart. They are also a type of involuntary muscle as they are constantly contracting and relaxing. It would not be possible for you to stop your heart beating at will!

Muscle structure

Figure 4.9 shows the structure of a skeletal muscle. You may also have the opportunity to look at some slides under a microscope to see the differences between the three different types of muscle.

The muscle fibres present in all voluntary muscles can be one of two types:

▶ *fast-twitch fibres* – these are white and work quickly for short-term power and strength activities

▶ *slow-twitch fibres* – these are red, with a good oxygen supply, and contract slowly for long-term endurance activities and events.

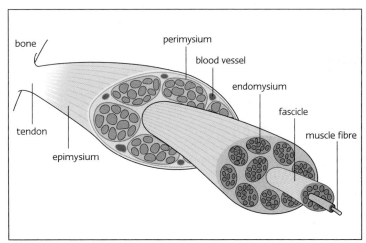

Figure 4.9 The structure of a skeletal muscle

The number of fast- and slow-twitch fibres in our bodies is hereditary, so no amount of training can affect their levels. This is why someone with a high percentage of fast-twitch fibres is likely to be a very good sprinter. Someone with a high percentage of slow-twitch fibres is more likely to be a good marathon runner.

Muscle function

The three different types of muscles have different functions.

▶ Voluntary (skeletal) muscles allow movement to occur.

▶ Involuntary (smooth) muscles contract automatically to allow vital bodily functions to continue.

▶ Heart (cardiac) muscles enable the heart to continue to beat and enable the cardiovascular system to function – see Topic 4.3 for full details.

Activity

The standing long jump is a power test. Each member of the group should perform a standing long jump to estimate who has the most fast twitch muscle in their quadriceps and gluteus maximus. Identify who in the group can jump the furthest.

Muscle movements

The only muscles that move to any great extent are the voluntary muscles. It is important that you understand how these movements occur and are able to identify them.

Figure 4.10 Muscle movements

Muscle	Location	Example of movement
Biceps	Upper arm, front	Bending and straightening at the elbow
Triceps	Upper arm, back	Bending and straightening at the elbow
Deltoids	Shoulder, front and rear	Raising and lowering the arm
Trapezius	Neck and upper back	Shoulder movement and raising and lowering the head
Pectorals	Front, upper chest	Raising the arms
Abdominals	Front of the stomach	Bending at the waist
Obliques	Both sides of the stomach	Sideways twisting movements
Gluteus maximus	Lower back by the bottom	Walking and running actions and bending and straightening the legs
Quadriceps	Upper front of the leg	Straightening the leg
Hamstrings	Upper back of the leg	Bending at the knee
Gastrocnemius	Rear of leg, at the back, bottom	Walking, running, jumping and pointing the toes
Erector spinae	Lower back	Bending – supports the spine

Antagonistic pairs

It is very important to remember that muscles can only pull, they cannot push. Because of this they are always arranged in pairs, so that one can contract (get smaller) and the other can relax (become longer) to allow a movement. The pair of muscles then reverse their roles to allow the opposite movement to happen (see Figure 4.11).

As the elbow bends (flexion) the bicep is the agonist, with the triceps as the antagonist. Then, when the elbow straightens (extension), the opposite occurs.

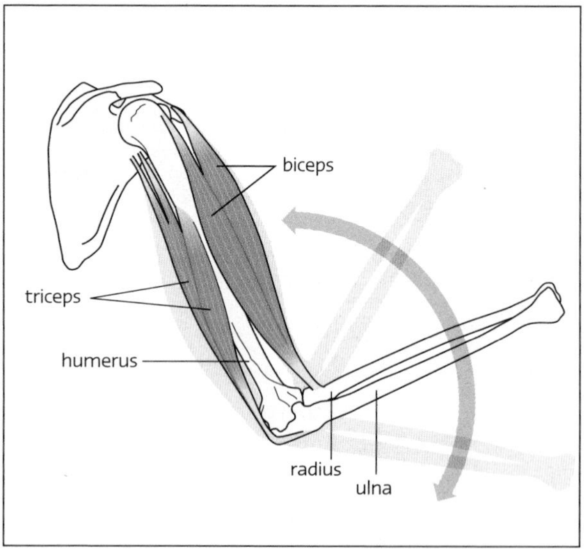

Some others specific terms that apply to muscle movements are:

▶ *antagonist* – the muscle which relaxes and lengthens

▶ *agonist* (or prime mover) – the muscle which contracts and shortens

▶ *synergist* – the other muscles that help in the movement, also sometimes known as the 'helper' muscles

▶ *origin* – the end of the muscle which is fixed to the bone that moves least in a joint

▶ *insertion* – the end of the muscle which is fixed to the bone that moves most, and which is at the opposite end of the muscle to the origin.

Figure 4.11 Movement at the elbow joint

Types of contraction

Muscles have to contract in order to allow movement. There are different types of contraction.

▶ Concentric contractions – the muscle shortens when performing an action, and the ends of the muscle move closer together.

▶ Eccentric contraction – the muscle lengthens under tension. and the ends of the muscle move further apart.

▶ Isometric contraction – the muscle stays the same length. There is tension in the muscle but the distance between the ends stays the same.

Case study

John is in the early stages of his training to become a health fitness instructor. He is working with a fully qualified colleague, presenting part of his first practical session. John has a group of ten people in the fitness suite where he has been given the job of explaining how to use some of the weight training machines. John's colleague is going to assess him on how well he explains how the musculoskeletal system is involved when training with weights. John has been asked not only to prepare a talk but also to produce some diagrams or other resources to help him explain.

1. What are the main points John needs to explain about the skeletal system?

2. What are the main points John needs to explain regarding the muscular system?

3. Suggest two diagrams, or other resources, John could bring along to the session to help explain his points.

4. How do you think John could fully prepare himself before he has to take this session?

Assessment activity 4.1 (P1, P2, P3, P4, M1, M2, D1)

You are training to be a health and fitness instructor, and know that it is important to have knowledge and understanding of the structure and function of the body systems. As part of your training programme, you are required to:

• Describe the structure and function of the skeletal system.

• Describe the different types of joint and the movements allowed at each.

• Explain the movements occurring at two synovial

joints during four different types of physical activity.

• Identify the major muscles of the body.

• Describe the different types of muscle and muscle movements.

• Give examples of three different types of muscular contraction relating to three different types of physical activity.

• Analyse the musculoskeletal actions occurring during four different types of physical activity.

Topic check

1 Name the three different types of muscle.
2 Identify the two different types of muscle fibre, and explain which type of activity they benefit most.
3 Which muscle acts to raise and lower the arm?
4 What are 'antagonistic pairs'?
5 Describe the function a synergist muscle performs.
6 Explain the difference between the origin and the insertion of a muscle.
7 What are the three different types of muscle contraction?

The structure and function of the cardiovascular system

The cardiovascular system is a combination of the circulatory system and the respiratory system working together. The respiratory system is dealt with in more detail in Topic 4.4, but it is important to understand that these two systems work together to enable your body to work effectively. This is particularly important during training and performing when the demands you are making are greater.

The most vital component of the cardiovascular system is the heart, which is clearly labelled in Figure 4.12.

When you have completed this topic, you should know:

- the structure of the cardiovascular system
- the function of the cardiovascular system.

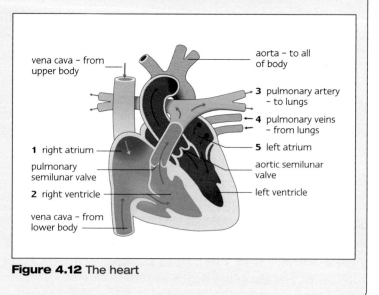

Figure 4.12 The heart

(Labels in figure: vena cava – from upper body; aorta – to all of body; 3 pulmonary artery – to lungs; 4 pulmonary veins – from lungs; 1 right atrium; 5 left atrium; pulmonary semilunar valve; aortic semilunar valve; 2 right ventricle; left ventricle; vena cava – from lower body)

🔑 Key terms

Haemoglobin: the part of the red blood cell that carries oxygen

Thermoregulation: the way the body maintains its temperature

Structure of the cardiovascular system

The heart is basically a pump. It works with the blood and the blood vessels to make up the circulatory system. You can see in Figure 4.12 that there are several main blood vessels leading into and out of the heart: the aorta, pulmonary vein, pulmonary artery and vena cava. Their main function is to supply the body with oxygen and remove carbon dioxide. In Figure 4.12 the red areas show the blood carrying the oxygen to the body and the blue areas show the blood carrying the carbon dioxide away from the body. Figure 4.13 (page 98) describes the flow of blood around the body, as per the numbered labels on Figure 4.12.

The blood

Your blood is made up of several different components:

▶ *Red blood cells* – these are extremely small and carry oxygen to where the body needs it. They are coloured red because they contain the pigment called **haemoglobin**.

▶ *White blood cells* – these are the body's main defence against infection and disease. They are not as plentiful as red blood cells. They are transparent cells in the blood plasma (see below) and some can produce antibodies that protect the body from infection.

▶ *Platelets* – these help the blood to clot. They are small fragments or particles of larger cells. They can help to seal the skin, and perform the same function on damaged blood vessels.

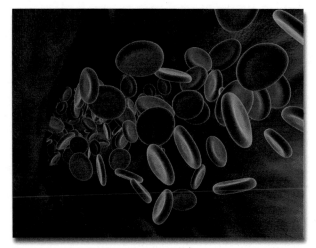
Red blood cells carry oxygen.

▶ *Plasma* – this makes up the remaining 55% of the blood. It is a liquid mainly made up of water. It also contains fibrinogen, protein (to assist in clotting) and nutrients such as glucose and some carbon dioxide and oxygen.

Blood vessels

All of your blood has to flow through blood vessels. There are different types of blood vessel:

▶ *Arteries* – these have relatively thick walls and carry the blood at high pressure away from the heart. They have no valves and have more elastic walls than veins. They subdivide into smaller vessels called arterioles.

▶ *Veins* – these carry venous, or deoxygenated, blood back to the heart and they have thinner walls than arteries. They are also far less elastic. Veins have valves to make sure that the blood is not able to flow backwards through the vein.

▶ *Venuoles* – these branch off the veins and link to the capillaries. They drain the deoxygenated blood from the capillaries and take it to the veins to return to the heart.

▶ *Capillaries* – these are microscopic vessels that link the arteries with the veins. They are very narrow and allow carbon dioxide, oxygen, nutrients and waste products to pass through their thin walls.

You will learn more about how the blood vessels link to the respiratory system in Topic 4.4.

Over to you!

You can get an idea about the rate of blood flow through your arteries by checking your pulse. There are four pulse points where you can do this. The easiest two are on the inside of your wrist or on the side of your neck. These points are where major arteries are closest to the surface, and the pulsing movement you feel is the blood flowing though at force.

Activity

Everyone in the group should find out their resting heart rate, a basic indicator of fitness. To do this, feel for your pulse and count the number of beats in 15 seconds. Multiply this by 4 to get your heart rate. Once everyone has done this, compare your results and see what the differences are. Find the class average and see how you compare.

Function of the cardiovascular system

The cardiovascular system has three main functions:

1. *Transport* – this is how the blood, water, oxygen and nutrients are carried throughout the body. It is also how the waste is transported and removed. The blood transports oxygen from the lungs to the body's tissues, and then carries carbon dioxide back to the lungs to be breathed out. Oxygen is a limiting factor in many sports performances – once a performer has taken on as much oxygen as they can their performance cannot improve any further.

2. *Temperature control and regulation* – the body temperature is controlled as the blood absorbs the body heat and carries it to the lungs. From there it is taken to the skin where it is released through the veins and capillaries. This is also known as **thermoregulation**. The blood vessels widen (known as vasodilation) to allow this process to take place, and then they return to their normal size and become narrow again (known as vasoconstriction). Sports performance can suffer if athletes cannot regulate their temperature properly, for example, in the marathon athletes sometimes suffer dehydration and heatstroke.

3. *Protection* – antibodies that fight infection are carried in the blood. This helps with the process of clotting blood to seal wounds.

The blood flow through the heart to the body and the lungs is shown in Figure 4.13. You can see that oxygen is taken up and carbon dioxide is 'unloaded' at point 3 (see label 3 on Figure 4.12).

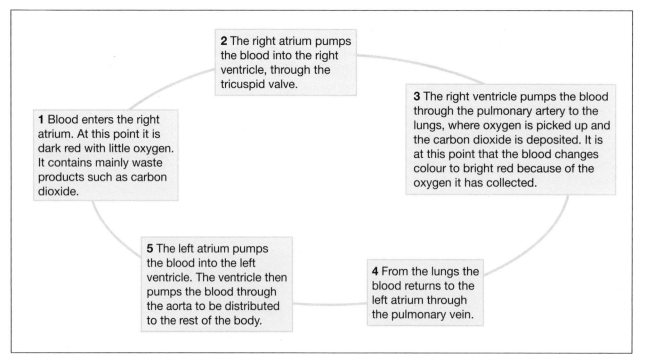

1 Blood enters the right atrium. At this point it is dark red with little oxygen. It contains mainly waste products such as carbon dioxide.

2 The right atrium pumps the blood into the right ventricle, through the tricuspid valve.

3 The right ventricle pumps the blood through the pulmonary artery to the lungs, where oxygen is picked up and the carbon dioxide is deposited. It is at this point that the blood changes colour to bright red because of the oxygen it has collected.

4 From the lungs the blood returns to the left atrium through the pulmonary vein.

5 The left atrium pumps the blood into the left ventricle. The ventricle then pumps the blood through the aorta to be distributed to the rest of the body.

Figure 4.13 Blood flow around the body

Activity

Search the internet for websites that show an animation of blood being pumped through the heart, flowing through the different blood vessels. Seeing this in action will give you a far better idea of what happens. Discuss reasons why people may have a better performance because of their cardiovascular system.

Topic check

1   How many chambers make up the heart?
2   What are the names of these chambers?
3   What type of blood flows through the aorta?
4   Where does the pulmonary artery take blood to?
5   Explain the main function of the heart.
6   Identify the four different components of the blood.
7   Which component carries oxygen within it?
8   Name the three different types of blood vessels.
9   Describe the three main functions of the cardiovascular system.
10 What is the difference between vasodilation and vasoconstriction?

The structure and function of the respiratory system

▶ Getting started

It is important to remember that the respiratory system works together with cardiovascular system, which is covered in Topic 4.3. It is the respiratory system which allows us to take in oxygen to be carried though the blood to provide all the energy we need to function properly. When you train or perform you will need greater amounts of oxygen, as the demand will increase. In order to meet this demand, your rate of breathing increases.

When you have completed this topic, you should know:

- the structure of the respiratory system
- the function of the respiratory system.

🔑 Key terms

Alveoli: tiny air sacs within the lungs where the exchange of oxygen and carbon dioxide occurs

Lung capacity: the amount of air (oxygen, nitrogen and carbon dioxide) that your lungs can hold

Structure of the respiratory system

Oxygen is initially breathed in through air passages. These consist of the following:

- ▶ *Nasal passages* – the air enters here through the nostrils.

- ▶ *Mouth* – air also enters here, but it is separated from the nostrils by the palate. It is this which allows you to eat and breathe at the same time.

- ▶ *Epiglottis* – this is a flap of tissue at the base of the tongue which keeps food from going into the trachea.

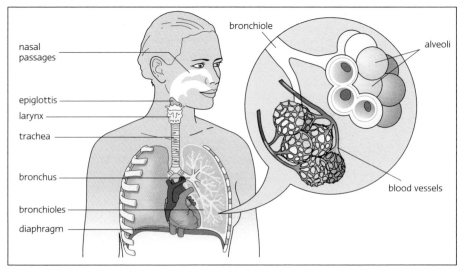

Figure 4.14 The respiratory system

▶ *Trachea* – this is commonly known as the 'windpipe'. It is made up of rings of cartilage.

▶ *Bronchus* – this is at the base of the trachea. It branches out into the two smaller tubes known as the right and left bronchus.

▶ *Bronchioles* – the bronchi in turn branch out into smaller tubes called bronchioles.

▶ **Alveoli** – these are the air sacs where the bronchioles subdivide. There are literally millions of alveoli, and it is here that the exchange of oxygen and carbon dioxide takes place.

While the air is being breathed in via the air passages, two muscles assist in the process:

▶ *The diaphragm* – this is a large, dome-shaped muscle sheet under the lungs, which seals the chest cavity from the abdominal cavity.

▶ *The intercostal muscles* – these connect the ribs and allow them to move. There are two types: the internal intercostal muscles and the external intercostal muscles.

The lungs are the main organs for breathing. They are protected inside the chest cavity by the ribs at the back, side and front. The diaphragm is situated below them. The lungs have a very large surface area, which enables oxygen to transfer quickly into the blood.

Function of the respiratory system

The primary function of the respiratory system is to allow breathing to take place and to take oxygen into the body and then remove the carbon dioxide.

Mechanics of breathing

There are two distinct movements in breathing:

1. *Inspiration*, breathing in, happens when the intercostal muscles contract, lifting the ribs upwards and outwards. At the same time, the diaphragm becomes flatter and moves downwards. This makes the chest cavity larger, which reduces the pressure inside the cavity and causes air to be sucked into the lungs.

2. *Expiration*, breathing out, is the reverse of the inspiration process. The diaphragm relaxes at the same time as the intercostal muscles. The chest cavity returns to its normal size and the pressure on the lungs is increased, forcing the air out.

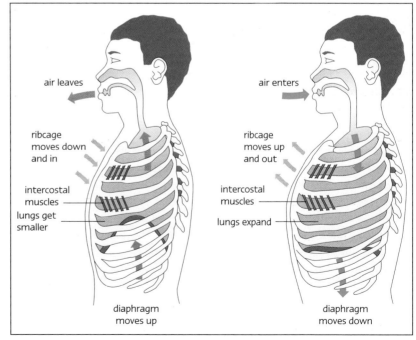

air leaves

ribcage moves down and in

intercostal muscles

lungs get smaller

diaphragm moves up

air enters

ribcage moves up and out

intercostal muscles

lungs expand

diaphragm moves down

Figure 4.15 How we breathe

Activity

Using balloons, identify who in the group can blow the largest balloon from one breath. What information does this reveal and how does this relate to sport? Is there a difference between genders? Are the people with the largest **lung capacity** the fittest people in the class?

Over to you!

Sit down and put your hands on the sides of your stomach, just below the bottom rib of your rib cage. Take a deep breath in, hold it for several seconds and then breathe out. You will feel your whole ribcage move upwards, pulled by your intercostal muscles. You will also feel your stomach move in as your diaphragm moves down. You will then feel all of this reverse as you breathe out.

Gaseous exchange

This is the process that allows oxygen to be taken from the air and be exchanged for carbon dioxide. You can see this process in Figure 4.16.

Over to you!

Examine your breathing rate at rest for a minute. The number of breaths you take may be an indication of your fitness level. Discuss your findings with the rest of the class. Is there a difference between your results and the class average? What do your results mean?

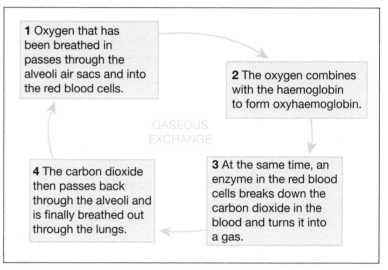

1 Oxygen that has been breathed in passes through the alveoli air sacs and into the red blood cells.

2 The oxygen combines with the haemoglobin to form oxyhaemoglobin.

GASEOUS EXCHANGE

4 The carbon dioxide then passes back through the alveoli and is finally breathed out through the lungs.

3 At the same time, an enzyme in the red blood cells breaks down the carbon dioxide in the blood and turns it into a gas.

Figure 4.16 The process of gaseous exchange

Case study

John is entering the second stage of his training to become a fitness instructor. Having successfully presented his first session, John now has the task of making a presentation about the cardiorespiratory system. John has decided that he will do this in the fitness suite using the aerobic exercise machines, including cross-trainers, treadmills and rowing machines. Once again, John is going to be assessed on how well he can explain the functions of the cardiovascular and respiratory systems. He has also been asked to prepare some resources to use with his group, and to demonstrate the different effects that using the machines will have on the two body systems.

1. What main points does John need to explain regarding the cardiovascular system?

2. What main points does John need to explain regarding the respiratory system?

3. What two resources would you suggest John puts together to help with his presentation?

4. What sorts of things do you think John is going to be able to demonstrate when using the exercise machines?

5. What additional preparation should John carry out before taking this session?

Assessment activity 4.2 (P5, P6, M3 and D2)

Your training as a health fitness instructor continues. Having studied and explained the musculoskeletal system, you are now required to demonstrate your understanding of the cardiorespiratory system. You should:

- Describe the structure and function of the cardiovascular system.

- Describe the structure and function of the respiratory system.
- Explain how the cardiovascular and respiratory systems work together to supply the body with oxygen.
- Evaluate how the cardiovascular system and respiratory system work together to supply the body with oxygen and remove carbon dioxide.

Topic check

1 Identify the three aspects of the respiratory system.
2 What immediate effect does training have on the respiratory system?
3 Explain the function of the epiglottis.
4 What is the windpipe more correctly known as?
5 Describe what happens in the alveoli.
6 What is the diaphragm and where is it?
7 Where are the intercostal muscles located?
8 Explain the difference between the right and left lungs.
9 Identify the two movements in breathing.
10 What is meant by 'gaseous exchange'?

Assessment summary

The overall grade you achieve for this unit depends on how well you meet the grading criteria set out in Appendix 1 (see page 294). You must complete:

- all of the P criteria to achieve a **pass** grade
- all of the P and the M criteria to achieve a **merit** grade
- all of the P, M and D criteria to achieve a **distinction** grade.

Your tutor will assess the assessment activities that you complete for this unit. The work you produce should provide evidence which demonstrates that you have achieved each of the assessment criteria. The table below identifies what you need to demonstrate to meet each of the pass, merit and distinction criteria for this unit. You should always check and self-assess your work before you submit your assignments for marking.

Remember that you MUST provide evidence for all of the P criteria to pass the unit.

Grading criteria	You need to demonstrate that you can:	Have you got the evidence?
P1	Describe the structure and function of the skeletal system	
P2	Describe the different types of joint and the movements allowed at each	
M1	Explain the movements occurring at two synovial joints during four different types of physical activity	
P3	Identify the major muscles of the body	
P4	Describe the different types of muscle and muscle movements	
M2	Give examples of three different types of muscular contraction relating to three different types of physical activity	
D1	Analyse the musculoskeletal actions occurring at four synovial joints during four different types of physical activity	
P5	Describe the structure and function of the cardiovascular system	
P6	Describe the structure and function of the respiratory system	
M3	Explain how the cardiovascular and respiratory systems work together to supply the body with oxygen	
D2	Evaluate how the cardiovascular system and respiratory system work together to supply the body with oxygen and remove carbon dioxide	

Always ask your tutor to explain any assignment tasks or assessment criteria that you don't understand fully. Being clear about the task before you begin gives you the best chance succeeding. Good luck with your Unit 4 assessment work!

5 Injury in sport (Unit 5)

Unit outline

Most people who participate regularly in sport will suffer some form of injury at some time. This unit will give you an understanding of the types of injuries that are most likely to occur in sport. The old saying 'Prevention is better than cure' is very true, so you will be given guidance on how to reduce the risk of injuries, as well as how to deal with some injuries if they do occur. The issues of health and safety and risk assessment are important aspects of prevention which you will learn more about in this unit.

It is important to remember that completing this unit is not going to make you an expert – injuries should always be dealt with by fully qualified people, such as paramedics or doctors. However, you should be able to identify an injury and then decide upon the correct course of action to take.

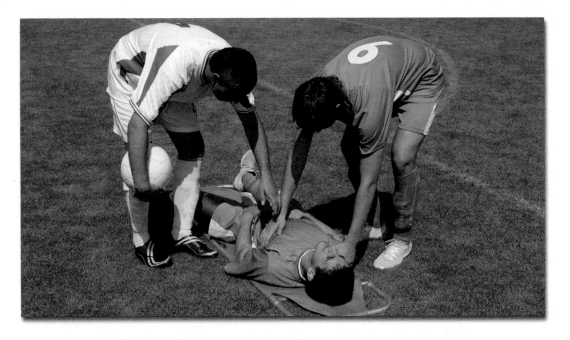

Learning outcomes

1 Know the different types of injuries and illness associated with sports participation.
2 Be able to deal with injuries and illnesses associated with sports participation.
3 Know the risks and hazards associated with sports participation.
4 Be able to undertake a risk assessment relevant to sport.

Types of injuries and illnesses associated with sports participation

Getting started

Completing this topic will give you some knowledge of possible injuries and illnesses associated with sports participation. However, it will not enable you to give a correct **diagnosis** every time. When you have completed this topic, you should know:

- some of the possible causes of injury
- some of the possible types of injury
- some of the possible types and signs of illness.

Key terms

Abrasion: a scrape on the skin, often the result of rubbing

Diagnosis: the identification of illnesses or injuries

Lever: a rigid bar which rotates around a pivot point

Ligaments: strong fibrous bands which stabilise joints and control movement

Load: any unit of weight

Muscle tone: tension that is maintained in the muscles, even at rest

Symptom: a sign or indication of a particular medical condition

Tendon: fibrous tissue which joins muscle to bone

Tennis elbow: an inflammation of the elbow joint, caused by repeated forceful movements causing microscopic tears

Vertebrae: the group of bones that make up the spinal column (backbone)

Causes of injury

There are some common causes of injury in sport.

Loading

Loading causes injuries by putting the body under too much stress during training. Loading might actually be considered as *overloading*. Overloading is one of the principles of training (see Topic 9.1). Using this principle, you deliberately increase the amount of training you do, but you must do this gradually and in stages (known as progression) so that it is safe.

Loading should be done gradually to avoid injury.

Trying to progress too quickly, or training too often, can lead to injury. For example, if you were to lift a medium weight and then go straight on to lift a very heavy one, this is likely to result in a loading injury. Overload can also be caused by activities such as running or jumping and changing direction. If the force of the activity exceeds the force that the muscle, tendon or ligament can take, this will result in injury.

Intrinsic factors

An intrinsic factor is a personal factor that may contribute to an injury. Intrinsic factors can be divided into three types:

1. *Basic* – This includes gender, age, growth, body type, body mass and height. For example, an older person tends to have more brittle bones, which increases the chances of breaking them in any form of impact injury. Someone who has a greater body mass tends to suffer from more joint problems and injuries due to the increased load being placed upon them — this is particularly the case with the knee joints. Taller people often find themselves prone to back injuries due to the increased length of their spine. You may have some control over your body mass and be able to regulate your weight, but all of the other factors cannot be controlled by you at all.

2. *Primary* – includes misalignments, differences in leg length, muscle imbalance and lack of strength or flexibility. Working on improving your posture and flexibility through regular stretching and mobility exercises reduces the chances of misalignments and muscle imbalance. There should be a strength balance between the quadricep and hamstring muscles. If the hamstrings are too weak they are likely to suffer a muscle tear during activity. If you have one leg longer than the other, this is a factor beyond your control, but you could increase the strength in your legs.

3. *Secondary* – includes any previous injuries or illnesses. You can take measures to reduce the chance of injury and illnesses, but they are not completely avoidable. If you have had an injury or illness which has had a permanent effect (e.g. a dislocated shoulder can make the joint 'loose' and prone to further dislocations), there is little you can do about it. Previous injuries heal with scar tissue. This is less flexible than the rest of the muscle. The previous injury is usually a weak area and is more likely to suffer a repeat injury if put under pressure.

You can influence some of the factors above, but you have no control over most of them.

Over to you!

Put together a questionnaire regarding intrinsic factors that may contribute to injury. Give the questionnaire to another member of your group to complete, then interview them to identify any intrinsic factors they may have. Discuss what effects they have experienced and any injuries they may be more prone to due to these factors.

Extrinsic factors

Extrinsic factors are external factors related to the environment. There are two types of environment to consider:

1. One of the most significant factors relating to sporting injuries in the uncontrolled environment (over which you have no control) is the weather, e.g. wet grounds can be dangerous because of a risk of slipping; dry grounds can be very hard and cause impact injuries; hot weather can cause dehydration and heatstroke. Other factors to consider include coming into contact with other players, particularly in team sports. Also, in ball games, the ball itself can cause injury (e.g. in basketball fingers are often injured when trying to catch or intercept the ball).

2. The controlled environment includes any environmental factors over which you have some control. Many of these can cause injuries in sport, such as:

- the state of playing surfaces, e.g. glass or sharp objects on grass pitches or in jumping pits (you can check for these); wet, slippery floors on indoor surfaces, such as sports hall floors (these should be kept dry where possible or clearly signposted if they are known to be wet)

- equipment, which should be: appropriate for the user (e.g. a hockey goalkeeper's helmet would not be correct for a cricket batter), worn correctly (e.g. a loose strap or fitting could be dangerous to an opponent) and in good condition (e.g. referees check players' studs before soccer matches as these can injure other players if they become sharp – these studs would have to be changed before the game).

Activity

Carry out a survey of all the protective equipment which needs to be provided by your centre for the different sporting activities which are offered. You can also carry out a survey with the rest of the group to find out how many different pieces of specialist equipment are owned by them which they need for the sports they participate in. How many items do you have?

Overuse

Overuse is when a particular part of the body is used repeatedly, in the same way, over a period of time. Injuries caused by overuse are often linked to regular training. There are four main causes of overuse injury:

- the **load** being too great for the individual, e.g. using too heavy a weight during a weight-training session using resistance machines

- poor technique or posture, e.g. not keeping the back straight and the legs bent when lifting or carrying in a weight-training session or when training pushing in a rugby scrum

- faulty or poor-quality equipment, e.g. if free weights are used without a training partner to help you lift and lower them correctly. This is why the better quality equipment would be considered to be the purpose built resistance machines

▶ anatomy or posture problems, e.g. a person who is very round shouldered would find it difficult to carry out some weight training exercises as they would not be moving the weights through the whole range of movement correctly.

Overuse is a common cause of injury. These injuries tend to come on gradually, as the combined factors of training and performing constantly put a strain on the performer. The majority of people who participate in an activity regularly and at a reasonable level will suffer from some form of overuse injury at some time.

Alignment

Alignment refers to your posture or body alignment. The body is correctly aligned when it is able to maintain the correct posture. When standing, you should have a straight back, with your shoulders upright (not hunched in and stooping, known as round shouldered), stomach held firmly in and head facing forwards. Maintaining a good posture helps to reduce the chances of injury as it prevents uneven strain being placed on the body. Injury can occur, for example, when a strain is put on the knees during running if the load exerted on each leg is not equal. This might be due to the runner getting tired, so their posture and **muscle tone** are not maintained by the tired muscles. Being round shouldered can result in poor or uneven weight distribution which the legs and knees have to counteract and adjust to. The poor posture itself can be caused by the overdevelopment of some of the muscles around the shoulders.

Most people who participate in an activity regularly will suffer from an overuse injury at some point.

Intensity

Intensity is the level at which you train. If you constantly train at a very high intensity without sufficient rest this is bound to put a greater strain on some of the body systems. High-intensity training can lead to gradual muscle tears or stress fractures.

Effects of levers

Most body movements performed during sporting activities are at the major joints, such as the elbow and the knee. The joints act as **levers**, and if too much load is applied to these levers an injury may result. For example, creating the power to kick a football involves a lever action at the knee. Constantly repeating this movement under a load (the kicking movement under the weight of the ball) in training can put the joint under a lot of strain. This can result in straining the muscles being used, spraining the joints involved in the movement or, in extreme cases, even fracturing a bone or dislocating the joint.

Effects of gravity

The force of gravity is constantly pushing us all down. Gravity adds an extra force on landing in any movements where we rise and fall (e.g. running, jumping). This might only be a small force when running, but landing at the end of a triple or long jump, or after leaping up to head a football, creates a greater force. Injuries caused by this force are called impact injuries. A common example is **ligament** damage to the knees as the force of a landing is absorbed. Overbalancing on landing can cause injuries to elbows, shoulders or head as they impact on the landing surface. This is why inflatable landing areas are provided in sports such as high jump and pole vault.

Resistance

Many training methods used in fitness training involve working against some sort of resistance: in weight training, the weights provide the resistance; in swimming, the water is the resistant force. If the amount of resistance is too great, then injury is likely to occur due to loading, as explained above. Muscle strain is the most common type of resistance injury, due to the muscle not being able to cope with the extra demand being placed upon it.

Types of injury

Some of the most common injuries linked to sporting activity are discussed below.

Overuse injuries

This type of injury is linked to overuse, explained above. Overuse injuries include:

▶ tendonitis, which is the inflammation and irritation of a **tendon**, which then causes pain and tenderness – **tennis elbow** is a common example of this

▶ shin splints cause tenderness and pain in the lower leg, which gets worse during exercise – it is very common problem with runners

▶ dislocation occurs at a joint when one bone comes out of its normal position against another – the most common place for this is the shoulder.

An overuse injury tends to be painful and annoying, and means that the sporting activity or movement cannot be performed correctly. A person suffering from shin splints will still be able to walk around but will find running painful. Similarly, tendonitis is aggravated when performing and pain levels increase. For both of these a period of rest is required to allow recovery to occur naturally. Dislocation will require hospital treatment and a fairly lengthy recovery period to allow the joint to recover properly.

Fractures

A fracture is a break in a bone. There are two types of fracture:

- In an open fracture the skin is broken, so there is a wound caused by the broken bone, which may be sticking out.
- In a closed fracture the bone has broken but it has not pierced the skin. This is the most common and straightforward type of fracture.

Many fractures are 'impact injuries', caused by receiving a blow or impact from something. A fracture is a serious injury that requires specialist hospital treatment and quite a lengthy recovery time.

Sprains and strains

Sprains occur where ligaments at a joint are overstretched or torn. They are usually caused by a sudden wrench or twist, and it is a very common injury at the ankle.

Strains are caused by overstretching a muscle. They can also be caused by a wrench or a twist. They are quite painful, and movement may be reduced or weakened where the injury has occurred. The **symptoms** for this would not be as serious as those for a sprain or a fracture. You should stop an activity immediately and seek medical advice if you are suffering from a strain or sprain.

Grazes

These are a form of cut or **abrasion** to the skin, where the skin is scraped off against a rough surface. Most grazes only take off the surface layer of the skin and then leave a raw, tender area underneath. Falls, scrapes and friction burns can all cause grazes. These are very common in team games if contact is made with the pitch. This is not usually a serious injury and will soon heal if kept clean and dry.

Over to you!

Carry out a survey with the rest of the group to see how many of the group have suffered these injuries. Which is the most common one?

Bruising

Bruises are very common in most sporting activities. They are the result of blood collecting beneath the skin. This is because the blood vessels have been damaged, but the skin has not been broken so the bleeding occurs beneath the surface. The first sign of a bruise is swelling, followed by discoloration of the area. It might go blue or purple at first and then green or yellow.

Concussion

This is a sudden loss of consciousness, often caused by a blow to the head. It does not have to be a particularly hard blow to cause concussion – being hit by a basketball could be enough. The sufferer may be unconscious for a few seconds or even for hours. There is also something known as delayed concussion, when a person loses consciousness after being injured. The signs to look for are:

- immediate unconsciousness
- very relaxed limbs with a very weak and irregular pulse
- slow, shallow breathing
- large (dilated) pupils
- bleeding from the ears.

Any suspected concussion injury is serious and must be dealt with as such. It requires expert and qualified treatment and it is very important that action is taken immediately.

Spinal injuries

These include any injury to the **vertebrae** in the back or neck. Your spinal cord runs along the inside of your vertebrae and any damage to this can result in paralysis. Anybody showing signs of a spinal injury must be left precisely where they are until medical help arrives.

Spinal injuries tend to occur in sports where physical contact is part of the game and allowed within the rules (e.g. in rugby), but can also be caused by falling awkwardly (e.g. after jumping, such as after heading a football, or falling from a horse when riding).

Blisters

A blister is a small pocket of fluid within the upper layers of the skin. This is usually caused by forceful rubbing (friction), but it can also be caused by burning, freezing, chemical exposure or infection. Most blisters are filled with a clear fluid called serum or plasma, which is known as 'blister water'. Sometimes blisters can be filled with blood (blood blisters) or pus if they become infected. Blisters can be extremely painful. Poorly fitting footwear is the most common cause of blisters for sports performers.

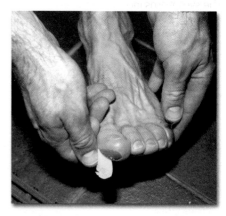

Blisters should always be left to heal naturally and should not be burst as this is likely to result in infection. In time the fluid within them will disperse and the skin will heal over.

Over to you!

Working with at least two other members of your group, list any injuries you have suffered from. Consider the ways in which the injuries were caused and the effects they had on you. Use the table below to record the information.

Injury	Cause	Effect

Types of illness and their symptoms

An illness is a medical condition (e.g. a disease or sickness) that affects the body or the mind. A few of the illnesses associated with sport are discussed below.

Asthma

This is probably the most common illness you are likely to come across in the context of sporting activities. It is a chronic (long-term) lung disease that inflames and narrows the airways. Asthma causes recurring periods of wheezing and difficulties breathing. Other symptoms include a whistling sound when breathing, tight chest, shortness of breath and coughing. This coughing often occurs at night or early in the morning. The airways become very swollen and sensitive and tend to react strongly to certain substances in the air, such as pollen. The sufferer will need to use an inhaler which allows a controlled dose of a drug to go straight to the affected airways. Asthma suffers have their own inhalers which they have to look after and keep with them. There are many different types so inhalers should never be shared with other asthma sufferers.

Paula Ratcliffe is an asthma sufferer.

Heart attack

This is a very serious condition. It occurs when part of the heart muscle dies because it has been starved of oxygen. This is usually caused by a blood clot forming in one of the arteries, which then blocks the blood flow to the heart. The symptoms include shortness of breath and a severe and crushing pain in the middle of the chest. This pain can travel from the chest to the neck, jaw, ears, arms and wrists. The person suffering may also feel nauseous, be cold and clammy and their skin might appear to be pale and grey coloured. This is clearly an extremely serious condition which requires immediate emergency treatment by qualified personnel such as a paramedic or doctor.

Activity

Paula Ratcliffe is not the only elite performer who suffers from asthma. Do some research to find out which other well-known athletes suffer with the condition.

Viral infections

A virus is a micro-organism that invades living cells and replicates itself there. There are many different types of virus, which cause many common infections, including the common cold. The most general symptom experienced is a high temperature, but each different virus can have particular effects on the body. A virus such as the common cold is unpleasant but not particularly serious. A virus such as 'flu can be more serious and will probably require several days in bed to recover – in extreme cases it can even be fatal.

Hypoglycaemia

This is a condition where the levels of glucose (sugar) in the blood drop below a certain point. It is usually a temporary condition, with the symptoms often disappearing after about 10 to 15 minutes. These symptoms can vary, but confusion is a common one. Other symptoms include trembling, perspiring, a feeling of weakness and difficulty concentrating. This is a condition that can usually be treated quite quickly and easily by taking some glucose tablets or sugar lumps.

Case study

Tolu has been asked to give a presentation to her group on injuries, describing two types of injury, and one type and symptom of a sports-related illness.

Tolu has suffered a few injuries in the past, and thinks that describing these might be the best thing to do in her presentation. She landed badly when performing the high jump, and broke her arm when she was 11. She has had various grazes and bruises, strains and blisters, and has also twisted her ankle several times when playing netball.

Tolu suffers quite badly from asthma and regularly has to use her inhaler. She contracted swine flu when she was in Year 10 and had nearly a week off school because of it.

Tolu considers herself to have quite good ICT skills and is thinking about using these to support her presentation.

1. Do you think it is a good idea for Tolu to use her own experiences for this presentation? Explain your answer.

2. Which two injuries do you think Tolu should concentrate on if she decides to talk about her own experiences?

3. What types of injuries are they?

4. Which illness would you advise Tolu to consider in her presentation and why?

5. How do you think Tolu could best make use of her ICT skills in this presentation?

Over to you!

Working with at least two other members of your group, list any illnesses you have suffered from. Consider the ways in which these were caused and the effects they had on you. Use the table below to record the information. Note that viral illnesses might be a large category on their own.

Illness	Cause	Effect

Assessment activity 5.1 (P1, P2, P4, P5, M1, M3, M4, D1)

You are on work placement at your local sports centre. As part of your induction you have been asked by the manager to produce information that could be given to customers regarding safe sports participation. The customers you will be dealing with should only be in small groups of a maximum of four, so prepare a presentation to give to them. This could include producing a basic explanatory leaflet or even a poster that you could use to help with your explanation.

Topic check

1 What is a symptom?
2 Explain the term 'diagnosis'.
3 Give the name of the type of injury caused by placing too much stress on the body.
4 What is the difference between an intrinsic and an extrinsic factor?
5 Identify three possible causes of an overuse injury.
6 What sort of injury might being 'round shouldered' cause?
7 Where does leverage occur?
8 Explain the difference between tendons and ligaments.
9 Name two different types of fractures.
10 What is the difference between a strain and a sprain?

Dealing with injuries and illnesses associated with sports participation

▶ Getting started

There will be first-aid procedures in place in any workplace, and particular members of staff will be designated with responsibility for giving first-aid treatment in an emergency. Working through this topic will not make you an expert first aider, but it is nonetheless important that you are aware of general first-aid procedures.

When you have completed this topic, you should know:

- about the procedures and treatments for some sports injuries
- some of the possible types of casualty
- some of the possible types of injury and illness.

🔑 Key terms

Dementia: a disorder of the brain which causes personality changes, loss of memory and difficulty carrying out normal activities

Procedures and treatment

Most organisations have clear first-aid procedures in place, with particular members of staff being responsible for these. You should know what the procedures are for treating casualties in the environment you are working in. Some guidance on dealing with illnesses and injuries is given below.

Protecting the casualty and others

Protecting the casualty from any further injury and from becoming ill should be a priority. For example, if the casualty is outside and the weather is cold and wet, you should cover them up with something warm and try to keep them dry.

You also need to protect other people who might be at risk. For example, if the casualty has an open cut, you should make sure that you and others avoid coming into contact with the blood as this could transmit disease or infection. There may also be some hazard in the immediate area, such as broken glass or sharp metal, which could constitute a danger. As a general rule, you should clear people away from the casualty.

Qualified assistance and organisational provision

All workplaces, including leisure centres and sports facilities, keep lists of qualified first-aiders. These would normally be the first people to call upon for help. In some circumstances there may be qualified medical staff available. At all professional sporting events, for example, there are medics and doctors attending, and ambulances and paramedics may be on standby. If these people are available you should contact them and inform them of the situation as soon as possible.

Another option is always to call the emergency services. The standard number to call is 999, and now it is also possible to use 112. Calls to 999 and 112 can be made from mobile phones even if the keypad is locked, it has no SIM card or if there is no credit on the phone.

It is a legal requirement for all organisations to make provision for medical emergencies, and to display the information relating to this. If you are working or helping out in an organisation, for example on a work placement, it is likely that you will be told about these procedures during your induction when you start work there. However, if you are not, be sure to ask about the procedures for first aid and dealing with an emergency.

Over to you!

Find out what the policies are for first aid and emergency situations in at least two organisations. One of these could be your school or college and the other could be a local leisure centre.

Dealing with a casualty

Ideally you should not leave the casualty alone. If you think the injury is serious and the casualty should not be moved, then you must decide what is the best way to get help. If you do not have a mobile phone with you, ask if anyone nearby has one you can use, or ask someone else to call for assistance.

You should try to comfort and reassure the casualty as best you can. Anyone who has been injured will be anxious and concerned, as well as probably being in pain. You should try to calm them down and let them know that help is on the way. Some people react very badly to the sight of blood, and if they have a broken bone sticking out of their skin they are likely to be feeling frightened and may also be in shock. Talk to them and try to take their mind off the injury. You will probably be concerned yourself, but it is important that you try to stay calm. Panic will only make the situation worse.

For something as simple as a minor cut, you might be able to clean the wound and apply a plaster. For a strained ankle you could offer to support the casualty while they walk to a treatment centre or somewhere warm and dry to wait for help. However, you should not attempt to give first aid unless you have some form of first-aid qualification.

Accident reporting

It is always a good idea (and sometimes compulsory) to report an accident. Make sure that you are fully aware of any accident reporting procedures, even if they are as basic as knowing where telephones are located.

It is important that you give clear and accurate information when reporting an accident, even if you are out in the middle of a playing field or half-way around a cross-country course. Some sporting events and activities take place in out-of-the-way locations, especially outdoor and adventurous activities. In extreme situations, emergency services such as the air ambulance or lifeboat service could be called. In these instances it is very important to be precise about where you are and the condition of the casualty.

Over to you!

With someone else in your group, carry out a role-play activity in which you report an accident and your partner takes the role of the emergency services operator.

Types of casualty

Casualties might be adults, children or people with different needs, and each of these groups will need to be treated slightly differently.

Adults

In many ways adults will be the easiest group to deal with. They are less likely to panic and you will be able to talk to them and reassure them more easily. However, they are also likely to be more aware of their condition, so could become quite distressed if they are in a serious condition. Also, most adults will be much larger and heavier than children and therefore more difficult to move, if moving them is a safe option.

Children

Very young children might not be able to speak yet, which will make it more difficult for you to establish what their condition is. They are also more likely to panic, cry and ask for their parents, so you will need to give plenty of reassurance and comfort. They will almost certainly be worried about being left alone, so it is doubly important that you stay with them and reassure them that you are not going to leave them.

People with particular needs

This group includes people with a great variety of needs. For example, the casualty may have a physical disability (e.g. sight or hearing impairment), a learning disability (e.g. Down's syndrome), or they may not speak English. These conditions are not always immediately apparent (e.g. someone suffering **dementia** may just seem confused), and may make communication more difficult. As with any other casualty, you should try to provide reassurance, and if necessary call for help as quickly as possible.

> ### Activity
>
> Carry out a role-play situation with another member of your group. One of you should be a hearing-impaired person who has been injured. This person could wear headphones or earplugs to enable them to imagine more clearly how it would feel not to be able to hear. Go through the process of dealing with the injury, finding ways to communicate with each other effectively.

Types of injury or illness

It is hoped that most of the casualties you come across in a sporting situation will have only a minor injury or illness. However, there may be times when you have to deal with a more serious (major) injury or illness, and you need to be prepared to deal with either situation. If you are ever in doubt about the degree of seriousness of the injury or illness, always assume that it is more serious and err on the side of caution!

Minor injuries

Minor injuries are those for which there are no ongoing symptoms and no ongoing treatment is required. They include minor cuts, grazes, bruises and clear strains and sprains. If you are certain that the injury is minor, then you will probably be able to deal with it on site, or wherever you happen to be. However, if you are in any doubt then it is safer for the casualty to stay where they are and for you to call for assistance from a qualified member of staff or the emergency services.

Minor illness

A minor illness is any condition that only lasts for a limited time, and does not prevent the patient from carrying on their normal functions for more than a short period of time. Examples include backache, a sore throat or eczema.

Faulty or damaged equipment

It is the responsibility of participants to make sure that the equipment they use is not faulty. Footballers should check their boot studs to make sure that they are not worn and sharp, as this could cause cuts on impact. A damaged hockey stick can result in splinters, and a worn landing mat will not absorb the impact of a landing properly. If the pads are not fixed securely to rugby posts they will not give full protection.

> ### Over to you!
>
> Think of three more examples of faulty or damaged equipment which could be hazards.

If you are certain of your diagnosis then minor illnesses can also be dealt with on site. Many people who have on-going health issues, such as asthma or diabetes, will carry medication with them. If this is the case, you will need to make sure the casualty has their medication with them and is able to use it. Do not, under any circumstances, give any medication to a casualty, not even something as simple as a paracetamol. Asthma inhalers are specific to individuals and do vary, so they should not be shared. For something like hypoglycaemia, the symptoms should pass quickly, so just sit the casualty down quietly for several minutes and then suggest that they have something to eat or drink. However, as with injuries, if you are in any doubt what the problem is, then it is safer for the casualty to stay where they are and for you to call for assistance from a qualified member of staff or the emergency services.

Injuries to noses are fairly common in some sports and are usually considered to be minor injuries.

 **Activity**

Make a note of all of the injuries and illnesses mentioned in this unit and put each one on a separate piece of paper. Working in groups, put each one into one of the following categories: minor injury, major injury, minor illness or major illness.

Major injuries and major illnesses

A major injury or illness is one that requires significant treatment and may even be life threatening (e.g. serious fractures, head injuries, deep cuts with heavy bleeding, a severe asthma attack). In many cases it will be clear if an injury or illness is a major cause for concern. In these instances you must call for help as quickly as possible from a qualified member of staff or the emergency services. Unless you are a qualified first aider it is safer not to try to help, as you may instead make the situation worse. Try to remain calm and patient until help arrives, and do your best to reassure the casualty.

Case study

Kelvin is on a work placement at his local leisure centre. He has been called over to one of the five-a-side pitches at the far side of the complex, where there has been an accident involving two footballers. They have collided in a tackle and one of them has a badly bruised shin and appears to have twisted his knee. The other casualty is clearly in pain and his shin seems to be broken as it is bent at a very strange angle. One of the junior players on the nearby pitch has fainted after looking over from the pitch he was playing on.

One of the players involved in the incident did not have proper grips on his trainer soles, and the other one was not wearing shin pads.

The main building of the centre is about 200 metres away. Kelvin does not have a mobile phone with him, but there is a main street right next to the pitch with pedestrians on it. When

Kelvin started his work placement he was fully briefed by the centre manager regarding the centre's procedures for accident situations.

1. What specific advice do you think the centre manager is likely to have given Kelvin during his briefing, which would help him in this situation?

2. What major injuries and what minor injuries is Kelvin faced with?

3. Who do you think Kelvin should prioritise to be treated first, and what should he do?

4. Who do you think Kelvin can turn to for help?

5. What is likely to be the quickest way for Kelvin to get through to the emergency services if he decides they need to be called?

Assessment activity 5.2 (P3, M2)

Throughout your time on placement at the sports centre you have to deal with a variety of different issues that arise while you are on duty. Plan in advance how you would deal with three separate injuries that you think are most likely to occur

during your placement. As you are likely to be in a situation where you will have to make initial decisions, consider who you would be able to turn to for help and advice in this situation and also what action you would decide to take.

Topic check

1 Describe two ways you might be able to initially protect a casualty.

2 Identify one hazard that might be a danger to a casualty and one that might be a danger to other people.

3 Give the two phone numbers you can use to contact the emergency services.

4 What sort of qualified help might be available at a sporting event or a sports facility?

5 Describe two things you would do when first dealing with a casualty.

6 When should you definitely *not* give first aid?

7 Explain two differences between dealing with a child and dealing with an adult casualty.

8 Identify two needs that would require you to help a casualty in a particular way.

9 Identify three possible minor injuries.

10 What action must you take if a casualty has a major illness or injury?

Risks and hazards associated with sports participation

There is inevitably an element of risk in most sporting activities, and for many people this is the appeal of taking part in them. It is impossible to make all sporting situations completely safe, but it is important that measures are taken to minimise the hazards and the risks.

When you have completed this topic, you should know:

- some of the possible risks and hazards to people participating in sports
- some of the possible risks and hazards to equipment
- some of the possible risks and hazards from the environment
- about the rules, regulations and legislation relating to risks and hazards in sports.

🔑 Key terms

Dehydration: excessive loss of fluids from the body, causing water level in the body to drop

Hypothermia: a condition where the body temperature drops to a dangerously low level due to exposure to extreme cold

Lactic acid: a waste product that can build up in the muscles after exercising

Legislation: laws that need to be enforced

Novice: a beginner who is new to an activity or event and has no previous experience

Over training: carrying out too much training or training at too high a level for your capabilities

Physique: your bodily structure or appearance

Sunstroke: also known as heatstroke, this is a condition that occurs due to too much exposure to the sun, causing a rapid rise in temperature, headaches, convulsions and even comas

Risks and hazards to people

Many of the hazards to people in sporting situations can be controlled and the risk of injury or accident reduced.

Inappropriate warm-up or cool-down

Warming up and cooling down correctly are dealt with in more detail in Chapter 9, Topic 9.1 (page 209). It is important to warm up thoroughly before any period of training or performance. Failure to do so increases the risk of injury. You are likely to develop a regular warm-up routine, but it is important that it is appropriate for the activity, the conditions and for you – an inappropriate warm-up can be as dangerous as not warming up at all. For example, if you planned to do some intensive sprint training outside on a cold day, you would do some gentle exercise first to loosen up your muscles and start to increase your heart rate. If you did not warm up first you would run the risk of straining or pulling a muscle. You would also need to carry out an appropriate cool-down at the end of the session, to stretch your muscles and lower your heart rate. Cooling down properly allows the **lactic acid** to disperse from the muscles, which reduces stiffness and soreness.

Physical fitness

You need to be 'fit for your sport'. This means that you must be properly physically prepared for the demands of the activity you are taking part in. It is no good setting off on a long-distance run if you do not have the levels of endurance to make it to the end. If you are training with free weights, using one that is too heavy is likely to cause damage and result in an injury. It is important, therefore, to be aware of the physical demands of the activity you have chosen and to take responsibility for ensuring that you are fit to do it at the levels required.

Physique

Your **physique** is unique to you! If you have a strong physique you may be well suited to activities requiring strength, but if you have a slight physique it is probably not advisable to join in a rugby scrum with people who are twice your size! Some aspects of your physique are beyond your control, such as height and basic body shape. Others, such as muscle bulk, you may be able to train and work on.

Alcohol

The simple fact is that alcohol and sport do not mix, so alcohol consumption should always be avoided before you participate in any sporting activity. If you do consume alcohol then you need to be sure that it is out of your body system before your train or participate in any sporting activity. Many people who go skiing have a lunch break during which they consume alcohol with their meal. They then go back out on the slopes to ski in the afternoon. Unfortunately, many have too much alcohol, which affects their judgement and coordination, resulting in accidents where they may injure themselves and other skiers whom they collide with.

Technique

Technique is an important aspect of all sports. Good technique will make you a better performer; poor technique can be dangerous. For example, if you do not use the correct technique for tackling in rugby, it is likely that you will injure yourself or someone else. You may also hurt someone else if, for example, you follow through too high with a hockey stick after hitting the ball.

All sports have particular techniques specific to them, and it is important that you are aware of the techniques you need to master in any sports you participate in.

Over to you!

Think of three different examples, from three different sports, where poor technique could be dangerous to either the performer or an opponent or teammate.

Skill level

You should train and compete at a skill level you are capable of and competent in. If a **novice** rugby player takes part in a high-level rugby game they are not likely to have developed the skills to tackle the opponents correctly. In a sport such as trampolining a beginner may try to move on to more complex skills (e.g. somersaults) before they have mastered the basics, and this could have disastrous consequences.

This applies equally to outdoor and adventurous activities. For example, a novice canoeist would struggle to cope with a demanding white water slalom course, as they would not have the paddling skills needed to manoeuvre safely down the rapids and to negotiate the gates.

C2 (two-person canoe) slalom racing

Over training

As well as being unfit through not training enough, it is possible to train too much. **Over training** will reduce your physical condition so that you are not 'fit for your sport'. It may make you too tired and weak to participate, and may even lead to injuries. Over training is also likely to make you less mentally alert due to tiredness, and this is an additional hazard.

Behaviour of other participants

People in sport can become aggressive, putting other people at risk. Some sports are naturally aggressive (e.g. rugby). However, managing the behaviour of players within the rules and regulations of play is important to minimising risk.

Jewellery

There are very specific health and safety rules which ban the wearing of jewellery in certain circumstances, but as a general rule jewellery should never be worn during training or performing. Wearing any item of jewellery, such as earrings, necklaces, watches or rings, is hazardous to those wearing them as well as others. For example,if you were wearing hoop earrings, you might easily catch one and pull it out.

Food

Eating food while taking part in physical activity is clearly unacceptable – you could easily choke if you were involved in a violent movement. Eating while exercising can also cause digestive problems and stomach pains. Eating chewing gum is also inadvisable, as it may be breathed in accidentally or knocked back into the throat on impact (e.g. in a rugby tackle) and cause choking, restricting the flow of oxygen. This can be very dangerous and even lead to death.

Activity

What action would you take if you were a coach in the following circumstances?

- A player walks on to the rugby field ready to play and is wearing earrings.
- A girl is performing on the trampoline and clearly has a 'belly bar' showing.
- A player in a hockey match can clearly be seen blowing bubbles with bubble gum.
- One of the best footballers, who has never played rugby before, volunteers to make the numbers up in the school rugby team, which is one player short in a vital match.

Risks and hazards from equipment

Most activities you are likely to take part in will use some form of specific equipment. In many activities it is within the rules that certain equipment must be worn (e.g. shin pads in soccer). There are several general areas related to equipment that may be considered as hazards or risks.

Inappropriate clothing

You should always wear clothing that it appropriate to the activity you are doing. For example:

▶ If you are hill walking you need to wear clothing that is appropriate to the weather, and to consider whether the conditions are likely to change, e.g. if it is fair when you leave, but may become cold or wet, then you need to take extra warm and waterproof clothing with you.

▶ For judo you would wear a judo suit, which is loose enough to allow the range of movement necessary, and has a thick jacket to withstand the stresses of the grappling involved in the sport.

Wearing the wrong clothing for the wrong activity always increases the risk of injury.

Lack of protective clothing or equipment

In many sports there is now a large selection of protective clothing and equipment which can be worn. A hockey goalkeeper has protective clothing from head (helmet) to toe (kickers), with plenty of additional items in between. A cricket batter is permitted to wear a helmet, chest protector, forearm guards, gloves, thigh pad, box and pads – and expected to run between the wickets wearing it all! Small, simple pieces of equipment, such as a gumshield in hockey and rugby, are equally important in providing protection.

Playing surface

These vary from sport to sport. Grass pitches tend to be quite soft, so falling on them or being tackled on them is less likely to result in injury than harder surfaces. Indoor surfaces are much harder and potentially more hazardous. The surface of many netball playing areas is tarmac based, and falling on these can cause cuts, grazes and abrasions. Professional tennis players will dive to play a shot on grass courts, but are less likely to do so on clay courts!

Risks and hazards from the environment

Apart from outdoor and adventurous activities, these are mainly related to extremes of weather. Other types of sporting activity are usually quite safe in normal weather conditions, but there are exceptions.

Cold weather

Sports such as rugby, hockey and soccer are played throughout the winter in cold conditions. However, if the ground is frozen the match may be cancelled as the risk of injury will be too high. Also, cold weather means that players require longer warm-ups to prevent injury. Many outdoor and adventurous activities are also done during the winter months and, as long as precautions are taken and the correct clothing is worn, the cold should not be a problem. The risk of **hypothermia**, associated with any activity in very cold weather, comes when inappropriate clothing is worn, weather conditions are not researched and accounted for, or other unforeseen factors lead to participants being out in the cold for too long without the appropriate clothing or equipment.

Rain

Rain in itself is not dangerous, but it can cause dangerous conditions. For example, it can make playing surfaces slippery, resulting in more injuries caused by players colliding, over-stretching or falling over. Heavy persistent rain may cause flooding. Football, hockey and rugby cannot be played on a flooded pitch, and a flooded river would be a hazard in cross-country running. Again, there is a risk of hypothermia if rain is combined with cold weather, particularly if you cannot dry yourself once you become very wet as your body temperature will drop.

Hot weather

Prolonged exposure to hot weather can result in **sunstroke** and **dehydration**, as well as sunburn. Very bright sunlight can also cause problems with visibility, for example in rounders, when catching a high ball which is coming down out of a very bright sky, or with the sun behind it.

Activity

Consider what might be the most likely main injuries to occur in wet slippery conditions. Try to describe exactly how they could occur in a particular sporting situation. Then do the same for dry hard conditions. Remember to describe an actual situation that could occur and the injury which would result.

Rules, regulations and legislation

All sporting activities have specific rules, regulations and legislation that apply to them, and you will need to be aware of those that apply to your sports. There is also some **legislation** (the process of making laws) that is more general and will apply to a range of sporting activities.

The ones you need to know about are:

▶ Health and Safety at Work Act 1974

▶ Management of Health and Safety at Work (Amendment) Regulations 2006

▶ Control of Substances Hazardous to Health (COSHH) 2002

▶ Health and Safety (First Aid) Regulations 1981

▶ Safety at Sports Ground Act 1975

▶ Children Act 2004.

This list might seem quite daunting, but as part of this unit you must find out about four rules, regulations and legislation relating to health, safety and injury in sports participation. The list above should help you to decide which ones to look at for this task.

In addition, if you are on a work placement, you need to ensure that you are aware of all of the organisational rules which apply there.

Activity

Using the internet, find the legislation documents listed on the left. The first one, for the Health and Safety at Work Act 1974, is included here to start you off: www.hse.gov.uk/legislation/hswa.htm.

Case study

Kelvin has been set the task of giving a presentation to the rest of his BTEC group. He has to choose four rules, regulations and legislation relating to health, safety and injury in sports participation and explain them. He has decided to choose two aspects from 'risks and hazards to people', and one each from, 'risks and hazards from equipment' and 'risks and hazards from the environment'. Kelvin has decided that the incident he had to deal with on the football pitch (see page 121) would be a good starting point for this, but is not sure what aspect regarding the 'environment' he will cover, as he did not experience any weather extremes when he was on his placement.

1. Which two of the ten identified areas for 'risks and hazards to people' would you advise Kelvin to cover?

2. Is there one of these which is likely to link most closely to the incident he had to deal with on placement?

3. Which aspect of 'risks and hazards from equipment' is Kelvin most likely to be able to link his report to?

4. Which 'weather' aspect would you advise Kelvin to consider? Why would you choose this one?

5. Which of the legislation documents is Kelvin likely to have to refer to?

Topic check

1 Give two risks associated with an inappropriate warm-up.

2 What is 'lactic acid'?

3 Give one aspect of your physique over which you have some control.

4 Name two problems which could be caused by over training.

5 Which legislation bans the wearing of jewellery when taking part in sport?

6 Why is it dangerous to chew gum when playing sport?

7 Which piece of protective equipment must be worn when playing soccer?

8 Describe the conditions that may make rain hazardous.

9 What is dehydration?

10 What is hypothermia?

Undertaking a risk assessment relevant to sport

▶ **Getting started**

In this topic you will have the opportunity to apply the knowledge you have gained in the earlier topics to carry out a risk assessment. When you have completed this topic, you should know:

■ the purpose of risk assessments

■ how to carry out and record a risk assessment.

Purpose

Risk assessment is an important area in sport and something that has to be done on a continuous basis. For example, a coach has to assess the risk every time they take a group onto a field for football or any other type of outdoor activity. This may involve walking the pitch and checking for sharp objects, checking the playing condition (e.g. frozen, too wet to play), and checking the players.

Risk can be seen as the likelihood of a **hazard** causing harm. The level of risk can be minimised by putting appropriate measures in place. Once these measures are in place, what was originally considered a high-risk activity becomes lower risk. Risk assessments are carried out for specific purposes, as discussed below.

🔑 **Key terms**

Hazard: a possible danger that might cause injury or harm

Risk: the possibility of suffering harm from a hazard; possible exposure to the chance of injury

To ascertain the level of risk

This means deciding if the risk of a particular outcome is low, medium or high. For example, if you are playing a contact sport, such as rugby, then the risk of an impact injury will be high. The possible hazards here would be the other players and the uprights of the posts. If you are playing badminton, where contact is not allowed, then the risk of an impact injury will be low, and the level and number of hazards is therefore less. When considering levels of risk, the important factors are:

▶ severity – how serious any injury is likely to be

▶ frequency – how often this particular risk occurs

▶ likelihood – the chance of the risk happening; how probable it is that it will occur.

To minimise injury

The possible level of injury can be reduced by identifying the type of risk and potential hazard, and then taking action. For example, in rugby, the goal posts are a possible hazard and the risk is that an injury will occur if a player collides with one. Once this is identified you can make sure that protective padding is placed around the post to reduce the seriousness of an injury if someone does hit it.

To maintain a safe environment

It is important that a safe environment is established and then maintained, so any action that has been taken should be reviewed regularly (e.g. the padding on rugby goal posts checked to ensure it has not moved or worn through). Also, weather conditions can change quickly and decisions might need to be made relating to these. For example, golf matches should be stopped if there are thunderstorms, because of the risk of lightning strikes. A loud siren rings to let golfers know that they should get off the course and move to safety.

To protect all participants

This includes the people who are leading the activity and spectators who might be in the area. All activities take place in a designated playing or performing area and only the participants are allowed within this area. As a performer, you know that you only have to avoid, or deal with, other performers. This is why professional football matches have large numbers of stewards to make sure the players, officials and fans are all safe at all times.

Risk assessment

It is important to carry out risk assessments for all activities, and to review these regularly to ensure that they are up to date and effective. Risk assessment has already been covered in some detail in Chapter 3, but not all risk assessments are the same – they will vary from activity to activity. For example, a risk assessment for a session of table tennis in an indoor gym is going to be far less complex than one for an outdoor and adventurous activity such as rock climbing. The following list considers the different aspects which could, or should, be taken into account when carrying out a risk assessment.

▶ Record sheets – these can be for any particular area of the assessment, including accidents, incidents, specific activity requirements.

▶ Types of hazards – these need to be identified and could be in categories such as fire hazards, environmental hazards, activity-specific hazards (javelin, for example, would have some very specific hazards!).

▶ Risk identification – risks need to be identified and then a level of risk (high, medium or low) allocated to them.

▶ Specialist equipment – initially this needs to be identified as being necessary and available, and then procedures need to be in place to make sure its use is enforced. An example would be corner flags in football, which should be light and only lightly placed in the ground so that they slide out easily on impact (heavy wooden posts firmly embedded in the ground might cause injuries).

▶ Reporting procedures – these must not only be in place, but it must be clear who reports to whom. Levels of reporting need to be established so that messages get through to the right people. The correct forms must be used to make these reports. There may also have to be a system in place for verbal reports.

▶ Contingency plans – this would be 'plan B'. You should always have a back-up plan for such things as weather changes, damaged equipment or different skill levels of participants.

Sport Risk Assessment Form

Club: _____   Date and time: _____

Activity or trip/event name: _____   Position and name: _____

Location: _____   Signature: _____

Score (1–5)	Location	Equipment	Transport	First aid *	Weather	
1	A managed and staffed centre catering specifically for your activity	No equipment or protective clothing required	Activity on site or local, no transport requirements for participants	First aid available. Access to emergency support. Persons qualified at appropriate level.	Change in weather will have no adverse effect on group	
2	A managed and staffed centre that is suitable for your activity	Minimal equipment or protective clothing required to undertake activity.	Use of hired coach or public transport	First aid not available. Access to emergency support. Persons qualified at appropriate level.	Change in weather will have minimal effect on activity	
3	A managed but unstaffed centre or site suitable for your activity	Some equipment or protective clothing required. No training required for use. Equipment failure may cause minor injury.	Local or regional movement of participants or large/heavy items, using self-driven vehicles	First aid available. Access to emergency support. No, or insufficient, persons qualified at appropriate level.	Change in weather could cause problems if the group is not adequately prepared with training or equipment	
4	Unmanaged and unstaffed site or centre suitable for your activity	Complex, delicate or extensive equipment or protective clothing required. Training in use of equipment required. Some reliance on equipment where failure may cause some injury.	National movement of participants using self-drive vehicles or including overnight stay	First aid not available. No access to emergency support. No persons qualified at appropriate level.	Change in weather could rapidly lead to serious problems if the group is not adequately experienced or equipped	
5	A remote location. Unmanaged and unstaffed site	Complex, delicate or extensive equipment and/or protective clothing required. Extensive training in use of equipment required. Direct reliance on equipment, failure is likely to cause serious injury.	Transportation of heavy or large items and many people. Use of minibuses and trailers or travelling abroad.	First aid not available. Persons not qualified at appropriate level. With or without access to emergency support.	Change in weather could have very serious repercussions for the group	
Score (1–5) **						Total score

* *First aid* – where a third party is qualified in first aid at an appropriate level, but not a member of an emergency service or your club, e.g. instructor, attendant at sports facility

Certain activities will have specific requirements with regard to leader–student ratios and leader qualifications/levels of experience.

Access to emergency support – where trained professionals (e.g. ambulance, mountain rescue, coastguard) could be called to an incident within 45 minutes of an incident

** Give each category (e.g. location) a score from 1 to 5 in the box at the bottom of its column. Add up the scores to find the total, which will give the risk rating for the activity.

7–11	12–18	19–24	25–29	30–35
Low risk	Medium risk	High risk	Extreme risk	Unacceptable risk

Figure 5.1 An example of a risk assessment form

Over to you!

Looking at the example of a risk assessment form, consider what you might need to include in a basic risk assessment for one of the practical sporting activities you are involved in on your course.

Case study

Kelvin has been in his work placement for six weeks and has been asked to carry out a risk assessment of the fitness suite. The fitness suite has free weights, which are kept in stands, and aerobic exercise machines including treadmills, rowing machines, cross-trainers and exercise bikes. It also has weight-training machines with built-in adjustable weights that can be selected by inserting pins.

Kelvin has been told that the facility is available for all users. This includes young people over 16, adults and people with particular needs, including those with learning difficulties and wheelchair users.

1. What would be the highest injury risk factor Kelvin might identify?
2. What 'maintenance of a safe environment' factors are likely to be most important?
3. What would be the main high-risk hazards in the fitness suite?
4. Are there any particular problems which might be associated with the specialist equipment?
5. What considerations is Kelvin going to have to give to the different groups of users of the facility?

Assessment activity 5.3 (P6, M5, D2)

Having nearly completed your placement, and having worked in all of the different environments (i.e. gym, sports hall, outdoor track and field areas), you have been asked to produce a risk assessment for one of the areas. Select one specific environment and carry out a risk assessment for it, considering all of the factors which would be most relevant to your chosen environment. Describe the contingency plans you would have to have in place and consider the use of any specialist equipment which might be needed to minimise the chances of injury.

Topic check

1 What is the main purpose of a risk assessment?
2 How might you minimise injury risk in a specific sporting activity?
3 Who would be considered to be participants when carrying out a risk assessment?
4 Give three examples of a type of record sheet which could be used for risk assessment.
5 Does all reporting have to be carried out in writing?
6 What is meant by a 'contingency plan'?

Assessment summary

The overall grade you achieve for this unit depends on how well you meet the grading criteria set out in Appendix 1 (see page 295). You must complete:

- all of the P criteria to achieve a **pass** grade
- all of the P and the M criteria to achieve a **merit** grade
- all of the P, M and D criteria to achieve a **distinction** grade.

Your tutor will assess the assessment activities that you complete for this unit. The work you produce should provide evidence which demonstrates that you have achieved each of the assessment criteria. The table below identifies what you need to demonstrate to meet each of the pass, merit and distinction criteria for this unit. You should always check and self-assess your work before you submit your assignments for marking.

Remember that you MUST provide evidence for all of the P criteria to pass the unit.

Grading criteria	You need to demonstrate that you can:	Have you got the evidence
P1	Describe four different types of injuries associated with sports participation and their underlying causes	
M1	Explain why certain injuries and illnesses are associated with sports participation	
P2	Describe two types and signs of illnesses related to sports participation	
P3	Demonstrate how to deal with casualties suffering from three different injuries and/or illnesses, with tutor support	
M2	Independently deal with casualties suffering from three different injuries and/or illnesses	
P4	Describe six risks and hazards associated with sports participation	
M3	Explain risks and hazards associated with sports participation	
D1	Give a detailed account of why participants are at risk of injury whilst taking part in sport	
P5	Describe four rules, regulations and legislation relating to health, safety and injury in sports participation	
M4	Explain four rules, regulations and legislation relating to health, safety and injury in sports participation	
P6	Carry out and produce a risk assessment relevant to a selected sport	
M5	Describe contingency plans that can be used in a risk assessment	
D2	Justify the use of specialist equipment to minimise the risk of injury	

Always ask your tutor to explain any assignment tasks or assessment criteria that you don't understand fully. Being clear about the task before you begin gives you the best chance of succeeding. Good luck with your Unit 5 assessment work!

6 Planning and leading sports activities (Unit 7)

Unit outline

Taking on a leadership role is a big responsibility, and requires certain skills and qualities. Thorough planning is necessary if an event is to be successful. This unit will give you the knowledge and skills to be able to plan and lead a sports event successfully. It will give you the opportunity to plan and lead a fairly short (about 10 minutes) activity session in preparation for the full sports event.

You will be required to carry out ongoing reviews and assessments of what you are achieving throughout this unit, which will then result in a final review of your main event.

Learning outcomes

1 **Know the skills, qualities and responsibilities associated with successful sports leadership.**
2 **Be able to plan and lead an activity session.**
3 **Be able to review your planning and leadership of a sports activity.**
4 **Be able to assist in the planning and leading of a sports event.**
5 **Be able to review your planning and leadership of a sports event.**

Skills, qualities and responsibilities associated with successful sports leadership

▶ Getting started

As part of this unit you will choose two sports leaders who you feel are successful and compare and contrast their skills and qualities. This will help you to identify skills and qualities required of a leader, and see them being put into operation effectively.

When you have completed this topic, you should know:

■ the skills associated with successful sports leadership
■ the qualities a person may need to be a successful leader
■ the responsibilities associated with successful sports leadership.

🔑 Key terms

Communication: the exchange of thoughts, messages or information

Etiquette: the unwritten rules and conventions observed in sporting activities

Inspire: to influence positively and make a person want to do well

Intonation: the pattern or pitch (high or low) of your speech

Motivation: encouragement or desire to achieve something

Qualities: distinguishing characteristics

Responsibility: a duty to perform or complete a task satisfactorily

Leaders all have to possess certain **qualities**, which you will need to consider. With leadership comes **responsibility**. The responsibilities of a leader are very significant, and it is essential that you also consider these.

Skills

There are certain skills you can acquire to help you successfully lead a sports activity. These are unlike many of the physical and technical skills you might have acquired elsewhere, but may be equally challenging.

Communication

Effective **communication** is vital. There are various forms of communication available.

▶ *Verbal communication* mainly involves talking to people. You will have to talk to many people on a one-to-one basis in the planning stages of your event. In the later stages, and when you are actually leading the event, you will have to talk to, and lead, a number of people. Communicating with a group can be quite difficult, so make sure that you observe how others deal with individuals and groups, e.g. the volume they speak at (how quietly or loudly), their body position (facing the group, quite close, far away) and **intonation**.

▶ *Written communication* can be equally important. You will have to write out plans, instructions, notes and possibly even produce diagrams. The written materials you produce (e.g. letters, information sheets) will need to be clear and easy to understand, so that everyone else involved is kept informed and has clear records to refer to. It is useful to compile a 'contact list' of everyone's contact details (e.g. email address, mobile phone number).

▶ *Electronic communication* (emails) can be an efficient form of communication, particularly when you want to communicate the same thing to a number of people (e.g. other sports leaders, your peers, sports organisations). Any email communication should be just as clear and well written as your letters, information sheets and other forms of written communication. Setting up a contact list of all the people you are involved with will help you to ensure that everyone involved is kept informed of all decisions and plans.

▶ *Mobile phones* can also be a useful way of keeping in touch with people. It is a good idea to compile a list of mobile phone numbers of everyone involved. You can then use texts and calls to update everyone and keep in constant contact with them. This is likely to be your most useful form of communication if any 'crisis' arises or if you need to get in touch with someone urgently.

Texts and emails can now be sent from mobile phones.

As you can see from the list, the different forms of communication are useful for different things. It is important that you choose the right form of communication for the situation or for the type of information you need to communicate. For example, texting is best for short messages and instant communication, whereas an email might be better for passing on more detailed information to several people at the same time.

Organisation of equipment

Depending on the activity or event you are planning, organising the equipment may prove to be quite challenging. You are likely to be involved in obtaining, storing, checking, transporting, giving out, supervising, collecting in and then replacing equipment. You need to be very organised in this task and make sure that you keep track of all the equipment at all times.

Over to you!

You will be in contact with the two sports leaders you have chosen to study (see page 140). Ask them if they would be happy for you to interview them about the forms of communication they use, and which ones they find most useful in different situations.

Figure 6.1 lists the various issues you need to take into consideration. You can use this to help you plan how you will manage the organisation of the equipment.

Figure 6.1 Equipment checklist

Equipment consideration	Possible issues
Obtaining	Is the equipment you need available anywhere? Will it be available when you want it?
Storing	Where is the equipment stored? Is it accessible? Do you need/have keys for the storage area?
Checking	Is it all in good condition and is there enough? If you are using any form of balls, are they all fully inflated?
Transporting	Has it got to be taken far? Are there any safety considerations such as the weight of the equipment or danger (e.g. javelins)?
Giving out	Where is this going to happen and when? To all at once or one at a time? Are there any safety concerns here?
Supervising	Can you supervise it all and all of the time? Is it all going to be in the same place? Do you have any spares/replacements?
Collecting in	When will you do this and where? Will you be able to be sure it all comes back in? Did you count the equipment when you gave it out?
Replacing	Can you get it back to where it originally came from? If anything has been lost, broken or damaged can you get it fixed/replace it?

Other considerations

The more prepared you are before you start planning your activity or event, the more successful it is likely to be, and the more likely you are to enjoy it. Here are some other areas for you to bear in mind:

▶ You must make sure that you know enough about the activity you are going to lead. This means knowing about the equipment, rules, officials, game/match formats and any specific safety considerations.

▶ Each activity will have a different structure. For example, sports such as football and rugby have five-a-side and sevens formats which could be used, as well as full-sided games. Different sports will also use different competition formats, such as leagues, knockouts, round robin or combinations. An athletics event, for example, would include a number of different events, all with different structures.

▶ It is important to set targets for the different stages of planning and the activity or event itself. For example, what do you want to have achieved by one week before the event? What do you want to achieve overall? What targets do other sports leaders prioritise?

▶ You may be used to talking to people of your own age and to adults. However, you may be working with much younger children in your sports event, so you will have to make sure that you talk to them in a way that they will clearly understand, possibly using more simple language. You are also likely to have

> **Over to you!**
>
> Would you add any other factors to either of the two columns in Figure 6.1?

to use some technical terms and language, so you must ensure that you know and understand these.

▶ All leaders need constantly to evaluate the sessions they deliver. They can use their evaluations to consider how they can make improvements for future sessions. They might consider these in the general categories of their strengths (what went well) and areas for improvement (what did not go so well), so that they can concentrate on these to make the next session better.

Athletics competitions often include a number of different events.

> ### ⚙ Activity
>
> Interview your two chosen sports leaders about the different activity structures they have to manage in their particular sport or activity. Ask about the different competition formats they use.

Qualities

Your **qualities** are related to your character and personality, but you can aim to develop the particular qualities that you need to become a successful leader. You will find it useful to look out for and identify the qualities that have made the sports leaders you've chosen to study successful.

▶ *Appearance* – It is very important that you 'look the part'. This will usually mean being dressed appropriately – smart for a planning meeting but wearing sports kit for leading a session. Your general appearance is also important (e.g. being clean and tidy). Again, look at the appearance standards set by your two chosen sports leaders and use these as good examples and standards to aim for.

▶ *Leadership style* – Different people have different styles of leadership, or may use different styles in different situations. The style used is often linked to the personality of the leader and their levels of experience and training. You will find it useful and interesting to compare and contrast the leadership styles of the two sports leaders you have chosen to study. Three main styles of leadership have been identified, as explained in Figure 6.2 on page 138.

▶ *Personality* – This is something that is unique to each individual. It is not necessary for you to try to change your personality and is probably not possible. However, it is good to consider some aspects of it. If you are a naturally shy person then you might need to try to be more outgoing. If you are very confident and outgoing you might need to restrain this aspect a little and make sure that you listen to others.

▶ *Enthusiasm* – It is vital that you remain enthusiastic throughout. If you do not, then it is unlikely that the groups you work with will become or remain enthusiastic. Keeping up your levels of enthusiasm may be a challenge when things are not going well, but this is exactly when you need to **inspire** others to stay keen and positive.

▶ **Motivation** – This links closely with your levels of enthusiasm. You must not only be motivated yourself, but you must motivate the young people you are working with. Giving praise and encouragement always helps to raise motivation levels. Having clear aims and targets will also help.

▶ *Humour* – It is always useful to have a good sense of humour. It is important to establish a serious working environment, but humour can add a balance to sessions you lead. However, you need to make sure any humour you use is appropriate.

▶ *Confidence* – It is important that you appear to be confident even if do not feel confident! You will feel more confident if you are well prepared and organised. Your confidence will also increase with experience.

Figure 6.2 Leadership styles

Style	Summary	Advantages	Disadvantages
Laissez-faire	A leader who minimises their involvement in decision-making. They allow the group to make the decisions but take responsibility for the outcome.	Works well when the group is capable and motivated in making their own decisions.	Can result in no one taking the lead. Groups with low levels of motivation make very little progress.
Autocratic	The leader makes decisions without consulting others and there is no real consultation with the group.	Very clear and definite plans for each session and clear aims laid out, resulting in swift action being taken.	Most likely to result in discontent among the group, especially if they have some knowledge and would like to contribute.
Democratic	The leader involves the group in decision-making. The leader may have the final say or the group may decide.	Often appreciated by the group as they feel they have an input.	Too many different opinions in the group can lead to problems making decisions and moving on.

Over to you!

Observe the leadership styles of your two chosen sports leaders. Use Figure 6.2 to decide which leadership style each uses most.

Activity

When you are observing your two chosen sports leaders, look specifically for examples of when, and how, they show enthusiasm and use motivation and humour successfully.

Responsibilities

With any form of leadership come responsibilities. These are very important and must be considered carefully.

▶ *Professional conduct* – This means behaving in a correct and proper manner at all times. As the leader, you must always set a good example and conduct yourself in a sensible and mature fashion.

▶ *Health and safety* – There are specific rules and regulations regarding responsibility for health and safety issues, and these must be complied with at all times. There are general rules that apply to all sports, such as not wearing any jewellery and only performing in safe conditions. There are also rules that are specific to particular activities, such as wearing shin pads in football and keeping nails short in netball.

▶ *Insurance* – This is likely to be dealt with by your tutor. However, it will be your responsibility to make sure it is in place. If you are also taking the Community Sports Leaders Award or Junior Sports Leaders Award then you may have insurance cover through your involvement with this.

▶ *Child protection* – This is a priority in any situation involving children. There are rules regarding 'safeguarding', which include checking that all adults working with young children have been officially checked out. This is known as a CRB (Criminal Records Bureau) check, which shows up any criminal convictions.

▶ *Legal obligations* – Anyone working with children has what is known as a 'duty of care'. This means you must check that all the legal requirements for working with children are in place and fully complied with. This includes checking such things as fire regulations being in force, and valid health and safety certificates being in place for any facilities used.

▶ *Equality* – This means that you must make sure that everyone is treated fairly, regardless of their gender, race, religion or any disability they may have. No one must be discriminated against.

▶ *Rules and regulations* – You must make sure that you know the rules and regulations for any activity or event you are leading. There may be a great number of these, so it could be quite challenging to find out about and learn them.

▶ *Ethics and values* – This means that you should encourage fair play and correct etiquette at all times. **Etiquette** is the unwritten rules and conventions that participants in particular activities usually follow, such as shaking hands with your opponents and thanking officials at the end of a match. Your values are the importance you place on behaving correctly and in a way that should be encouraged.

Sports leaders

As has already been mentioned, you will need to choose two successful sports leaders to study so that you can compare and contrast their approaches. You can choose sports leaders who are:

▶ school or college coaches

▶ local club coaches

▶ national club coaches.

It is important that these people are accessible to you, as you will have to observe them both in their work. You will need to contact them to see if they are happy to be your chosen subjects, and also to arrange when it would be convenient for you to observe them or interview them.

Case study

Jermaine is in the process of selecting two sports leaders to compare and contrast. He considers himself quite fortunate because he has a list of four people he might choose from. Jermaine's elder brother is a personal fitness coach, and Jermaine attends a karate club every Thursday evening which has two sensei's (leaders) in charge. Jermaine's main sport is basketball and he goes to his local club to train every week. He also plays in the team at least once a week. Jermaine has been selected for the national development squad for basketball and attends squad training about twice a month. These sessions are organised and run by a team of national coaches. Jermaine still manages to find time to play for the school basketball team as well!

1. Explain the possible advantages and disadvantages to Jermaine of choosing his brother.

2. Explain the possible advantages and disadvantages to Jermaine of choosing one or both of his karate club leaders.

3. Explain the possible advantages and disadvantages to Jermaine of choosing his local basketball club coach.

4. Explain the possible advantages and disadvantages to Jermaine of choosing one of the national squad coaches.

5. Which two leaders would you advise Jermaine to choose?

Assessment activity 6.1 (Unit 7 P1, M1, D1)

You are assisting a sports coach at your local club and gaining valuable experience from observing established coaches in action. Produce promotional material for sports leadership using examples to promote the skills, qualities and responsibilities required. Your materials should:

- Identify two successful sports leaders who have contrasting leadership styles.

- Describe and explain the skills, qualities and responsibilities associated with sports leadership, comparing and contrasting your two chosen sports leaders.

- Evaluate the skills and qualities of your two sports leaders, commenting on their effectiveness.

Topic check

1 Name three different types of communication you might use when organising your event or activity.

2 What challenges might you face when communicating with children?

3 Describe the problems you might face in obtaining equipment.

4 What problems might you face in transporting and giving out equipment?

5 Identify three different areas of knowledge you might need to acquire for your particular event or activity.

6 Why would leaders carry out an evaluation after every session they take?

7 Name the three different leadership styles.

8 Which type of leader encourages the group to make the decisions?

9 In what ways are motivation and enthusiasm closely linked as qualities?

10 What is meant by 'safeguarding'?

Planning and leading an activity session

▶ Getting started

This topic will help you to plan and lead a short activity session. You might be given the option of planning and leading a particular phase of a longer session as part of a team. This will be a very useful 'rehearsal' for the main event which you will be planning and leading later.

When you have completed this topic, you should:

- know what you need to consider when planning an activity session
- understand that you may have to adapt your leadership style to the activity and ability level of the group, and demonstrate skills
- know the different components of a session and their importance
- know the options for recording information for later review.

🔑 Key terms

Aim: what you want to achieve overall

Environment: external surroundings, conditions or influences

Gender: the sex of an individual, whether they are male or female

Objective: the ways in which you plan to achieve an aim

Portfolio: a file or folder containing documents and papers

Planning

There are a large number of factors to consider when planning an activity session.

Participants

You need to take into account various factors relating to the people who will be participating in the activity. These include the following:

▶ *Age* – For this session you are likely to be dealing with people of the same age as you or slightly younger. If you are dealing with much younger people in your later event, they will not be as physically developed or capable as the group you are leading here.

▶ *Ability* – Most groups you deal with are likely to be what is known as 'mixed ability'. This means that there is a spectrum of ability within the group. This could range from being very able to having very low ability levels. Planning to lead a group with this range of abilities can be very challenging – but it must be planned for.

▶ **Gender** – You are likely to be dealing with a mixed group of males and females. If this is the case, they will need to have separate changing facilities. You might also find that there are certain sports and activities in which mixed groups are not allowed to participate. This certainly applies to football and rugby for older age groups. This is because physical contact is allowed within the rules, and it is considered dangerous to allow females to play with males due to the natural differences in their size and strength.

It is important to consider the age group of the group that will be participating in the activity.

▶ *Numbers* – You will need to know how many people are going to take part in the activity. This will enable you to provide enough equipment for everyone and ensure that there is enough space available. For many activities there are rules about ratios of leaders to group members (e.g. in the majority of outdoor and adventurous activities you would not be expected to work with a group of more than ten people), so you need to check if this is the case for your activity. If it is, you will need to ensure that you have enough leaders for the number of participants.

▶ *Medical conditions* – You must be aware of any medical conditions in members of your group that might affect their performance or require any specialist treatment (e.g. asthma – if any of your group suffers from this you should make sure they have their inhaler with them). All schools, colleges and centres hold this information, so make sure you have it before you work with a group.

▶ *Specific needs* – This refers to any disabilities, such as poor vision or hearing, or mobility problems. You should always ask the person who is usually in charge if anyone in your group has a special need that you should be aware of.

Aims and objectives

Your **aims** are what you want your session to achieve overall (e.g. to lead an effective warm-up), and your **objectives** are the ways in which you will achieve that overall aim (e.g. the different stages within that warm-up to make it effective, such as using pulse raisers and stretching). These need to be set out fully and clearly. It is a good idea to get advice from your tutor regarding these in the planning stage, to check that they are appropriate. Inappropriate aims and objectives often lead to poorly led sessions.

Activity

Interview your two chosen sports leaders about the specific factors of age and numbers. Find out the issues relating to these that you might have to consider in your planning for your activity session.

Resources

You will need to consider the following when planning your session:

▶ *Equipment* – As explained in Topic 6.1 you will need to consider what equipment you will need, how many of each thing, and so on. Look back at Figure 6.1 on page 136 to remind yourself about all the possible equipment issues.

▶ *Time* – This session is only supposed to last for about 10 minutes. However, you will find that this probably still requires a great deal of planning. The session is likely to include different activities or 'phases' within it, so you must plan out exactly how long each one will last and the order in which you present them. Time management is one of the greatest challenges any leader faces, and is something you will get better at with experience. Remember that this is your rehearsal for a longer event later.

▶ **Environment** – Sporting sessions will often take place in more than one environment. However, for this brief session you are likely to be taking a group that is already in its performing environment. This could be a classroom, gym, sports hall, fitness suite, swimming pool, outdoor ball court, astroturf pitch, playing fields, dance studio or any other type of sporting environment. Larger events may involve several different environments. For example, there could be an initial assembly point, changing areas, travelling points (from changing to performing) and then the performance environment. You will have to think about the practicalities of moving between environments when planning the event. Maintaining high levels of health and safety will be very important when you are considering the use of resources and the environment you will be working in. Remember that this was one of your responsibilities identified earlier.

Target setting

You will have to have clear targets for this session and these are going to be at the core of your planning. For this short session you may want to have just one or two basic targets. When it comes to your final event you are likely to be asked to consider more targets.

Expected outcomes

These are what you want to have happened by the end of your session. Just like your target setting these might be quite brief for this session and just consist of one or two. When you have your final event with more content you are likely to have a greater number of expected outcomes.

> 💡 **Over to you!**
>
> Start to get the planning process underway for leading a session by discussing your options with your tutor.

Leading

You are going to lead this session on your own – it will be solely your responsibility. This can be quite a nerve-racking experience the first time you do it, and you need to know exactly what is going to be required of you.

Demonstration of skills

There are likely to be specific skills you will want to cover in your session, and which you will want the group to practise. A good way of starting to teach a skill is to demonstrate it. There are three possible ways of doing this:

▶ demonstrate yourself
▶ choose a member of the group to demonstrate, preferably an able performer
▶ show an example demonstration such as a video clip.

Over to you!

Consider what skills you are planning to teach in your session, and which will needed to be demonstrated. Start to practise these skills yourself, to be sure you are competent at them before the session. If you plan to use a video clip, sort this out now and decide exactly how you are going to incorporate it into your session.

Appropriate content

The content of your session needs to be appropriate to what you are covering in the session and to the ability level of the group.

▶ You should consider issues that are specific to the activity, such as wearing the right kit (e.g. being barefoot for gymnastics). Your leadership style may also be influenced by the nature of the activity. For instance, an athletics throwing event might need a more autocratic style to ensure that safety standards remain high.

▶ You will have to identify what development stage the group is currently at, and tailor the session to fit this. Younger people may have lower levels of coordination or understanding. If you do not take this into consideration, you may be the only one capable of achieving the task. On the other hand, if you set a task which is too easy for the group they may become bored.

Activity

You will have to plan carefully the content of the session – the different stages and how you are going to present them.

Warm-up and cool-down

It is very important that you include a warm-up and a cool-down in all sessions, mainly to prevent injuries. Wherever possible they should be appropriate to the activity as well. For example, a badminton session where players can perform actions such as clears , drives and lifts to warm the muscles that will be used in the game itself.

For an outdoor games session on a cold day, plenty of pulse-raising movements to raise the body temperature would be advisable.

Structure and components of an activity

For most activities the following are common options that can be used:

▶ *Skill introduction* – Introduce the specific skills that are to be used, and practise them with the group. These may be skills they already have, or there may be opportunities to teach and practise new skills.

▶ *Development* – This could mean adding new dimensions to the skills, which might mean participants trying them out with a partner or in small groups. The development stage involves placing the skill in a realistic game environment. For example, the skill of performing a lay-up in basketball can be developed from an individual practice, into a practice against an opponent who is passive (does not move) and then active (moves to defend).

▶ *Conditioned games* – These are commonly used. They are when rules or conditions for playing are altered or adjusted so that particular skills or objectives can be concentrated on. For example, to develop passing skills in basketball the condition could be added that no dribbling is allowed. In football and hockey only two touches could be allowed before a pass has to be made.

▶ *Competition* – Finishing off the session with some form of competition is a good idea. This concludes the focus of the session and can often be the most enjoyable phase for the participants.

Recording

You need to carefully consider how you are going to record the planning stages and various other aspects of your session. The main choices you have are:

▶ keeping a diary – this could record all of your planning sessions in detail

▶ filling in a logbook – this might contain the specific details of the content you have planned

▶ putting together a **portfolio** – this would be where you keep all of your records

▶ keeping video records – getting someone else to record your actual session from start to finish

▶ keeping audio records – you could interview some of your group after the session has ended

▶ an observation record – a non-participant could note down what happens in your session

▶ witness testimony – a statement written by your tutor, sports leader or even one of the group

▶ feedback sheets – you could produce a comment sheet for each member of the group to fill in.

What is most likely is that you will use a combination of the above.

Case study

Chrissie is at the planning stage of the activity session she is going to lead. She does not consider herself to be a particularly confident person or a very strong sports performer. Chrissie's tutor has told her that she can work with three other girls in her group to take one phase of an organised school session each. The group they will be working with are infant school children who are being brought to the school specifically for this session.

The activity is going to be gymnastics, which is not one of Chrissie's strongest or favourite sports. However, one of the other girls in the group is a strong club gymnast.

1. Because of Chrissie's lack of confidence, which particular phase would you suggest she leads and why?

2. What age factors should Chrissie take into account with this group?

3. Are there likely to be any environment issues with this group which Chrissie and her friends should consider?

4. Will there be any equipment-related issues the girls should consider?

5. What are the most sensible options available to Chrissie with regard to demonstrations?

Topic check

1. What is meant by the term 'mixed ability'?
2. Why might gender reduce the options of activities available?
3. Identify three other issues related to participants that you will have to consider in your planning.
4. State at least four different environments in which you might be asked to present a session.
5. What is a reasonable number of targets to set for this short session?
6. Identify the three main options for providing demonstrations.
7. Why might an autocratic leadership style be most suitable for an athletics throwing event session?
8. Why is it essential to include a warm-up and cool-down in every session?
9. What are the four activity phases most commonly included in an activity session?
10. Name five different recording options available to you.

Reviewing your planning and leadership of a sports activity

▶ Getting started

This is the first of two review topics in this unit. The purpose of a review is to enable you to reflect on what you have done so far, and use this information to help you plan the next stage.

When you have completed this topic, you should:

- know about a range of reviewing methods and how to use them
- be able to set targets for improvement and development
- understand how to use the results to carry out some comparisons.

Review

As mentioned in Topic 6.2, you must record information about the planning of your short activity session and the session itself. You can then use this information to **review** how it went and identify areas for improvement.

Feedback

This is any form of information or comment you can get back from other people regarding how your short activity session went. You should consider all of the following:

▶ *Participants* – If possible, you should get **feedback** from everyone who took part in your session. Ask for 'constructive criticism' and encourage them to be very honest with you. This means that, rather than just making a negative comment about something they thought didn't go too well, they should suggest how it might have been better.

▶ *Supervisor* – There will have been a tutor or member of staff in overall charge of the session. Ask them for their comments as well. They are likely to be qualified, so they will be able to give your more technical feedback on your content and delivery.

▶ *Observers* – There may be others who were not directly part of the session but who watched it in progress. You can ask them for their comments too.

Consider any criticisms to be 'constructive', directing you to areas you can improve. Most people find it easier to concentrate on what did not go so well, so try not to feel demoralised – the rest of your group are likely to experience the same thing. Make sure that you also take note of any positive feedback on the aspects that went well.

The feedback you receive will probably be more useful if you plan some prompts. This means you should consider what questions you are going to ask one or all three of these groups.

🔑 Key terms

Agenda: a list, plan or outline of things which need to be done

Feedback: information received back as a reaction or response

Review: the process of going over something again, or producing a report looking back on what was achieved

Strengths and areas for improvement

When you have received your feedback you will be in a better position to consider your strengths and areas for improvement. Remember to include your own thoughts and reflections in this as well. It is likely that you will have noted these in one of your recording methods (e.g. diary, logbook). You will find it useful to consider the following headings when you review your records:

▶ planning
▶ content
▶ organisation

▶ health and safety
▶ style and personal qualities
▶ achievements.

Achievements are something that was not specifically included in your planning. You need to compare these with the aims and objectives you set at the start of this unit. This will give you some idea of how well the session went overall, and whether or not you were able to achieve what you set out to.

Setting targets for improvement and development

Based on what you have found out from reviewing your short activity session, you can now set yourself some targets for improvement and development. Try to be realistic with your target setting. It is likely that this was the first time you have had to plan and lead a session, so there might be quite few areas you would like to improve and develop. Some ways to help you with this process are discussed below.

A team review meeting.

Activity

Meet with the rest of your group and put together an outline **agenda** for your meetings. It should identify all of the key issues you are going to address at each meeting.

Targets

Make sure that your targets are SMART:

▶ **S**pecific – identify particular targets

▶ **M**easurable – make sure you can measure how successful you have been at achieving them

▶ **A**chievable – you must be able to do them in the time you have available

▶ **R**ealistic – they must be possible both in terms of your ability and the time you have available

▶ **T**ime-bound – you need to give yourself a time limit by which you will achieve your target.

Development plans

You will be encouraged to have regular planning meetings, which will form part of your assessment. These will be overseen by your tutor and, particularly in the later stages, will include other people involved in the event you will be leading. These meetings will give you the opportunity to start considering phased plans, looking at different stages and developing them as you go along.

Development opportunities

You must identify opportunities that will help you to develop your planning, leadership and other skills. For example, you may identify a particular area for improvement and look to attend a course related to it, or receive specific training. This would be something to discuss at length with your tutor, as they should be able to help you with this.

Activity focus

You will find it very useful to review how the delivery of each of the different stages of the activity itself went. It is useful to do this even if you did not deliver all of them yourself. You can work with the people who did deliver other stages to review these. This will help you with your planning in the future. The phases you should review are:

▶ warm-up

▶ skill introduction

▶ development

▶ conditioned game

▶ competition

▶ cool-down.

You will have kept records of how the activity went, to which you can refer back to review it.

Assessment activity 6.2 (Unit 7 P2, M2, P3, M3)

This assessment activity focuses on planning and leading a sports activity. You are required to:

- Plan and lead a sports activity session.
- Review and explain your own performance in planning and leading the activity, commenting on your strengths and areas for improvement and development.

The evidence you produce for this assessment activity should include a session plan, witness statements or forms describing and assessing your leadership of the sports activity, and a written review of your performance, strengths and areas for improvement.

Topic check

1 What is the purpose of carrying out a review?
2 Identify three different sources you could receive feedback from.
3 What does SMART stand for?
4 How would you review your achievements?
5 Give three other areas you might identify as strengths or areas for improvement.

Assisting in the planning and leading of a sports event

Having completed Topic 6.2 and carried out a review of planning and leading your activity session, you should now be able to help with planning and leading a sports event. This topic will guide you through the processes and help you to build on the experiences you have already had.

When you have completed this topic, you should:

■ know all the areas you have to consider when planning an event
■ understand what is required to lead an event successfully
■ have considered a variety of events you might lead
■ know the options for recording information for later review.

Key terms

Contingency: something that might happen if another unlikely event happens
Risk assessment: the determination of the level of risk in a particular course of action or activity

Planning

You will find that your planning for this has to be in far more depth than your planning for the activity session. There are more issues to consider for a large event than for a short activity session.

Over to you!

Find out if a sports event is planned within your school in the near future. Ask if you can be involved in, or at least observe, the planning and delivery of this event.

Roles and responsibilities

Your roles and responsibilities, and those of others, will depend on the type of event you are involved with planning and leading. Figure 6.3 gives you an example of the roles and responsibilities that would be included in an athletics meeting – something like your school sports day.

Figure 6.3 Roles and responsibilities in an athletics meeting

Role	Responsibility
Overall leader/organiser	All aspects of the event. This includes planning for and managing all of the other people identified below.
Track events co-ordinator	This would be the person in overall control of the various track events. These would normally include the 100 m, 200 m, 400 m, 800 m and 1500 m races. It could also include hurdles. These would then be subdivided into age and gender groups.
Field events co-ordinator	This would be the person in overall control of the various field events. These would normally include the long jump, high jump, triple jump, discus, javelin and shot. It could also include hammer throw and pole vault. These would then be subdivided into age and gender groups.
Announcer	To announce all events as they are programmed to take place, plus results of races and events and any other information for the spectators.
Starter	To start all of the races in the track events.
Track judges/timekeepers	One judge/timekeeper for each lane for any sprinting events that are run in lanes. Place judges/timekeepers for longer events.
Finishing judge	To decide finishing places and the order of finishing.
Field judges/measurements	One judge for decisions on foul throws and no jumps, and another judge to measure the distance thrown or achieved. In the case of the high jump this means measuring and placing the bar.
Recorders	Taking times, scores and results and filling these in on score sheets.
First aiders	To deal with any injuries, accidents, over exertion etc. in various areas around the event.

You can see from the table above that in any event there are a great number of roles and many responsibilities. For many of the roles identified it is not just one person. For the sprint events you need eight lane timekeepers/judges alone!

You might decide to organise a school sports day.

Over to you!

Complete a roles and responsibilities table like Figure 6.3 for another type of event.

Other planning considerations

There is a range of other areas you will have to take into consideration when planning your event, including the following.

▶ *Health and safety* – This will vary with the type of event you are involved in. Specific events will have specific health and safety considerations. For our sports day event example above, there will be many health and safety considerations relating to the throwing events, and the throwing areas in particular. If you had a swimming gala you would need qualified lifeguards, and for any outdoor event you would have to check all pitches for broken glass, stones etc.

▶ *First aid* – This is one of the roles and responsibilities identified in Figure 6.3. First aid cover has to be in place for all events and you need to make sure that you have qualified first-aid personnel available who hold a current award/certificate.

▶ **Risk assessment** – The area of risk assessment is covered in detail in Unit 5, Topic 5.4 (page 128). It is essential that a full risk assessment is carried out before any event takes place.

▶ **Contingency** *planning* – This means having alternative plans in place which will enable you to cope with any changes in circumstances. For example, if you are planning an outdoor event, what will you do if the weather is bad?

▶ *Other bookings of the facilities* – Other people may be using the same facilities as you, so you may have to share them. This might raise the issue of clashes of usage, e.g. using changing rooms at the same time.

▶ *Rules* – These must clearly relate to the rules in place on the day. A written copy of the rules must be handed out to everyone involved.

▶ *Letters* – You must ensure that all letters regarding the administration of the event, and formal letters of invitation are sent out in plenty of time to all the relevant people. You will need to include reply forms for people to send back to you so that you know who has accepted the invitation.

▶ *Structure of the competition* – You must decide on the structure the competition will take and make sure that everyone understands this. For example, you may be using a combination of league and knockout formats, but competitors need to know what will happen if there are draws or ties.

▶ *Scoring systems* – You may use the recognised system for scoring, or may decide to adapt it for your event. In many events shortened scoring versions are often used, e.g. in tennis it is common to play shorter sets.

▶ *Refreshments* – If large numbers of people are expected to attend then you will have to provide refreshments for everyone: the competitors, spectators and for the staff/coaches accompanying them. You will have to consider where they will be distributed, what they will be, how much you will provide and what it will cost.

▶ *Organisation of equipment* – Refer back to Figure 6.1 (page 136) to see the type of things you will have to consider in relation to this.

▶ *Presentations and rewards* – Your event is likely to have a winner or winners, so you will have to decide what sort of award is to be given and who will present it.

Over to you!

You should have an idea of the event you are intending to lead. Look at Figure 6.1 (page 136) and check how many of the issues identified there are going to need to be taken into consideration.

Leading

Once you have done all of the planning and preparation, you will have to actually lead the event on the day. Leading the event will require similar considerations to those for leading your sporting activity (see Topic 6.2), but on a much larger scale and involving far more responsibility in the following areas.

Organised warm-ups are important.

▶ *Skills demonstrations* – These could be over a range of skills if it is something you have decided to take responsibility for (e.g. showing the correct way to perform an action in the warm-up)

▶ *Qualities and responsibilities appropriate to your role* – As the leader you may have to carry out all of the introductions and give out full instructions regarding the organisation of the event.

▶ *The warm-ups and cool-downs* – If you are not going to do these, who is?

▶ *Officiating* – You are unlikely to officiate everything yourself, but you will have to lead your team of officials.

▶ *Timekeeping* – You should be able to control the overall timings of the programme, but individual matches/games/performances might have to be left to others.

▶ *First aid* – You must check that all of the first-aid arrangements you have made are in place, that the first-aid station is set up and that everyone knows what the first-aid arrangements are.

▶ *Presentation ceremony* – You will probably want to choose someone else to make the actual presentations, but you should consider running the ceremony.

▶ *Refreshments* – You must check that all of arrangements you have made regarding refreshments are in place. You will need either to oversee these yourself or have delegated someone else with the responsibility of supervising them.

▶ *Equipment* – You will have overall responsibility for this. One of the biggest challenges can be collecting it all in and putting it back where it belongs at the end of the event.

Event type

It will be up to you to decide what type of event you plan and lead. However, you will have to work very closely with your tutor regarding this. It is probably going to be easier for you to take over an event which has been provided before or which is already in the PE programme/calendar. You may have the option to come up with one of your own if this is possible.

 Activity

Take the opportunity to practise leading by volunteering to lead parts of PE lessons, or training sessions such as the warm-up phase.

The main options which are usually provided consist of the following:

▶ *Sports day* – This was considered in some detail earlier in the topic. See page 153 and Figure 6.3.

▶ *Festival of sport* – It is possible to include a variety of sports in a festival. You could cater for both genders by having a netball and football tournament running at the same time. You could also mix age groups as well as activities.

▶ *Sports tournaments* – These are commonly activities such as five-a-side football, mini-rugby, netball and rounders. Most sports can be adapted to a tournament format, which is very popular.

Recording

This is something you must consider very carefully and make sure that you do it properly. You will use your records of the event to carry out a review, so you must make sure that you have all the information and data you need.

Here is a reminder of the formats you can use for this:

▶ diary
▶ logbook
▶ portfolio
▶ observation record
▶ video
▶ audio
▶ witness testimony
▶ feedback sheets.

Remember that on the day you are going to be very busy. You will need to set up your recording system well in advance. If you are going to use feedback sheets then these must be produced in advance and handed out on the day. If you are going to use a visitor for witness testimony, they must complete the statement and hand it back in before they leave, so you must ensure that there is a system in place for this.

Case study

Chrissie has decided to form a team with her friends to plan and lead a sports day. They are going to carry it out with the infant school they worked with previously. Chrissie and her friends have been told that they can use their own school facilities for this during the summer term. Four year groups from the infant school are going to be invited along and the event will take place in an afternoon.

The team Chrissie has formed has been told that they will have to adapt the day to suit the age of the children. They have also been told that parents should be invited along, and to cater for them as well as for the children taking part.

1. How big a team do you think Chrissie needs? What particular roles can you identify?

2. What responsibility do you think Chrissie is likely to take on?

3. Are there any particular issues relating to the age group being invited to the event?

4. Suggest at least five specific events which Chrissie and her team could include in this sports day.

5. What sorts of things should the team plan to involve the parents in?

Topic check

1 What is meant by 'risk assessment'?
2 Why is contingency planning needed?
3 Identify any issues that could arise from other people being booked into the chosen facility.
4 Why would you need to prepare reply forms as part of your invitation letters?
5 For one particular sport, what options are available to you in terms of scoring systems?
6 Name three groups you may need to provide refreshments for.
7 What two aspects of timekeeping will you have to consider?
8 Name three different types of event you might choose to lead.

Reviewing your planning and leadership of a sports event

▶ Getting started

This topic revisits many of the aspects covered in Topic 6.3. The lessons learnt from that review should have been taken into account for your planning and leadership of the sports event.

In this topic you will carry out a more detailed review of the event you planned and led in Topic 6.4. You will have recorded a large amount of information which you can use for this review, on which you will be assessed.

When you have completed this topic, you should:

■ know more about a range of reviewing methods and how to use them

■ be able to set targets for improvement and development based on your leadership of the event.

Review

The same reviewing methods are available to you as were discussed in Topic 6.3, but the data you have gathered from leading your event will be different from that you recorded for your earlier activity session.

Feedback

Due to the number of people involved in this large-scale event you are likely to have received a great deal of feedback. One of the skills you now need to use is interpreting that feedback. Try to find consistent comments about particular areas or issues which are most important. You are unlikely to be able to consider every aspect if you have a large amount of information, so prioritise areas for consideration. Remember that the three groups you should have received feedback from are:

▶ participants

▶ supervisors

▶ observers (there might be some spectators/parents who could be added to this category).

💡 Over to you!

Look back at the feedback you received at the end of Topic 6.2 and compare that with this latest feedback.

Strengths and areas for improvement

You will already have identified some strengths and areas for improvement after the activity session you led. You now need to do the same in relation to leading the larger event. As before, consider these in terms of

▶ planning (clearly, far more of this will have been needed for the large event)

▶ content

▶ organisation

▶ health and safety

▶ leadership style and personal qualities

▶ achievements.

Setting targets for improvement and development

Once again, these will match those you considered in Topic 6.3. You should remember that this is likely to be an area which you will be called upon to plan and deliver in the future, so setting longer-term targets is still important.

SMART targets

Remember that targets you set yourself should always be SMART (see Topic 6.3, page 150). You can review whether or not you have achieved the targets you set yourself at the end of Topic 6.3. How effective was this target-setting approach? If you find that you are repeating areas you identified previously, this indicates that your earlier target setting was poor. Think carefully about all the elements of using SMART targets, and make sure that the targets you set really do fit in with this approach.

Development plans and opportunities

Due to the higher-level demands of leading the larger event, it is likely that you will have identified more areas for development. Did you find the development plans you made in Topic 6.3 were useful and did indeed help you to develop your planning and leadership skills? Can you identify any new development opportunities (specific training or courses)?

This area of sports leadership is a growth area in terms of career opportunities. Completing this topic might be a first step towards finding volunteer work in schools, youth centres, sports centres, crèches, hospitals and hospices. These may then lead on to paid career opportunities.

Over to you!

Look back at the strengths and areas for improvement that you identified in Topic 6.3. Compare these with the strengths and areas for improvement that you have identified this time. Have they changed? Do you feel that you learnt from the activity you led earlier, and have achieved improvements in the areas you identified?

Activity

Find out about any National Governing Body awards which you could obtain in the areas and sports which interest you most.

Over to you!

Compare your overall findings and summary for this topic with those you had after completing Topic 6.3.

Assessment activity 6.3 (Unit 7 P4, P5, M4, D2)

The final assessment activity in this unit requires you to contribute to the planning of a sports event. You will need to plan and deliver the event as part of a group and then review your performance. Your evidence for this assessment activity should include:
- an event plan and associated evidence of event planning

- a written report describing how you contributed to the planning and leading of the sports event
- an evaluative review of your own performance, identifying strengths and suggesting areas for improvement and ways of developing your skills as a sports leader.

Topic check

1 What is meant by the term 'feedback'?
2 Name three groups of people you could receive feedback from.
3 Identify two specific categories you should include in your development plan.
4 Where might you be able to obtain work which involves aspects of sports leadership?

Assessment summary

The overall grade you achieve for this unit depends on how well you meet the grading criteria set out in Appendix 1 (see page 296). You must complete:

■ all of the P criteria to achieve a **pass** grade
■ all of the P and the M criteria to achieve a **merit** grade.
■ all of the P, M and D criteria to achieve a **distinction** grade.

Your tutor will assess the assessment activities that you complete for this unit. The work you produce should provide evidence which demonstrates that you have achieved each of the assessment criteria. The table below identifies what you need to demonstrate to meet each of the pass, merit and distinction criteria for this unit. You should always check and self-assess your work before you submit your assignments for marking.

Remember that you MUST provide evidence for all of the P criteria to pass the unit.

Grading criteria	You need to demonstrate that you can:	Have you got the evidence?
P1	Describe the skills, qualities and responsibilities associated with successful sports leadership, using two examples of successful sports leaders	
M1	Explain the skills, qualities and responsibilities associated with successful sports leadership, comparing and contrasting two successful sports leaders	
D1	Evaluate the skills and qualities of two contrasting leaders in sport, commenting on their effectiveness	
P2	Plan and lead a sports activity, with tutor support	
M2	Independently plan and lead a sports activity	
P3	Review the planning and leading of a sports activity, identifying strengths and areas for improvement	
M3	Explain strengths and areas for improvement and development in the planning and leading of a sports activity	
P4	Contribute to the planning and leading of a sports event	
P5	Review own performance whilst assisting with the planning and leading of a sports event, identifying strengths and areas for improvement	
M4	Explain strengths and areas for improvement in assisting with the planning and leading of a sports event, making suggestions relating to improvement	
D2	Evaluate own performance in the planning and leading of a sports activity and event, commenting on strengths and areas for improvement and further development as a sports leader	

Always ask your tutor to explain any assignment tasks or assessment criteria that you don't understand fully. Being clear about the task before you begin gives you the best chance of succeeding. Good luck with your Unit 7 assessment work!

7 Technical skills and tactical awareness for sport (Unit 8)

Unit outline

In this unit you will investigate the technical and tactical requirements of a sport and the methods of improving your own technical and tactical ability in a selected sport. You will look at elite performers as examples of excellence in these areas. An example of an elite performer is given, but you will need to select one who performs in your chosen sport.

This will prepare you to plan and undertake a six-week programme designed to develop your own technical skills and tactical awareness. At the end of the programme you will review it and set targets for further development.

Learning outcomes

1 **Know the technical and tactical demands of a selected sport.**
2 **Understand the technical skills and tactical awareness in a selected sport.**
3 **Be able to plan and undertake a six-week programme to develop your own technical skills and tactical awareness.**
4 **Be able to review your own technical and tactical development and set goals for further development.**

The technical and tactical demands of a selected sport

Getting started

In order to become a better performer in your chosen sport, you must know its technical and tactical demands. You then need to look at the ways in which you can improve your levels in both of these areas.

When you have completed this topic, you should:

- know the technical demands of your chosen sport
- know the tactical demands of your chosen sport when defending and attacking.

Key terms

Strategy: An overall plan of action against an opponent or team that includes a variety of tactics

Tactic: A play or plan, for attack or defence, to achieve victory

Technical demands

Different sports have different technical demands. You must make sure that you understand those associated with any sport you are participating in, observing or assessing. The technical demands can be considered in relation to three different types of skill:

▶ *Continuous skills* – as the name suggests, these are skills that you use continuously – you carry on doing them (e.g. running, swimming).

▶ *Serial skills* – these are made up of a combination of skills, for example in the pole vault, where each phase of the jump involves a separate skill, which have to be put together to achieve the final successful jump. Other examples include the triple jump, with a hop, step and jump, and the lay-up in basketball, with the dribble, jump and shoot phases.

▶ *Discrete skills* – these are clearly identified specific skills needed in a particular sport, such as a golf swing, a hammer throw, kicking a football or passing a netball.

Tactical demands

Some tactical demands are fairly general and can apply to most sports in both attacking and defensive situations. Others can be specific to the activity, in the same way as some skills are. Some general tactical considerations that can be applied to a variety of sports are:

▶ *Positioning* – this can include the positioning of an individual (where you would position yourself in an activity such as tennis) as well as players' positions (defensive, attacking) and how they use the space in a team activity. In a sport such as netball, your position also dictates where on the court you are allowed to go.

▶ *Choice and use of correct/appropriate skills* – this includes things such as what stroke you choose to play in cricket or tennis. In every activity you have to decide what tactics to play and how to make the best use of your skills.

▶ *Conditions* – these will vary a great deal. Your activity could be indoors or outdoors; the weather could be wet or dry, cold or hot, sunny or foggy. Other factors that can affect conditions include pressure from spectators/the crowd, and even the type of equipment you are using. For example, if you are playing rugby in very wet conditions, the ball will be very slippery and difficult to catch and pass. Figure 7.1 gives some indication of how conditions can affect sporting activities.

▶ *Use of **strategies*** – for example, a rugby team may identify that their forwards are much stronger than the opposition's. Their strategy for the game would be to keep the ball with the forwards as long as possible and only release the ball for the backs when the opposition have committed extra people to defending the forwards' progress. The team will have a variety of **tactics** they can use to carry out their strategy, e.g. they can 'ruck' and 'maul' the ball, use the number 8 and flankers for a variety of back-row moves, or just use the props and locks to physically drive forward, trying to punch a hole in the opposition's defence.

Figure 7.1 Possible effects of conditions on activities

Condition	Possible effects
Indoors	This could be positive, as it is likely to be warm and dry, or negative if there was insufficient space to play the sport properly.
Outdoors	This could be positive, as large pitches and playing areas can be provided outside, but negative if there are poor weather conditions.
Wet	This is likely to have a negative effect. For activities such as tennis or rounders, wet conditions could make the playing area slippery and dangerous, so it is likely that the activity would be cancelled. Thunderstorms with lightning can be very dangerous – golf matches are always stopped in these conditions.
Dry	In general the effect will be positive, as outdoor activities are more likely to take place. However, if there is a prolonged dry spell then outdoor playing areas can get very hard. For a sport such as rugby this could mean that the ground is too hard to play on.
Cold	Extreme cold can be dangerous. It can also cause frosts, which can result in hard, icy ground conditions which can make playing too dangerous.
Sunny	In general the effect will be positive, as outdoor activities are more likely to take place and be enjoyable. However, very bright sun can cause problems when catching a high ball in rounders, softball, rugby or soccer, or serving in tennis. Very high temperatures can also cause problems such as dehydration and sunstroke.
Foggy	In some team games, such as hockey, rugby and soccer, thick fog can mean games have to be abandoned. Players and officials will not be able to see what is happening!
Spectators/crowds	These can encourage players to do better, but they can equally put players off if they are making negative comments.

Case study

Rashid is a very keen basketball player and is a member of the school squad. Basketball is a high-profile and successful sport in Rashid's school. However, he is not usually included in the starting five in matches, but tends to be brought on as a substitute towards the end of matches when other players have been fouled out of the game. Rashid is aware that other players are chosen before him because they have better technical skills and tactical awareness, so he has chosen these areas to work on and improve. Fitness levels are not a concern for Rashid, as he already does regular fitness training, but he would like to improve his shooting (lay-ups and free throws in particular) and dribbling skills, as well as 'man-to-man' and 'zone defence' tactical skills.

1. Rashid has identified dribbling as an area he needs to improve. What type of skill is dribbling?

2. Can you think of any continuous skills which are important in basketball?

3. Identify at least one serial skill used in basketball.

4. What sort of conditions is Rashid going to have to consider and take into account, when playing?

Over to you!

Can you think of any other effects which you could add to any of the conditions in Figure 7.1?

Topic check

1 What is a continuous skill? Give one example.
2 What is a serial skill? Give one example.
3 Identify a third type of skill and give an example.
4 Name at least two different playing positions in your chosen sport.
5 Explain how having a particular position might restrict which areas you can play in.
6 How might very wet conditions affect how a game is played?
7 Identify two problems that might be caused by very dry conditions.
8 How could bright sunshine affect someone's performance?
9 Explain what is meant by playing a 'zone defence'.
10 What do you understand by the term 'man-to-man marking'?

Technical skills and tactical awareness in a selected sport

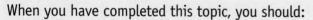

▶ Getting started

In this unit you will choose a specific elite performer and consider your own levels of performance compared with theirs. In order to do this you must first identify your own strengths and areas for development. This topic will help you to develop the skills necessary for effective analysis and assessment.

🔑 Key terms

Peer: someone who is the same age and status as you

When you have completed this topic, you should:

- be aware of the different types of analysis available
- understand the analysis model
- know how to identify your strengths and areas for improvement
- understand the level of an elite performance
- be able to select from and use a variety of assessment methods.

Performance analysis

All levels of sport performers must be able to analyse their strengths and weaknesses against a desired coaching model. Most sports have developed specific information for how to perform a variety of skills with success. This could include coaching points for the best smash, set shot or forehand drive in cricket, or somersault in trampolining. These techniques have often been tested rigorously to see if they are the optimum (best) level of performance and the most efficient movements for the activity.

To be able to compare performances and levels you will often be required to video an athlete's or team's performance and analyse the results. Playing the results back in slow motion will often help you identify the problems that the performer has and enable you to provide future training solutions and targets.

Alternatively, you can carry out observational analysis by keeping a checklist of skills and identifying and recording people's current level of performance by watching them play.

You can also use notational analysis, which is writing things down as they happen. This is a method of recording number details such as how many shots were on target and how many off; how many passes were accurate and how many were intercepted. For example, in badminton you could record the percentage of smashes that were successful and the percentage of errors in completing the shot. Figure 7.2 is an example of notational analysis for a badminton match.

You could analyse a badminton match using notational analysis.

Figure 7.2 Notational analysis for a badminton match

	Front			Middle			Back		
	Effective	Ineffective	Normal	Effective	Ineffective	Normal	Effective	Ineffective	Normal
Drop shot				1	1	1		2	2
Push		2	2	3	1	5		2	1
Block									
Smash	1			1				3	
Clear				1	1	5	1	2	4
Net		2	2						
Lift	1	3	1	2	2	4	1	2	4

The court can be divided into three sections: front, middle and back. Effective shots are outright winners. Ineffective shots are points lost from the rally. Normal shots are shots that are returned. Lifts are regarded as bad shots. Smash, net and drop shots are potential winners.

To enable you to score this you can either video the match and play it back in slow motion, or involve other people to help you score each shot. For example, a group could be split into seven to record drop shot, push, block, smash, clear, net and lift for a performer, in a game in real time using observational analysis only. The results can then be analysed after the game to identify strengths and weaknesses. In the example in Figure 7.2 it is easy to see that the player is lifting the shuttle too much, allowing the opponent to attack. Also, smashes are only effective at the front. When the player is smashing at the back of the court their smash becomes ineffective. This would be a weakness requiring additional coaching.

> **Over to you!**
>
> For your chosen sport, consider which type of analysis will be most useful: observation, video analysis or notational analysis. You can also consider using a combination of all three.

Analysis model

Using an analysis model means following the sequence listed below to analyse your performance:

1. Analyse
2. Evaluate
3. Plan
4. Perform
5. Observe

You will have to carry out an initial *analysis*, which you will then go on to *evaluate*. This could include the necessary skills and coaching points for specific performances such as throwing a javelin. Javelin throwing can be broken down into the run up, the transfer and the throw. This will give you an initial idea and model to compare performances with. From this you will *plan* what you should do next. You put the plan into action by doing another *performance*, which is then *observed* again. Strengths and weaknesses can then be determined by comparing the differences between the two performances.

When you carry out your analysis, make sure that you do not 'overload' yourself with too much information. You should focus your attention on identifying your particular strengths and areas for improvement.

Over to you!

Test out this analysis model in a particular sporting situation relevant to you. Go through the five steps to see what effect this is likely to have on your performance. To help you do this, follow the steps in Figure 7.3.

The release phase of the javelin throw.

Figure 7.3 Notational analysis

O	Organise yourself. Make sure you are ready and have everything you need (e.g. observation sheet, clipboard, something to write with). Make sure you are in the right place.	A	Arrange what you are looking for into separate parts (e.g. the phases of the performance: warm-up, skills practice, actual game or performance).	A	Aim to gather specific material so that you can advise the performer at the end of the performance.
B	Begin observing as soon as the session gets underway. Make sure you do not have any distractions.	N	Note down what you see.	S	Start observing the performance.
S	Select the person you are going to observe. Make sure you know exactly what they are going to do. Are they in a special position? Are they going to be doing the same as the other members of the group?	A	Apportion the different elements of the performance into their different categories (e.g. skills, techniques, tactics, strategies etc.).	S	Specify the particular aspects of the performance you are assessing.
E	Ensure you know what you are looking for (e.g. specific skills or advanced techniques, particular successes).	L	Look for specific details.	E	Estimate the value and importance of the different components of the performance.
R	Record what you see by noting it all down.	Y	You should start to distinguish the separate parts of the performance.	S	Sort out the information you have gathered from your analysis.
V	Verify what you are watching. In other words, check that you are doing what you set out to do.	S	See if you can find any solutions to problems that may have occurred.	S	State what you have seen in order to give advice and guidance to the performer.
E	Evaluate — at the end of your observation, make some judgements and comments about how successful the person you were observing was. Be fair and honest with your comments as you may have to discuss and justify them later.	E	Evaluate with an overview of how successful the whole performance was.		

Strengths and areas for improvement

Strengths and areas for improvement need to be identified as these will be central to any assessment. You have to develop the ability to identify these. You should take the following into account:

▶ What were the specific demands of the performance? See Figure 7.4.

Figure 7.4 Factors affecting performance

Demand factor	Possible effects
Level of opposition	Opponents who are at a lower level than you might not prove to be enough of a challenge, while higher-level opponents might prove too difficult and result in a short or failed performance.
Conditions	The playing conditions (as considered in Topic 7.1) could make your performance more challenging, e.g. a strong wind when playing tennis may affect a performance.
Equipment	The equipment you use might not be of particularly high quality, e.g. a basic badminton racket is much heavier than one designed for elite performers — the weight will slow down reactions and limit performance as it can reduce racket head speed.
Physical state	You might have to perform when you are not at your physical best, e.g. when you're tired or slightly injured. This is bound to have a negative effect on your performance.

▶ Performance profiling identifies the particular aspects of your chosen sport which you most need to consider overall. It involves assessing the level of each skill necessary to complete a competent performance.

▶ What technical skills are required? You should have identified these in Topic 7.1. You might need to concentrate on some particular skills rather than try to cover them all.

▶ What are the tactical awareness requirements for the activity? You should also have identified these in Topic 7.1, so now you can consider how effective they are proving to be. What options are available to you?

> **Over to you!**
>
> Consider what other demand factors you could add to Figure 7.4. Try to make them specific to your chosen sport.

> **Over to you!**
>
> As a starting point, start to consider what you think are your strengths and areas for improvement. Identify two of each which you consider are the most important ones.

Elite performance

You will be asked to complete this unit by comparing and contrasting your own technical skills and tactical awareness with an elite performer in your chosen sport. Elite performers would be considered to be anyone in the following categories:

▶ professional athletes

▶ national representatives

▶ national record holders

▶ world record holders

▶ national champions

▶ Olympians.

> **Activity**
>
> Consider the categories which are listed on the left. Find out about performers in your chosen sport who you could use for your comparison. If at all possible observe an elite performer actually performing.

Player profile

Andy Murray's second serve was considered to be weak in comparison to his first serve as it lacked pace and spin. He also did not hit through the ball on his forehand and his grip on his forehand was often wrong. This caused the shot to fall short and allowed his opponents to attack.

As a professional tennis player, Murray continues to practise the technical skills required, and his decision to improve specific areas of his fitness led to the most successful phase of his career to date.

Methods of assessment

There are different methods of assessment to choose from. These include:

▶ Analysis and observation, which you can do yourself or ask a friend or teammate (**peer**) to do for you. If you are working with a coach or a trainer, you could ask them to help. They could assist you by breaking down the skills and observing technical ability.

▶ You could carry out an interview with one of your teammates to obtain some feedback. This will help you to identify potential strengths and weak areas.

▶ You could make a formal presentation of your skills and abilities to an audience and get feedback from them.

▶ You could carry out a SWOT analysis. This would include identifying the necessary skills and coaching model required, comparing these skills with the identified coaching model and then explaining the following points:

- **S**trengths
- **W**eaknesses
- **O**pportunities to develop and improve
- **T**hreats to improvement and long-term performance.

▶ You could use performance profiling. This involves examining the skills required for a particular position in a team sport or event in an individual sport.

> **Over to you!**
>
> Decide which methods of assessment you are going to use in connection with your chosen sport.

Case study

David has chosen tennis as his sport for this unit. He plays for the school tennis team and is a member of the junior section of his local club, where he shares a trainer/coach with some of the other juniors. His club coach uses video recording and analysis regularly with the junior players and gives them copies of their performances to keep. As a member of the regional junior squad, David considers himself to be a fairly high-level player, but he would like to get into the county squad as well.

David has chosen Andy Murray as his elite performer to contrast his own technical skills and tactical awareness with. He attended a school trip to a Davis Cup tennis match and saw Murray in action. Like Murray, David is quite tall, but he is quite light in weight for his height and finds it difficult to perform consistently over longer matches. However, his height enables David to get good angles on his service, which he considers to be one of his best shots.

1. What advantage do you think David might have gained though watching Andy Murray perform live?

2. What sort of performance analysis would you advise David to make best use of?

3. Is there anyone else you think David could use to help him with his assessment?

4. What do you think David is going to identify as his particular strength?

5. What is David likely to identify as his area for development?

Assessment activity 7.1 (Unit 8 P1, P2, M1, M2)

This assessment activity focuses on the technical and tactical demands of a selected sport and on a performance analysis. Imagine that you are an aspiring sports coach who aims to take a recognised coaching qualification. In preparation for this, you will need to study the technical and tactical demands of a selected sport and know how to analyse performance. To complete the assessment activity, you need to:

• Choose a sport to focus on.

• Investigate and observe the technical and tactical demands for your chosen sport.

• Identify an elite performer in your chosen sport.

• Observe and assess the technical skills and tactical awareness of the elite performer, identifying and explaining their strengths and areas for improvement.

• Produce a report that describes and explains the technical and tactical demands of your chosen sport and which profiles the technical skills, tactical awareness, strengths and areas for improvement of an elite performer in the sport.

Topic check

1 Identify the two main ways in which you can use video playback to help with analysis.

2 What is meant by 'notational analysis'?

3 List the five steps in the 'analysis model'.

4 Give an example of a demand factor and the effect it could have on a performance.

5 What do you understand by the term 'performance profiling'?

6 Name three different categories of elite performers.

7 What might be the possible advantage of getting a peer to carry out an observation analysis?

8 What do the letters SWOT stand for in relation to analysis?

A six-week technical skills and tactical awareness programme

▶ Getting started

In this topic you will plan and undertake a six-week programme to develop your technical skills and tactical awareness in your particular selected sport. When you have completed this topic, you should have:

- set your aims and objectives
- set yourself some SMART targets
- planned and carried out your training schedule
- decided on areas for technical and tactical development and practised these
- recorded your planning and completion of the six-week programme.

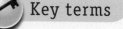

Key terms

Mentor: wise and trusted adviser or teacher

Tactical awareness: your ability to identify suitable available tactics and implement them in your performance

Aims and objectives

You need to set yourself aims and objectives that are based firmly on all of the analysis work you carried out in Topics 7.1 and 7.2. You should particularly focus on:

▶ Strengths and weaknesses identified from your player analysis. This will initially focus on the technical skills you have been looking at (e.g. the level of accuracy of shooting and hitting the target in any invasion game activity, such as hockey, netball or football).

▶ Looking at your **tactical awareness**. In invasion games this could be your ability to mark attackers in a set-play situation such as a re-start (in hockey), a free pass (in netball), a free kick (in football) or any of the particular 'game plan' strategies you have decided to use.

Your plan should include a daily schedule of technical and tactical areas that need development. You also need to include areas of strength that you want to maintain. This could include specific practices to assist in maintaining and improving performance. For example, if your sport is basketball you may want to focus on three-pointers and long-range shooting as your weakness, but you will also want to maintain your free throw and lay-up skills. Zoned defence may be a strength, but man-to-man defence is let down because of your fitness level.

You should be allocated a **mentor** to help you put together this programme. This could be a team coach or trainer rather than your tutor, as your tutor will be monitoring your programme.

Targets

You will be asked to set some specific targets to achieve over the six-week period. In order to do this successfully and appropriately you should make use of SMART targets. In this instance this means:

▶ **S**pecific – you need to identify the particular aspects you will be working on. For instance, it would not be specific enough just to say you want to 'be a better player'. You need to be clear about any skills or tactical aspects of your performance you want to improve in order to be better.

▶ **M**easurable – you need be able to identify where you are at the start of your programme so that you can measure how much you have progressed by the end of it. This means you must choose skills and tactics that you can clearly measure. Having been specific in the first place will help you with this. For example, if you identified 'accuracy of passing' as a specific area for improvement, you could record and add up how many times you achieved an accurate pass in a performance.

▶ **A**chievable – do not be too ambitious regarding what you want to achieve in six weeks – this is a fairly short time period. There is only a certain amount of progress you can make in this time, so make sure you discuss this fully with your mentor.

▶ **R**ealistic – as well as having time to achieve your targets, you must also make sure that you have the resources and ability to achieve them (remember that you need to be able to measure your progress). You should discuss this with your mentor too.

▶ **T**ime-bound – your programme is already time-bound; you know you have six weeks to carry it out and that you will have a daily schedule. You must consider how much time you are going to allocate for this each day. You might choose to have longer sessions some days than others – especially if you have other commitments, such as playing other sports or matches.

> **Over to you!**
> Identify which technical and tactical aspects are weaknesses that you need to improve. Also, identify strengths that you want to maintain.

> **Over to you!**
> Before finally deciding what your targets are, test out whether they are measurable.

> **Over to you!**
> Reconsider your programme, in discussion with your mentor, to make sure that your targets are achievable and realistic.

The following table can serve as a checklist to make sure that you have included everything you need in your programme.

Figure 7.5 Aims and objectives checklist

Inclusion aspect	Aims and objectives
Technical demands	Focused on skills: continuous, serial and discrete
Tactical demands	Focused on: tactics, strategies, 'game plans' etc.
Identified strengths	Related to both technical and tactical demands
Identified areas for improvement	Related to both technical and tactical demands
Daily schedule	For the six-week period (42 days in total)
Using SMART targets	Specific, measurable, achievable, realistic and time-bound

Training

Training is an essential element of your programme. You must ensure that you:

▶ Plan your training well. The plan needs to be clear and concise and include all of the elements identified in the checklist in Figure 7.5. Remember that you are putting together an overall plan that will consist of many individual sessions.

▶ Structure your plan, including details of what you will be covering, e.g. all the phases of the individual training sessions you have decided upon, such as skill phases, fitness training and game play.

▶ Include an appropriate warm-up at the beginning of each session and an appropriate cool-down at the end of each session in your plan (see Chapter 9 for more details about this).

Over to you!

Draft an outline plan of what a typical training session is going to consist of in your particular programme.

Technical and tactical development

You will already have identified your areas for improvement, but you may need some help from your mentor to come up with appropriate practices and methods to improve your technique. For example, if you identified accuracy of passing as a technical weakness, you might have to specify the distance involved, whether it was using the right or left foot/hand, whether you were stationary or moving, and so on. The more precise and specific you are the easier it will be to come up with exercises/practices to help you improve.

You will develop tactically through participating against different levels of participants in a variety of practices. You cannot use the same opponents every time you practise, so you will have to organise your tactical development carefully in advance to ensure that it can be scheduled into your plan.

Recording documentation

The checklist in Figure 7.5 considers all the elements you have to include in your programme, but must also keep a record of what you actually do and when. The easiest way to do this is probably to use a diary specifically for this six-week (42-day) period, making sure you link it to your plan. Use this to record exactly what you do each day, making sure you keep it up to date – set yourself the task of filling it in every day.

Case study

Becky is a high-level competitive swimmer in the individual medley event and is a member of the national swimming squad. She is the only person in her school who performs at this high level. Becky has to attend squad training sessions and has a coach who is assigned to work with her. Becky has to arrange her own training schedule and is allowed to use her local pool for early morning sessions before it is open to the public. Her coach is not able to attend these individual training sessions but has been able to consider Becky's strengths and weaknesses and has given her a detailed SWOT analysis. With all of her other commitments, Becky is a little unsure how she is going to be able to complete her six-week programme.

1. Will the fact that Becky is the only person at her school performing at this level cause any particular problems?

2. Becky is often likely to be training on her own, without an expert coaching. How can she monitor her own performance?

3. Becky is likely to have more strengths than weaknesses, given the level she competes at. How will she reflect this in her SMART targets?

4. Are there any tactical developments Becky could include in her training programme?

5. What will be the best way for Becky to record/document her programme?

Topic check

1 Why is it important to include working on your strengths in your programme?

2 Who could you consider using as a mentor to help you plan your programme?

3 Which of the two targets do you really need to consider together, almost as one?

4 Name the five different aspects you need to consider as a minimum to include in your programme.

5 Identify the three elements of training you need to consider in your programme.

6 Give two types of documentation you could use to record the details of your programme.

Reviewing development and setting goals for further development

In this topic you will evaluate and review the training programme from Topic 7.3. You will consider how you can improve further, setting long-term goals.

When you have completed this topic, you should have:

- reviewed your six-week training programme
- reflected on your progress
- have set yourself some short- and some long-term aims.

Review

To review your training, you must carry out a self-analysis and obtain feedback from other sources. This will enable you to assess your performance against the targets and objectives you set at the beginning of your programme. You must provide your completed log/diary demonstrating how you monitored your progress against these targets and objectives. This will be considered against the following criteria:

- *Your performance against targets* – You will have considered your targets in your SMART planning and will have come up with some very specific ones.

- *Factors affecting your tactical and technical development* – You may have been unable to achieve your goals and targets for various reasons (e.g. a minor injury or illness), which is obviously a negative effect. However, there may be some factors which had a positive effect and enhanced your opportunities (e.g. specific advice from an experienced and skilled mentor).

- *Recommendations for future plans and activities* – These have to be considered together with actual timescales. There is an expectation that you will carry on developing the progress you have made during your six-week training period.

💡 Over to you!

What were your two main achievements in relation to your targets for both technical and tactical development?

💡 Over to you!

Can you identify any factors that prevented you from achieving your goals? Were there any factors that enhanced your opportunities?

Goals

You will be expected to explain your development in your chosen sport, saying why and how you think you developed through following your six-week programme. From this you must decide on some short- and long-term goals and how you intend to achieve these using the SMART process.

Long-term goals

You will have a much longer period in which to achieve your long-term goals than the six weeks of your training programme. You can plan for months or even years into the future, which will give you the opportunity to set some quite ambitious goals. Elite performers can plan their development over 4 years (e.g. for the Olympics) or over shorter periods (e.g. for the Six Nations rugby tournament or the European Championships.) You will not have time to achieve any long-term goals in your training programme, but you can identify the areas that you need to focus on and provide recommendations on how you will achieve this.

Over to you!

Come up with one long-term goal you would like to set yourself to improve the level at which you perform in your chosen sport.

Over to you!

Think of at least one short-term goal you would set yourself after this review process which you did not identify in your original programme.

Elite athletes will plan for the future, setting themselves long-term goals.

Short-term goals

These may be similar to the targets you set yourself for the areas you identified for improvement in your six-week programme. It is hoped that they will not be exactly the same (you will want to have achieved most of them), but it is likely that six weeks was not quite long enough for you to have completely achieved all of them. As you will have been through the process of setting and implementing short-term goals already, this should be a fairly straightforward task to do again.

Other considerations

You will have been working with other people over the course of this unit (e.g. your coach, tutor, mentor), and they can help you to review your training programme and negotiate your new goals. They will have been involved in the planning and monitoring process, so they can be very useful in helping you to think about how to move forward in the future.

You will have set yourself some SMART targets when planning and implementing your programme, but you might need to look at these again in more detail now. Your SMART targets can be put into two categories: targets specific to you as a performer and those specific to a particular situation. For example, you may have made significant progress in relation to a technical demand by greatly improving a **discrete** (separate) skill. You might also have identified that you play less well against weaker opposition due to lack of motivation in those circumstances.

Over to you!

In relation to your chosen sport, think of one target you can set that is specific to you as a performer and one that is specific to a particular situation.

Case study

Becky has completed her six-week swimming training programme and is now reviewing it and setting goals for further development. She managed to improve against her targets, but found that the progress she made was quite limited. The main factor affecting her technical development was a minor injury (muscle strain) she suffered in the second week, which prevented her from training as intensively as she wanted to. Becky only had two competitive races in this six-week period, so she was unsure about being able to measure her tactical development very accurately.

Becky is currently in discussion with her coach, negotiating her short- and long-term goals.

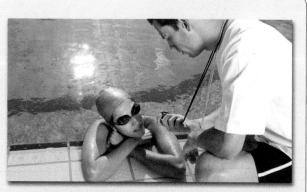

1. Can you think of any particular reasons why Becky feels she has made limited progress, other than the injury?

2. Is there anything else Becky could have added to her programme to test her progress in tactical awareness?

3. What is likely to be the most important short-term goal Becky sets herself?

4. What is likely to be the most important long-term goal Becky sets herself?

5. Apart from her coach, who else could Becky go to for advice related to her SMART targets?

Assessment activity 7.2 (Unit 8 P3, M3, D1, P4, M4, D2, P5, P6, M5, D3)

This assessment activity is based on the production and completion of a six-week training programme and a self-assessment of your technical and tactical awareness in a selected sport. You are required to:

- Select a sport or sporting activity to focus on during this assessment.
- Produce a six-week training programme that identifies aims and objectives, targets for development and training needs and activities that will improve your technical and tactical development.

- Carry out the programme, keeping a diary of achievements, successes and barriers during the programme.
- Review the success of the programme by analysing your own performance and obtaining feedback from other sources to assess your performance against the targets and objectives you set.
- Complete a development plan that identifies future targets for your own technical and tactical development in your chosen sport.

Topic check

1 Identify a negative factor and a positive factor which could affect tactical and technical development.
2 What is the main purpose for carrying out a review?
3 What sort of time frame would be appropriate for setting short-term-goals?
4 What sort of time frame would be appropriate for achieving long-term goals?
5 Who could you approach and negotiate with regarding setting targets for further development?

Assessment summary

The overall grade you achieve for this unit depends on how well you meet the grading criteria set out in Appendix 1 (see page 297). You must complete:

- all of the P criteria to achieve a **pass** grade
- all of the P and the M criteria to achieve a **merit** grade
- all of the P, M and D criteria to achieve a **distinction** grade.

Your tutor will assess the assessment activities that you complete for this unit. The work you produce should provide evidence which demonstrates that you have achieved each of the assessment criteria. The table below identifies what you need to demonstrate to meet each of the pass, merit and distinction criteria for this unit. You should always check and self-assess your work before you submit your assignments for marking.

Remember that you MUST provide evidence for all of the P criteria to pass the unit.

Grading Criteria	You need to demonstrate that you can:	Have you got the evidence?
P1	Describe the technical and tactical demands of a chosen sport	
M1	Explain the technical and tactical demands of a chosen sport	
P2	Assess the technical skills and tactical awareness of an elite performer, identifying strengths and areas for improvement	
M2	Assess the technical skills and tactical awareness of an elite performer, explaining strengths and areas for improvement	
P3	Assess own technical skills and tactical awareness in a chosen sport, identifying strengths and areas for improvement	
M3	Assess own technical skills and tactical awareness in a chosen sport, explaining own strengths and areas for improvement	
D1	Compare and contrast own technical skills and tactical awareness with those of an elite performer and the demands of a chosen sport	
P4	Produce a six-week training programme, with tutor support, to develop own technical skills and tactical awareness	
M4	Independently produce a six-week training programme to develop own technical skills and tactical awareness, describing strengths and areas for improvement	
D2	Evaluate the training programme, justifying suggestions made regarding improvement	
P5	Carry out a six-week training programme to develop own technical skills and tactical awareness	
P6	Review own development, identifying goals for further technical and tactical development, with tutor support	
M5	Independently describe own development, explaining goals for technical and tactical development	
D3	Analyse own goals for technical and tactical development, suggesting how these goals could be achieved	

Always ask your tutor to explain any assignment tasks or assessment criteria that you don't understand fully. Being clear about the task before you begin gives you the best chance of succeeding. Good luck with your Unit 8 assessment work!

8 Nutrition for sports performance (Unit 10)

Unit outline

A well-balanced diet is very important for everyone and is even more important for sports performers. This is because they place additional demands on their bodies. Poor nutrition can cause problems and fatigue, so it is very important to ensure you have a balanced and adequate diet that provides your body with enough energy. Your body weight is also important in most sports activities. It needs to meet the requirements of the activity. Athletes also need to make sure that their body weight does not significantly change during and after the activity (usually from dehydration).

Learning outcomes

1 Know the nutritional requirements of a selected sport.
2 Be able to assess own diet.
3 Be able to plan a personal nutritional strategy.
4 Be able to implement and review a personal nutritional strategy.

Knowing the nutritional requirements of a selected sport

This topic will help you to understand the important role nutrition plays in health and fitness. Poor nutrition can lead to illnesses, injuries, poor training and poor competitive performances. A healthy diet will help you to stay fit and competitive.

When you have completed this topic, you should know:

- what the main nutrients are
- the importance, value and contribution of different nutrients
- what constitutes a healthy diet
- what sort of diet a particular sports performer might have.

Key terms

Basal metabolic rate: the number of calories your body burns at rest to maintain normal body functions

Macronutrient: an essential nutrient that is required in large amounts (e.g. carbohydrate)

Micronutrient: an essential nutrient (e.g. vitamin C) that is required in minute amounts

Nutrients: substances in food which provide nourishment and energy for growth and metabolism

Rickets: a bone disorder caused by a lack of vitamin D, calcium and phosphate which leads to softening and weakening of the bones

Scurvy: a disease caused by vitamin C deficiency, which can cause spongy and bleeding gums, bleeding under the skin and extreme weakness

Nutritional requirements

Before going on to consider a specific sport, it is important to understand what makes up a balanced diet that meets your nutritional needs. The following are the essential **nutrients** that everyone needs to live.

Carbohydrates

Carbohydrates are **macronutrients**. There are two types of carbohydrate, simple and complex.

▶ *Simple carbohydrates* are found in foods such as sugar, milk and fruit.

▶ *Complex carbohydrates* are found in foods such as bread, pasta, potatoes, rice and pulses/beans.

Carbohydrates are the main suppliers of energy to the body and they are stored as glycogen in the liver and muscles. This glycogen can be used to provide energy during exercise. Many endurance athletes (e.g. marathon runners) load their bodies with carbohydrate (known as carbo-loading) in preparation for a particular event or competition. This increases their energy levels to sustain them through a performance that is going to last for a long period of time.

Fats

Fats are a major source of energy for the body. They also help to insulate it and keep the body temperature at the right level. It is important to control the levels of fat in the body, because too much fat can cause an increase in overall body weight and can contribute to heart disease. Excess fat can also decrease athletic performance. Fats contain a mixture of three types of fatty acids:

▶ saturates – found in meat, meat fats and dairy products

▶ monounsaturates – found in olive oil

▶ polyunsaturates – found in margarines and oils made from seeds and nuts, e.g. sunflower, soya and corn.

Fats are important because:

▶ they provide a concentrated energy source

▶ they are stored under the skin to help to keep the body warm

▶ they are stored around the heart and help to protect it

▶ foods with a high fat content also contain fat-soluble vitamins

▶ essential fatty acids cannot be made in the body so must be provided by food.

Proteins

Proteins are also macronutrients, and are often known as 'building blocks' because they are so important in the growth of new tissue. When they are digested they are broken down to amino acids that go straight into the bloodstream. The body needs 20 different amino acids for good health.

Proteins are found in animal sources, such as meat, fish, eggs, milk and cheese. These contain all of the essential amino acids. Other sources, such as beans, lentils, cereals, bread, pasta and rice lack one or more of the essential amino acids.

Proteins are needed in the diet:

▶ for the formation, growth and repair of tissues such as muscle, hair and skin

▶ to make enzymes and hormones.

If you are physically active you need a good supply of proteins and you are likely to need slightly more if you train hard or for long periods.

Water

Water is the most important nutrient because a lack of it can cause illness, or even death, more quickly than the lack of any other substance. Water is lost naturally through urine and sweat, expired air and faeces. The rapid loss of water is known as dehydration. This is a very serious condition, and one which sports performers should be aware of and try to avoid.

When you are exercising, more water is lost from your body than when at rest. Some of this is through sweating and some through water vapour when breathing out. The following will affect how quickly water is lost:

▶ the intensity of work or exercise being carried out

▶ the amount of time spent exercising

▶ the temperature and humidity of the environment.

It is therefore very important to replace water when you are exercising, especially if you are exercising in hot conditions or for a long time.

Activity

Weigh, in kg, each member of the class before an activity. Then complete an hour of exercise. The exercise can take any form, from five-a-side football to running, rowing or cycling. At the end of the activity, weigh each member of the class again. The difference between the start and finish weight should be the amount of water lost.

• 1 kg of weight loss = 1 litre of fluid lost in sweat.

Calculate the percentage weight loss.

• A 2% loss = a decrease in performance level.

Vitamins

You only need vitamins in small amounts (they are **micronutrients**), but they are essential to good health. A normal balanced diet will usually contain enough vitamins. There are two types:

▶ fat soluble – these can be stored in the body (e.g. vitamins A and D)

▶ water soluble – these cannot be stored, so you need a constant daily supply (e.g. vitamins B and C).

The functions of vitamins are to:

▶ protect the body and maintain the body chemistry

▶ enable growth and maintenance of bones, teeth, skin and glands

▶ help with digestion

▶ help with the stability of the nervous system

▶ help tissue growth

▶ increase resistance to bacteria and disease.

If you suffer from a vitamin deficiency, it is possible that you will suffer certain diseases. For example, a deficiency of vitamin C can cause **scurvy**; a deficiency of vitamin D can cause **rickets**.

Minerals

You take in minerals through eating vegetables and meats. They are important because they:

▶ help to build tissues

▶ are the main constituents of bones and teeth

▶ help to release and use energy in the body

▶ provide soluble salts in the body fluids

▶ help with the correct functioning of cells and muscles.

The most common minerals are:

▶ *calcium* – mainly found in milk and milk products, salmon, sardines, beans, broccoli and green vegetables; needed for bones and teeth

▶ *sodium* – mainly found in salt, seafood, processed foods and celery; needed to maintain body fluids

▶ *iron* – mainly found in liver, meat, egg yolk, wholegrain or enriched breads and cereals and green vegetables; needed for the transportation of oxygen by red blood cells

▶ *iodine* – mainly found in dairy products, seafood and drinking water; needed for hormone formation, notably from the thyroid gland.

Most people manage to take in sufficient minerals in their normal balanced diet but you may need slightly more of some minerals if you are exercising or training regularly. Some minerals (e.g. iron, copper and molybdenum) are only required in small amounts, and these are known as trace elements.

A healthy diet

A well-balanced diet is the basis for maintaining good health. The proportions shown on the plate in the diagram represent the correct daily intake for a balanced diet, as recommended by the government.

You will have different requirements at different times. If you are expending more energy (e.g. if you are training hard or taking part in some form of competition) you will need to take in more energy by eating more or higher-energy food, so that your body can cope. Your **basal metabolic rate** (BMR) is the amount of energy you need for important processes such as breathing and keeping your heart beating. This needs to be balanced against the energy you need for other activities. If you eat too much or too little you can suffer from:

The eatwell plate

Use the eatwell plate to help you get the balance right. It shows how much of what you eat should come from each food group.

A balanced diet

▶ obesity – being extremely overweight

▶ anorexia nervosa – being extremely underweight

▶ malnutrition – a lack of the right sort of nutrition.

All three of these conditions pose serious health risks and can lead to serious medical health problems.

Over to you!

Compare your 'normal' diet with the recommendations on the 'healthy food plate'. Can you identify any areas where you need to improve your diet?

Activity

Work out your metabolic weight using the following method:

$1.3 \times 24 \times$ body weight in kg.

Using the information, discuss why people have different BMRs.

The different stages of food preparation are also very important. You should consider the following:

▶ *Storage* – some foods can be kept in ordinary cupboards, in tins or containers, while some may need to be refrigerated or kept in a freezer.

▶ *Initial preparation* – check the use-by dates on products (this is different from the sell-by date). Frozen foods may need to be defrosted before being used. Proper hygiene standards need to be maintained when food is handled, cut and prepared (always wash your hands before preparing food).

▶ *Cooking* – most fruits and vegetables can be eaten raw, but any food that is cooked must be cooked properly, for the correct amount of time. This will vary between different types of food. You must also be careful when reheating food, ensuring that it is safe to reheat and, if so, that it is thoroughly reheated. Cooked food should be refrigerated or frozen if it is not going to be eaten immediately.

Over to you!

Do you currently take any responsibility for preparing your own food? If so, is it just your snacks, or do you get involved in preparing any of your main meals? Try to take a more active role in the preparation of your food.

Sports-specific requirements

Everyone needs to have a healthy diet, but some sports performers may need to make adjustments to their diet to make them more effective in their particular sport or activity. For example:

▶ A female gymnast needs to be small and light, so needs to avoid too much fatty food.

▶ A weightlifter needs to be quite large and bulky, so additional fats and proteins may be needed.

▶ A soccer player needs to eat sufficient energy-providing food to maintain their energy levels through a 90-minute game.

▶ A marathon runner may have a high carbohydrate diet, and specifically carbo-load for several days just before a race.

There are some very specific guidelines regarding when to eat as well as what to eat.

▶ Before activity, a snack should provide enough fluid to maintain hydration, and be high in carbohydrate to provide energy.

▶ During exercise, it is important to replace fluid losses and provide carbohydrates for energy. This is especially important for endurance events.

▶ After exercise, you need to provide enough fluids, energy and carbohydrates to replace muscle glycogen and ensure rapid recovery. A carbohydrate intake equal to about a banana during the first 30 minutes and again every 2 hours for 4–6 hours will be enough to replace glycogen stores. Protein eaten after exercise will help with building and repairing muscle tissue. Examples of food that can be consumed after exercise include isotonic sports drinks, pieces of fruit (two to three), dried fruit, cereal bars.

Remember that planning a diet for a sports performer is a long-term exercise. The actual content of the diet and meal planning needs to be thought through carefully. In some instances, supplements may need to be added to the diet. An example of this is creatine, which is often taken to improve muscular performance by helping to increase short-term strength for short bursts of energy. This has been a very popular supplement with many tennis players.

Case study

Joanne is a 30-year-old professional marathon runner. She runs a few competitive marathons each year, for which she has to train almost constantly. Joanne controls her diet very carefully and plans it around her training and then more specifically before each competitive race. Joanne does most of her training around her home area, but when she has to go away to race, often abroad, she has to stay in hotels where it is far more difficult for her to prepare her own meals. Joanne also competes professionally in races over the shorter distance of 10,000 metres throughout the year.

1. Which type of nutrient is most important to a marathon runner such as Joanne?

2. Is Joanne's age going to affect her diet?

3. How different is Joanne's diet likely to be when she is running competitively compared with when she is training?

4. What sports-specific requirements might Joanne have to consider in the period just before a competition?

5. How important are fluids to Joanne as a marathon runner? What arrangements regarding this need to be put in place for a marathon race?

Assessment activity 8.1 (Unit 10 P1, M1, D1)

Your sports coach has asked you to look at your diet and nutritional intake and check that this is appropriate for your sports training and performance. You are required to:

• Identify a sport for which you train and perform.
• Describe and explain the nutritional requirements of your chosen sport.
• Evaluate the nutritional requirements of your chosen sport, describing suitable meal plans.

Topic check

1 Name the two different types of carbohydrates.
2 Which category of carbohydrates are pastas in?
3 Identify three different functions of fats.
4 Name the three different types of fatty acid.
5 What are proteins also known as?
6 Identify three different sources of proteins.
7 Explain dehydration.
8 What are the two different groups of vitamins?
9 Describe a condition that can result from eating too little.
10 What is the recommended time gap for eating both before and after activity?

Being able to assess your own diet

▶ Getting started

It is important that you become more aware of your eating habits. The best way to do this is through keeping a food diary. You then need to assess what you have eaten, and complete a report summarising strengths and areas for improvement.

When you have completed this topic, you should know:

- what sort of information to gather in your food diary
- what the guidelines are for a healthy diet
- how to calculate what your dietary intake is
- how to assess your diet and write a report highlighting strengths and areas for improvement.

Collecting and collating information

In this topic you will collect information about your eating habits, then **collate** it and assess it. You should gather the information under the following four headings:

1. *The type of food being eaten* – looking back at Topic 8.1 will help you to identify this. Details will also be included on the packaging of many foods.

2. *The amount eaten* – you will have to find ways to 'measure' your food. This could be done using scales, measuring spoons or weight guidelines on the packaging of the food.

3. *Timing* – record the actual times you eat under this heading. Remember to include everything you eat – even snacks!

4. *Feelings* – under this heading you should record your feelings. For example, are you eating because you are really hungry, because someone has prepared food and put in front of you, or simply because somebody else is eating?

Using a table like Figure 8.1 in your diary will help you to record all the necessary information. You can see that it includes the four headings explained above.

🔑 Key terms

Calorie: a measure of energy – an active teenager can use up 2800 calories a day

Collate: to examine and compare information

Figure 8.1 Nutritional intake diary

Time	Meal	Food and drink	Amount	Environment (e.g. home, meal out)	Feelings (e.g. hunger pangs, snacking)
7 a.m.	Breakfast	Orange juice	1 glass	Home	Hungry
		Toast with jam	2 slices	Home	Hungry
11 a.m.	Snack	Packet of crisps	1 bag (small)	School	Snacking (not really hungry)

Time	Event	Activity undertaken/ type	Duration	Environment (e.g. school, club)	Intensity
1 p.m.	PE	Football	40 mins	School	Moderate
7 p.m.	Club	Badminton	1 hr 30 m	Leisure centre	Light

Make sure that you are totally honest about the information you include in this diary as it is primarily for you! Also, when you implement and review your personal nutritional strategy later, the process will be easier and more accurate if you keep your diary up to date.

Assessing and reporting

Once you have gathered information about your eating habits, you need to assess it. You should be able to find out the recommended daily allowances of the different food types and nutrients for someone of your age, gender and size. You can compare these with the information you've recorded in your diary and carry out some basic paper-based calculations using the information below.

Women: BMR = 655 + (9.6 × weight in kilos) + (1.8 × height in cm) – (4.7 × age in years)

Men: BMR = 66 + (13.7 × weight in kilos) + (5 × height in cm) – (6.8 × age in years)

However, if at all possible you should use dietary analysis software, which will help greatly with the assessment process.

Activity

Look at the website www.weightlossresources.co.uk and see what benefits this sort of software can bring.

Over to you!

- Using the calculations on the left, work out your recommended dietary allowance before exercise. Don't forget that you may also need to assess exercise. Your total **calories** for a day will include your BMR and the amount you burn up from exercise. This will show the total amount of energy you have used.

Calories used during moderate intensity exercise lasting 30 mins

Walking	120
Cycling	280
Running	400
Aerobics	200
Weights	140
Tennis	200
Swimming	225
Rowing	280
Golf	140
Circuit training	280

- Using the table above (approximations based on someone weighing about 155 lbs), and the previous information on BMR, calculate how many calories you needed for yesterday.

Once you have assessed your information, you must compile a report to summarise your findings and any conclusions you've come to. You might also be asked to design and present a poster. In your report you should consider some of the strengths and areas for improvement you have identified in your diet, and suggest any changes you might make. These might include:

▶ *Eating more or less food* – Generally speaking, eating more food is likely to result in gaining weight and eating less in reducing weight. You may have decided when assessing your own diet that you need to do one or other of these things.

▶ *Eating less or more of a particular food group* – You learnt in Topic 8.1 how the various nutrients contribute to your overall health. In analysing your diet you may have realised that you need to cut down on some food types (e.g. crisps and chocolate) and increase others (e.g. fresh fruit and vegetables). You might also decide to increase a food type because of the types of sporting activities you are involved in (e.g. increasing your carbohydrate intake for more efficient energy levels).

▶ *Eating at different times* – You may find that you do not have set eating times, or that you have got into bad habits (e.g. eating just before training or performing). You might decide, as a result of your assessment, to stick to more regular meal times, following the traditional pattern of breakfast, lunch and dinner without snack breaks in between. Alternatively, you may decide that snacking suits the type of activity you do (e.g. tennis players often eat a banana as an energy source during the turnaround between sets).

💡 Over to you!

You should already have a record from your food diary of your current eating times. You can use this information to consider any changes you might like to make in your eating times.

▶ *Preparing food in a different way* – The way in which some foods are cooked has an effect on their nutritional value. It is sensible to look at the options available in terms of preparation methods. For example, grilling food is often a healthier option than frying it. If you prepare the food yourself, rather than buying it ready-made or prepared by someone else, you will have more control over what you eat (e.g. not having mayonnaise in a sandwich).

▶ *Drinking water and fluids* – If you are taking part in strenuous activity it is likely that you will need to increase your fluid intake. This could be simply through drinking more water, but there are other options such as energy drinks.

Case study

Liam has been collecting and collating information using a food diary, and has assessed his findings. He is now starting work on his report, considering in particular the strengths and areas for improvement in his diet. Liam has found that he is eating more than his recommended dietary allowance and that on average he eats at eight different times during the day. Two of Liam's main meals are prepared for him by his mum (breakfast and his evening dinner), but he tends to eat snacks at the other meal breaks he has during the day. Liam always carries a water bottle with him when he is training and performing, and he always has a couple of chocolate bars during half-time intervals when he is playing a game of football.

1. Explain the likely result of Liam eating more than his recommended dietary allowance.

2. What would you suggest Liam does about this?

3. Would you have any advice for Liam regarding food preparation?

4. Identify the main strengths Liam is likely to put in his report.

5. What areas for improvement do you think Liam is likely to identify in his report?

Assessment activity 8.2 (Unit 10 P2, P3, M2, D2)

Your sports coach has asked you to monitor your diet in detail over a two-week period. You have been asked to:

• Collect and collate information on your own diet for a two-week period by completing a personal food diary.

• Describe and explain the nutritional strengths of your own diet.

• Identify areas for improvement and justify the recommendations you make for improving your own diet.

You should produce a written report and a poster presentation summarising your dietary intake and recommendations for improvement as evidence for this task.

Topic check

1 What should be included in a food diary?
2 Explain what is meant by 'collating information'.
3 What sort of 'feelings' are you likely to refer to in a food diary?
4 Explain why it is important to be totally honest when recording items in your food diary.
5 What is a 'recommended dietary allowance'?
6 Where might you find details regarding food portion content?
7 Give one likely effect of eating more food.
8 Why might you increase your carbohydrate intake if you were performing in games activities?
9 Explain why the way in which foods are prepared is important.
10 If you are taking part in strenuous activity, what effect is this likely to have on your fluid levels?

Being able to plan a personal nutritional strategy

 Getting started

In this topic you will plan your own nutritional strategy. You will need to consider all of the work you have done and the knowledge and understanding you have acquired so far in this unit.

When you have completed this topic, you should:

- understand what a nutritional strategy is
- know what a meal plan is and the options which are available to you
- know who you can go to for advice regarding your nutritional strategy.

Key terms

Creatine: a compound made by the body (also available as a supplement) and used to store energy

Nutritional strategy

A strategy is a plan of action designed to achieve a particular goal, so you have to come up with one which is going to be appropriate for you. When you are doing this you need to consider all of the following factors.

▶ *Food groups* – You learnt about the different food groups in Topic 8.1. You have also gathered information in your food diary about the quantities of each of the food groups you consume regularly. Based on this information, you can now decide whether you consume the correct quantities of each food group (see pages 182–185) and how much of each to include in your plan.

▶ *Balance of good health* – You should already understand the importance of a balanced diet to maintain general good health, and you should bear this in mind when planning your strategy. If you try to adjust your diet too drastically, you could affect your intake of essential components of your diet, which could lead to health problems.

▶ *The need for rehydration* – Rehydration is the process of restoring lost water to the body tissues and fluids. It is very important that you do this to avoid dehydration. Taking part in training or a sporting activity will to lead to fluid loss, so you need to plan how and when you are going to rehydrate.

Over to you!

Find out what energy drinks are available and what else is recommended other than water to replace fluids. Are any particular drinks recommended for your chosen sports?

It is very important to keep hydrated when participating in sports activities.

▶ *The preparation process* – This can include buying the ingredients and then preparing the food for eating or cooking. If you are going to cook the ingredients, you will have to choose which cooking method to use (e.g. meats can be stewed, roasted, grilled or fried). You must bear in mind that if someone else is involved in your food preparation then you have to let them know what you want.

Over to you!

Find out what different benefits there are to be gained by preparing/cooking foods in different ways. Link this to the food groups you will be including in your meal plan.

▶ *Food quantities* – You will have to decide exactly what quantities you will eat and find accurate ways of measuring them. This might get quite complicated when there are several ingredients involved, and you will have to be prepared to spend some time on planning and implementing this.

▶ *Meal/intake timings* – You will have to decide when you are going to eat. You may be able to set up a daily routine or you might have to plan around weekdays and weekends. In a normal week you will be attending classes, so timings will be less flexible, but you can plan a different routine for weekends – although you will have to bear other family members in mind at the weekend, especially if you have family meals.

▶ *Energy intake* – As you know, the more energy you expend the more you need to take in (the energy equation). You need to work out how much energy you are going to be using, so that you can factor this into your plan to ensure that you will be supplying your body with sufficient energy to meet its demands.

▶ *Substances that might have a negative impact* – These generally fall into the category of 'unhealthy options' (e.g. sweets, chocolates and crisps). Substances that have a negative impact are generally products that have a high proportion of fats. You may have to decide to reduce the amount of these you eat or to cut them out altogether.

▶ *Using supplements* – A large number of dietary supplements are now available, including energy bars, vitamin and mineral supplements, **creatine** and protein powders. With any of these supplements it is very important that you use them wisely, check all of the instructions provided and consider any side effects they may have.

> Creatine is sold as a dietary supplement and is commonly used by athletes to help to increase muscle bulk. There has been some concern about the long-term safety of using creatine. Before you decide to use this or any other supplements you should discus them with your adviser.

Meal plans

When putting together a meal plan you need to be very sure why you are doing it and what you want to get out of it. For this unit it is primarily about making you a more successful sports performer. You will have gathered a lot of knowledge and information from the previous topics, but you might now want to gather some information about your body fat percentage. You will also need to plan your meals around your activity levels, bearing in mind the guidance you were given in Topic 8.1 relating to eating before, during and after training.

You need to consider the following factors when you are putting your meal plan together:

▶ *The type of plan* – You might come up with a daily plan, a weekly plan or even a block plan (that covers a specified period). You may have a specific target, e.g. to lose weight; to 'bulk up' to increase your strength; to improve your stamina and endurance levels by carbohydrate loading. This will be the starting point and will help you to be clear about what you want to achieve.

▶ *The number of meals you want to include* – This will depend on the type of plan you make. You may want to vary the number of meals you have depending on the amount of activity you will be doing during a particular day or over a particular period.

▶ *Food preparation* – Responsibility for your meal preparation might vary – sometimes you may be responsible and at other times it might be someone else. You will have to include details of this in your plan.

▶ *Fluid intake* – You might decide that you just want to rehydrate with water, or you may want to try out some of the energy drinks are available. Whatever you decide, you must include the details in your plan.

You probably have a mealtime and snacking routine and may not previously have thought too much about your diet. You might be surprised at the amount of work you have to put into designing your meal plan, which must be very detailed and carefully considered. It is also very important that you stick to it properly once you start to use it. It is only going to be for a fairly short period, but you might find that it is a real benefit to you and that you want to carry it on for longer.

Advisers

You are not going to become an expert on diet and dietary control over the course of this unit, so it is very important that you get some expert help and advice before, during and after undertaking this unit. If you have any particular medical conditions you must make sure that you consult your doctor before radically altering your diet. The adjustments you make should not be too severe, but should be specifically aimed at the particular outcome you are trying to achieve.

You may be able to approach the following people for advice:

▶ *Coaching staff* – Coaches for specific sports and activities are very aware of the dietary demands for their particular activity, so they may be able to give you some very good guidance. If you have worked with them for some time they may also be familiar with your particular requirements. If you will be working with them while you carry out your strategy they may also be able to monitor you.

▶ *Nutritionists* – These are experts specifically trained in the field of nutrition. You probably won't be able to work with a nutritionist on an ongoing one-to-one basis, but it might be possible for one to come to speak to your group, giving you the opportunity to ask them specific questions.

▶ *Tutors* – Your tutor or other teaching staff may have some expert knowledge they can share. If food technology is delivered as part of the curriculum you may be able to get advice from the staff who teach this. There may also be a member of staff actively involved in any 'healthy eating policy' the school or college has, and they may be able to help too.

Nutritionists are trained to give advice on eating a healthy, balanced diet.

⚙ Activity

Find out if there is anyone on the staff at your school or college who has particular knowledge or expertise in diet and nutrition.

Case study

Kelly takes part in a lot of gymnastics and is going to plan her strategy with the aim of losing weight. She lives in a very close-knit family and her mother takes great pride in preparing and cooking all of the meals for the family. Kelly always has breakfast before leaving home in the morning, and her mother prepares a lunchbox for her. In the evening Kelly's mum cooks a family meal. The same routine happens at the weekend, except Kelly normally makes her own lunch arrangements on Saturday. On Sunday lunchtime the whole family always has a traditional roast dinner.

1. What challenges might Kelly face when trying to work out the exact quantities of food she needs?

2. Discuss whether Kelly is likely to be able to do anything about the actual timings of her meals.

3. What advice would you give Kelly about becoming more involved in the preparation of her food?

4. Are there any supplements Kelly might be advised to consider using?

5. Who would you consider to be the best type of person for Kelly to go to for some expert advice?

Assessment activity 8.3 (Unit 10 P4, M3)

Using the information gained from your food diary, your sports coach has asked you to:

• Create a personal nutritional strategy.

• Produce individual meal plans using your personal nutritional strategy for a two-week period.

You should produce a written report that includes a two-week menu and snack plans as evidence for this task.

Topic check

1 What is meant by a 'nutritional strategy'?

2 Explain the difference between micronutrients and macronutrients.

3 Why is rehydration important?

4 What is meant by the 'energy equation'?

5 What types of substances would be likely to have a negative effect on your diet?

6 Why is it important to check out the effects of supplements?

7 Explain what creatine is and what effects it can have.

8 What is a calorie?

9 For what reasons might you be wise to consult a doctor before starting a nutritional strategy?

10 Identify two different types of people who might be able to advise you on this topic.

Being able to implement and review a personal nutritional strategy

▶ Getting started

In this topic you will implement your personal nutritional strategy over a two-week period. You will have to monitor this process so that you can review it and make any adjustments or alterations necessary. You can then make a judgement on whether or not it has been successful.

When you have completed this topic, you should:

- be able to implement your strategy before, during and after training
- be able to implement your strategy before, during and after competition
- know how to monitor your strategy
- know the best way to review your strategy.

Implementing your strategy

Implementing your strategy means putting it into effect or carrying it out. There are particular areas you will need to focus on for this.

Before, during and after training

You will need to consider all three phases of your training separately. How easy was it to use your strategy as you planned? In topic 8.1 you looked at sports-specific requirements for these three stages, so you might like to compare your experiences with those. You should also consider if there were any problems implementing the strategy in relation to one of the phases in particular.

Before, during and after competition

There are three phases here too, but the demands of competition will be different from those of training. When you are training you are in control of exactly what you are doing, but when you are competing you do not always know how difficult it might be. The level of opposition and amount of effort you need to put in will be factors you might have to take into consideration and adjust your implementation accordingly. For example, if you are in a particularly tiring game of hockey, in very hot conditions, you might have to adjust your planned levels of fluid intake. Similarly, if you are particularly weary after competing, you might have to re-think your energy input to replace the energy you have used.

Food diaries

It is important to keep an accurate and up-to-date food diary throughout the two weeks during which you are implementing your nutritional strategy – what you ate and drank when, how you felt, whether you had to adapt the plan to particular circumstances. You will need to refer back to this to review and assess the success of your strategy.

Monitoring and reviewing your strategy

Over to you!

It is important that you will be training and competing during two weeks when you implement your nutritional strategy. Think about this now and make sure you include it in your forward planning.

Much of this will be an ongoing process during the two-week period when you are carrying out your strategy. To help you with this, here are some guidelines and areas for consideration.

How the nutritional strategy is meeting your needs

You will have planned your strategy in relation to what you thought your needs would be, and you may find that this is working perfectly. However, you may find that it is not working as well as you would have liked. It is important to be able to identify where your needs are being met and where they are not. You can then consider how you might adapt and improve your strategy in the future. Whether your strategy was right or not does not really matter – you will not lose marks for this. You are more likely to gain marks for having noticed any weak areas and suggesting how they could be improved.

Adopting the strategy

You will have to look at the ways in which you were able to follow through what you planned. In your strategy you probably had to change some things from your 'normal' diet. How easy was it to make these changes?

How your strategy fitted in with your likes, dislikes and lifestyle

This will depend upon how much you had to change your dietary habits. You may have decided to give up something you particularly like (e.g. fast foods), or you may have decided to eat foods you don't really like, because they are the healthy option. You should include this sort of detail, and how you felt about it, in your review. Also, the meal timings and food preparation issues may have affected your normal lifestyle. Were any lifestyle changes you had to make good or bad?

The cost of following your strategy

Cost may be an important factor in the success of your strategy. If you have included fresh foods instead of frozen foods, and you are preparing your own meals instead of using ready-made ones, the financial cost is likely to be higher. Fresh fruit and vegetables can be expensive, particularly if they are organic.

Changing from eating cheaper, unhealthy options may increase the cost of a meal. For example, a steak pie for four is likely to be cheaper than buying enough fresh steak for four people. There might also be costs in terms of time spent shopping, preparing and cooking meals. Supplements and sports drinks can also increase the cost of your diet.

Modifications made or considered

You will be able to modify your strategy at any time during the implementation if you find that it is not working the way you had hoped, or if conditions or circumstances change. However, try not to change it too much or you will be in danger of not achieving any of your intended outcomes.

The results of following your strategy

At the end of the two weeks you will have to judge whether your strategy was successful. Two weeks is a relatively short time, but you should still have some results you can include in your review. You should be able to assess whether you have achieved your overall aim, and how easy or difficult it was to implement your strategy. You should also be able to think about how practical it might be to continue with the strategy.

Over to you!

Did you modify any of your strategy as you went along? If so, what and why? If not, is there anything you wish you had modified?

Case study

Josh is a Year 11 BTEC First in Sport student. He filled in his food diary for two weeks and then collated this information so that he could use it to plan and implement his personal nutritional strategy. Josh was very surprised to see how many different times during the day he eats, and he realised that he does a lot of unnecessary snacking. When Josh filled in the activity section of his food diary, he was also surprised to see how little activity he does, and how short the duration is of the activities he does do. When it came to analysing the types of food eaten, Josh was concerned about how many of the foods he eats fall into the category of 'substances with a negative impact'! Josh made sure that he had three training sessions and two competitive rugby matches during the two weeks he implemented his strategy.

1. Which times of the day do you think it is most likely that Josh discovered that he was eating food which he was unaware of before starting the food diary?

2. Josh seems to have had a few 'surprises' and 'concerns'. Which do you think is the most crucial one and why?

3. What are the most likely 'substances with a negative impact' that Josh has been eating?

4. What are the main changes Josh is likely to have made to his 'normal' diet for his nutritional strategy?

5. How is Josh likely to react to increasing his activity levels over the two-week implementation phase?

Assessment activity 8.4 (Unit 10 P5, P6, M4)

This task requires you to implement and evaluate your personal nutritional strategy. You should:

- Implement your personal nutritional strategy, monitoring and reviewing your plans.
- Describe and explain the strengths of your personal nutritional strategy.

- Identify areas for improvement and make recommendations as to how your nutritional strategy could be improved.

You should produce a written report as evidence for this task.

Topic check

1 Explain the term 'implementation'.
2 In what ways are the demands of the three phases of competition likely to be different from the three phases of training?
3 What training and competition considerations do you need to plan for the two weeks of implementation?
4 What is meant by 'adopting the strategy'?
5 Identify two different costs which might be involved in your strategy.
6 When are you are able to modify your strategy?

▮▮ Assessment summary

The overall grade you achieve for this unit depends on how well you meet the grading criteria set out in Appendix 1 (see page 298). You must complete:

- all of the P criteria to achieve a **pass** grade
- all of the P and the M criteria to achieve a **merit** grade
- all of the P, M and D criteria to achieve a **distinction** grade.

Your tutor will assess the assessment activities that you complete for this unit. The work you produce should provide evidence which demonstrates that you have achieved each of the assessment criteria. The table below identifies what you need to demonstrate to meet each of the pass, merit and distinction criteria for this unit. You should always check and self-assess your work before you submit your assignments for marking.

Remember that you MUST provide evidence for all of the P criteria to pass the unit.

Grading criteria	You need to demonstrate that you can:	Have you got the evidence?
P1	Describe the nutritional requirements of a selected sport	
M1	Explain the nutritional requirements of a selected sport	
D1	Evaluate the nutritional requirements of a selected sport describing suitable meal plans	
P2	Collect and collate information on own diet for two weeks	
P3	Describe the strengths of own diet and identify areas for improvement	
M2	Explain the strengths of own diet and make recommendations as to how it could be improved	
D2	Justify recommendations made regarding improving own diet	
P4	Create a personal nutritional strategy, designed and agreed with an adviser	
M3	Contribute own ideas to the design of a personal nutritional strategy	
P5	Implement a personal nutritional strategy	
P6	Describe the strengths of the personal nutritional strategy and identify areas for improvement	
M4	Explain the strengths of the personal nutritional strategy and make recommendations as to how it could be improved	

Always ask your tutor to explain any assignment tasks or assessment criteria that you don't understand fully. Being clear about the task before you begin gives you the best chance of succeeding. Good luck with your Unit 10 assessment work!

Development of personal fitness (Unit 11)

Unit outline

Everyone has the capacity to develop their personal fitness. This unit looks at the methods of training available to you. You will formulate your own training goals and put together a 6-week fitness training programme that takes into account your personal fitness information. You will not use all of the training methods included in this unit – rather, your aim must be to see which ones are most suitable for your programme. You must be realistic about what you can achieve in 6 weeks, and make sure that you get the maximum benefit from your programme. The topics covered in Chapters 1, 2, 4, 5, 8 and 11 will also help your understanding of this unit.

Learning outcomes

1 **Be able to plan a personal training programme.**
2 **Know personal exercise adherence factors and strategies.**
3 **Be able to implement and review a personal fitness training programme.**

Planning a personal fitness training programme

▶ Getting started

In this topic you will plan a personal fitness training programme for yourself, considering the options available to you and bearing in mind the principles of training. You may choose a particular method, such as circuit training, or you might have a more mixed programme. There is no right and wrong way to do this – the important thing is that you plan a programme to achieve a particular goal. In order to set realistic goals, it is important to know your level of fitness when you start – look back at Chapter 1 for details on how to test this.

When you have completed this topic, you should:

- understand the importance of goal setting and have set some goals for yourself
- understand the relevance of personal information in planning your fitness programme
- have gathered the personal information required to plan your own training programme.

🔑 Key terms

Aerobic activity: activity requiring a constant intake of oxygen

Flexibility: the range of movement around a joint

Lactic acid: a by-product of exercise that causes muscle fatigue

Repetitions: the number of times you move weights

Sedentary: sitting down or being physically inactive for long periods of time

Sets: the number of times you perform an actual weight activity

Station: the specific parts, or areas, of a circuit

Goal setting

Goal setting is all about considering what you want to achieve and the ways in which you might achieve it. Without goals you will have no real aim or purpose to your training. A goal could be as straightforward as being faster, stronger or more flexible, but faster, stronger or more flexible for what? Goals are more helpful if they are more specific (e.g. being faster at dribbling with a ball, stronger to push hard in a rugby scrum, more flexible to be more efficient in hurdling). You need to set yourself short-, medium- and long-term goals.

💡 Over to you!

Look back at the components of fitness discussed in Chapter 1, Topic 1.1. Then revise Topic 1.3, which considers the various fitness tests available. Think about how this will be relevant when you plan your fitness training programme.

Short-term goals

These will be goals that you are able to achieve quite quickly (e.g. within two weeks), but the principle of progression (page 208) means that you should aim to improve gradually. For example, you might find that over a two-week period you can increase the number of sit-ups you can do in one minute by one or two – to expect much more would be unreasonable. Your short-term goals will also be dependent upon the type of training/exercise you are doing. If you are trying to improve your **flexibility**, improvement in the short term will probably be very small and possibly difficult to measure. Do not be over-optimistic with these short-term goals.

In the short term it might be difficult to measure improvements in flexibility.

Medium-term goals

Goals that you aim to achieve by the end of your 6-week training programme will be medium-term goals. You should set some specific and measurable goals which you aim to achieve in this time. Again, make sure that you are realistic with these. Even 6 weeks is not a particularly long period when it comes to training programmes. You might find that you are able to achieve some of your goals, while others may be more difficult to achieve. For example, if you weight train regularly it may be harder to increase by one repetition, than to take 5 seconds off your run time. Components of fitness that are well developed may be difficult to improve, and improvements may happen slowly. Components that have not been trained previously may show significant improvement quite quickly.

Long-term goals

You will not be able to achieve any long-term goals by the end of your 6-week fitness training programme, but you should still set yourself some. You can progress towards these aims and this in itself can be measured as success. For example, if you were a basketball player:

▶ Your short-term goal could be to increase your speed and agility test time from 19.7 seconds to 19.5 seconds within a two-week period.

▶ Your medium-term goal may be to focus on sprint training and decrease this to 18 seconds by 6 months.

▶ Your long-term goal may be to increase your speed and agility in basketball, making you a more effective player by the end of the season, or for a specific county trial. Your long-term target is to improve your agility test time, reducing it from 19.7s to 16.5s.

If you were 5000 m runner, you could focus on your long-term fitness level. You could set a target of increasing your aerobic fitness on the multi-stage fitness test, from level 7.7 to level 11.2. The timescale to achieve this could be 1 year, as it may take you a long time. Again, this time period might be targeted for county, national or international competitions. Don't forget that for some athletes the Olympics may be their long-term target, and this happens every 4 years!

Information

Before you start planning your fitness programme, you need to gather some specific information about yourself. You can then use this information to help plan your programme more effectively. It is important that you consider all of the categories identified below, although some may be more important and relevant to you than others.

Personal goals and lifestyle

Your personal goals will link in with your goal setting, but can also be more specific to you as an individual and less directly related to fitness training. For example, you might feel that you are slightly overweight. This may not directly affect your sporting performance (e.g. for a golfer, body fat has little effect on skill), however, it may be something that you would like to improve for your own health.

You will have established a particular lifestyle that suits you. You may have a very active lifestyle or a more **sedentary** one. See Chapter 1, Topic 1.2 for more about this and other lifestyle factors that may affect your fitness training programme.

Body fat has little effect on golfing skills.

Medical history and physical activity history

You may not have had any particular medical problems in the past, in which case your medical history is unlikely to affect the goals for your personal training programme. However, you should always consider checking with your doctor before taking part in a strenuous training programme if you have had any previous medical problems, or recent or recurrent injuries. If you have a medical condition, such as asthma, you need to take this into consideration. You should also seek advice straight away if you develop any medical problems once you have started your programme.

Another consideration is how much physical activity you are used to doing. You may be used to regularly taking part in a lot of physical activity. If this is the case then you can probably set yourself quite challenging goals. However, if you have not been particularly active up to this point, you should bear in mind that your levels of general fitness (see Chapter 1, Topic 1.3) may not be very high. Make sure that you set realistic goals in relation to the amount of physical activity you usually do and your current levels of fitness. Setting yourself over-optimistic goals might lead to injury or disappointment.

Dietary history, preferences and supplement use

Diet and nutrition are dealt with in detail in Chapter 8, so you might find it useful to read through that chapter again. You may find that you need to adjust your diet, or preferences, to achieve some of your goals. You should not do this without making sure that you understand what this involves and the possible effects of making these dietary changes.

There are many dietary supplements available that you might consider taking. However, you should consider this very carefully and seek advice from a tutor or other expert before making a decision about this. You should be absolutely certain that any supplement you are taking is both safe and suitable for you to use.

Attitudes and motivation

You must be honest and reflective about your attitude towards fitness training. Since you are taking this course, it is likely that you have a generally positive attitude, but you may not have undertaken this kind of fitness training before. It requires real commitment to plan and complete this unit, so you need to make sure that you approach it with the right attitude.

Your main motivation should be that completing this unit well is going to count towards your final qualification! It is hoped that you will also gain some personal satisfaction from completing the programme, and that you will feel better for feeling fitter. Consider whether you think of yourself as a particularly motivated person. If you think you lack motivation, try to think of ways of that you might be able to improve your levels of motivation.

Over to you!

Fill in the table below to help you prioritise the information you will use to set your goals. Tick the box that applies to each information factor listed.

Information factor	High importance	Medium importance	Low importance
Personal goals			
Lifestyle			
Medical history			
Physical activity history			
Dietary history and preferences			
Supplement use			
Attitudes			
Motivation			

Physical fitness training programme

You now have to consider what your fitness training programme will actually consist of. There are several areas to bear in mind when planning the programme, to ensure that you include all the important elements. You will also need to consider the training methods you will use.

Aims and objectives

It is important to set yourself aims and objectives. They will be an extension of the goals you identified earlier. Your aims will be the way in which you are going to set about achieving your goals. Your objectives will be the final result you are aiming for. The table below illustrates this with an example.

Goal	Aim	Objective
Increase running distance to 6 miles by week 6	To improve endurance levels	To be more effective in a full hockey game

Principles of training

In order to plan and perform your programme successfully, you must make sure that you understand and take into account the principles of training. Paying particular attention to these principles will also ensure that your training is as safe and effective as possible.

An easy way to remember the principles of training is using the SPORT acronym:

S = specificity

P = progression

O = overload

R = reversibility

T = tedium.

> ### Over to you!
>
> Use the table above as the basis for a table of your own. Start to fill it in, linking your goals to your aims and objectives.

▶ *Specificity* means choosing a particular kind of activity or exercise to build up or improve certain body parts or skills. To start with, consider your fitness levels, body type etc. Think about what you are actually going to be training for and choose exercises that are specific and appropriate to your goals.

▶ *Progression* means gradually increasing the amount of training you do, so that you avoid injury or over-tiredness by doing too much too soon. You must build this into your programme. What are your initial levels of general and specific fitness? You may have to start very gradually and build up slowly. You might find that you level out at a particular stage of training, and are unable to progress further – this is known as 'plateauing'.

▷ *Overload* is making your body work harder than normal in order to make it adapt and improve. The acronym **FITT** will help you to understand what overload is and how it works:

- **f**requency – how often the training takes place
- **i**ntensity – how hard you train
- **t**ime – the duration of your training
- **t**ype – of training or exercise.

▷ *Reversibility* refers to the fact that if you stop training you will lose the positive effects you have achieved through training – in other words, the results will reverse and you will go back to being as you were before the training. The positive effects you gain can be lost very quickly. A beginner loses effects at a faster rate than a regular, trained performer. Different factors of fitness may be affected in different ways and at different rates.

▷ *Tedium* refers to boredom during training, which is something you should try to avoid. If you become bored with your training you will become less motivated, less effective and less likely to continue with it. Try to build variety into your programme so that it remains interesting and enjoyable.

Warm-up and cool-down

It is very important for you to perform a warm-up at the beginning of each training session and a cool-down at the end. Figure 9.1 gives you some indication of the amount of time you should give to each phase of a training session.

The warm-up is essential in any training session because:

▷ It prepares the body for the activity. It raises the heart rate and breathing rate and stimulates the nervous system so that you are psychologically prepared.

▷ It reduces the possibility of injury, especially muscle injury.

Your warm-up should consist of the following:

▷ a pulse-raiser – this is a continuous movement activity

▷ light exercises – these should be targeted at particular muscle groups

▷ mobility exercises – such as stretches aimed at particular muscle groups and major joints.

The time spent on the warm-up phase and the type of content you include will depend on the following:

▷ the type of activity you are preparing for – gymnastics might require extra stretches

▷ the environment you are in – a cold outdoor environment might need additional pulse-raisers and plenty of active movement.

The cool-down is also essential and is often neglected. The cool-down is essential in any training session because:

▷ It allows the body to return to its normal temperature.

▷ It allows the pulse rate to return gradually to its resting level from its working level.

▷ It helps to prevent stiffness and soreness in the muscles by dispersing **lactic acid**.

The activities you perform in your cool-down can be similar to the activities that you included in your warm-up.

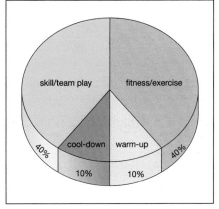

Figure 9.1 Warm-up and cool-down as a proportion of a training session

Training methods

There is a variety of training methods that you can use. These can focus on one aspect of fitness (e.g. power training using weights), or can combine components of fitness (e.g. strength and endurance in circuit training).

You can choose different aspects from different methods or you can opt to follow one particular one. Remember that this has to be linked to the goals, aims and objectives which you considered earlier in this topic. Types of training suitable for four different areas of fitness are discussed below.

1 Flexibility training

It is important to remember that none of the following stretches should be done before a thorough warm-up has been performed. There are three types of flexibility training:

▶ *Static stretching* involves slow but sustained stretching of a joint. This can be active or passive. Active is where your muscle is lengthened in a set position but needs other muscles to hold it in position. Passive is when the muscle is helped to stretch by some other form of force such as an object (e.g. pushing against a wall), a partner or a coach. Examples of these can be hamstring, quadricep and pectoral stretches.

▶ *Ballistic stretching* is sometimes referred to as 'dynamic stretching'. It involves performing bouncing or jerking movements to increase the range of your stretch. This can be effective at increasing your range of movement but it is also associated with injury, so you must perform these with great caution! An example of this could be a dynamic hamstring stretch, involving a kicking action, swinging your leg backwards and forwards.

▶ *Proprioceptive neuromuscular facilitation* (PNF for short!) is a more advanced form of stretching where the muscle group is stretched under tension. You then have to contract the stretched muscle for 5–6 seconds while a partner (or an immovable object) supplies enough pressure to stop any other movement occurring. The controlled muscle is then relaxed and a controlled stretch is applied for about 30 seconds. The muscle group is then allowed 30 seconds to recover and the whole process is then repeated over again between 3 and 4 times.

2 Strength training

This can be targeted specifically at muscular endurance, strength or power. There are several ways in which this can be achieved.

Resistance machines

Resistance machines are commonly found in gyms and fitness suites. The different machines are designed to work on specific muscles or muscle groups. You can easily adjust the machines to the particular weight (resistance) required for your level of training.

Over to you!

Go to the following website to find out more about stretching: www.thestretchinghandbook .com/archives/pnf-stretching.php. Which type of flexibility training do you think would best suit your needs at your current level of fitness and flexibiity?

There are two important terms which you must understand when weight training. **Repetitions** are the number of times you move the weights when you are training. **Sets** are the number of times you do a particular weight activity. So, you might do four sets of six repetitions (reps) each. The way you vary both of these factors is the basis for any weight training or strength training session.

To improve muscle tone and general levels of endurance you should use fairly light weights and do 12–15 reps for about three sets. For more specific strength improvement you should use heavier weights and do 10–12 reps and an increased number of sets. For power you should use very heavy weights and do 4–6 reps for about three sets.

If you are lucky enough to have access to a fitness suite with these machines you will find that they are all labelled with instructions. It is easy to identify which muscles, or muscle groups, can be exercised.

Free weights

Using free weights is an alternative method of weight training if you do not have access to resistance machines, or if you prefer not to use them. The principles are the same as for resistance machines, but you will have to select specific weights and possibly use benches or tables to position your body. You should also have a 'training partner' to work with you and help you with the weights on some of the exercises.

Circuit training

Circuit training is one of the most popular forms of fitness training. One of its main advantages is the flexibility and variety of options it offers.

Circuit training makes use of a variety of different exercises and equipment. The exercise areas and pieces of equipment (each called a **station**) are arranged around an area. Often each station is labelled with instructions for the exercise to be performed there. You start at a particular station and perform that activity for either a set period of time (e.g. 30 seconds) or for a particular number of repetitions (e.g. 20 press-ups). Once you have completed this activity, you move to the next station and do that exercise. When you have done each activity once, you have completed a circuit. You may perform several circuits in the same order, or may make each circuit different (e.g. changing the work time, the number or repetitions or the rest time between stations). You can have a fitness circuit (using exercises such as press-ups and sit-ups), a weights circuit (using resistance machines or free weights), or even a skills circuit (performing set skills for a particular sport), but they are quite often a combination of two or more types.

Plyometrics

You can see from Figure 9.3 that plyometrics involves jumping and bounding movements. These movements put a load on the muscle, which has to contract in a rapid movement. This helps to increase the speed of muscular contractions to help you jump higher, run faster, throw harder or hit harder. It is one of the best ways to increase power.

An example of a plyometrics exercise.

3 Aerobic endurance

Aerobic activity is activity that requires a constant intake of oxygen. Aerobic endurance training is designed to help you keep going for long periods of time. There are different ways you can train for this.

Continuous training

This is a type of training which keeps your heart and pulse rate high. You can do this by continuously running, jogging, cycling or swimming, or even by taking part in an organised exercise session. The intention is that you make sure your body's demand for oxygen is matched by its oxygen intake. It is easy to vary the level at which you train simply by starting slowly and increasing your speed, e.g. walking, increasing this to brisk walking, then jogging and running. The intensity of your training should be 65–85% of your maximum heart rate. Your maximum heart rate is worked out using the following equation: 220 – age. So, for someone aged 16:

220 – 16 = 204

65% of 200 = 133 and 85% of 200 = 173

Training should be completed between 130 and 170 heart beats per minute.

Fartlek training

This is a Swedish word meaning 'speed play'. It originated in the Scandinavian countries where it often involved running up hills. It involves walking, then brisk walking, then running, then jogging and finally fast steady running. You can also alternate speed at regular intervals. For example, people who struggle to run continuously for 20 minutes because of their fitness level can gradually improve by alternating between walking and jogging at regular 100 m intervals.

Interval training

This is a form of training which consists of periods of work followed by periods of rest. It usually involves some form of running. It can be varied by adjusting the work time duration, the intensity of the work, the number of repetitions performed and the recovery time allowed (e.g. 8 repetitions of 50 m sprints). A rest period of 1 minute can be included between each interval. Intervals can also cover longer distances.

Activity

Find out what form of training a top level, elite performer in your main sport uses. Remember that it is likely to be combination of different methods, rather than a single one.

4 Speed training

The most effective form of speed training is to use Fartlek and interval training, as outlined above, but to concentrate on bursts of speed rather than longer distances or times. You should also include sprint work. In order to improve, you should aim to maintain a high speed for longer than 6 seconds or produce repeated sprints with minimal rest periods in between.

Over to you!

Carefully read about all of the training methods and make sure you understand what each one does. Then choose which method, or combination of methods, you think will be best suited to helping you achieve your goals, aims and objectives.

Case study

Amy is starting to plan her personal fitness training programme. However, she is struggling to come up with reasonable short-term and medium-term goals. She wants to be a better netball player in the end, and considers this to be part of her long-term goal. Amy has studied the principles of training carefully and has decided to opt for circuit training as her chosen training method. She is not sure if this is all she should be doing, but cannot decide what else might help her. Amy has not really undertaken any form of formal fitness training before and does not exercise much in her spare time. She is a committed vegetarian and is unsure if this is a factor she should include in her dietary history information.

1. What advice you would give Amy regarding her short-term and medium-term plans?

2. Are there any particular lifestyle factors Amy should be considering more carefully?

3. Is the fact that Amy is a vegetarian likely to have any significant effect on her planning or her ability to complete her programme?

4. Is there anything you would suggest that Amy should do in addition to circuit training?

5. Do you think circuit training is the most appropriate training method for Amy? If not, what would be the best alternative?

Assessment activity 9.1 (Unit 11 P1, M1, P2, M2, D1, P3, P4, M3, D2)

This assessment activity requires you to show that you can design a 6-week personal fitness training programme. This should improve your fitness levels to enhance your sports performance and overall health and wellbeing.

- You need to plan, design and agree a 6-week personal fitness training programme with a coach, contributing as many of your own ideas to the planning and design of the programme as possible.

- You should produce a written training programme as evidence for this assessment activity.

Topic check

1 Why is goal setting important?
2 Give two examples of medium-term goals.
3 What do you understand by the term 'supplements'?
4 How might motivation affect the way you carry out your training programme?
5 What does the SPORT acronym stand for?
6 What does the FITT acronym stand for?
7 Identify three elements of a good warm-up.
8 Explain what lactic acid is and the effect it can have.
9 What does PNF stand for?
10 Explain the difference between repetitions and sets.

Personal exercise adherence factors and strategies

This topic is concerned with making sure that you are able to stick to the personal fitness training plan you have decided upon. It outlines some factors you need to consider and suggests some strategies for you to use.

When you have completed this topic, you should:

- understand the exercise adherence factors you may come across
- know some strategies that will help you to stick to your training plan.

Key terms

Adherence: sticking to something

Motivation: a stimulus, or incentive, to encourage and improve

Reinforcement: information that confirms or verifies and a stimulus which strengthens behaviour

Exercise adherence factors

These will depend on the fitness programme you have planned – not all of them will necessarily apply to you and your programme. Some might have a greater effect than others.

Overcoming barriers

It is likely that there will be a few barriers to consider when planning your fitness programme. You may have to accept that there is very little you can do about some of them, but you will be able to overcome others. There are various types of barriers you may come across.

Access to facilities

If you plan to use a gym, weights room or swimming pool, you will be restricted to using them during opening hours when they are available to the general public. With many gyms you have to become a member in order to be able to use the facilities, and you will have to pay for this. Some gyms allow non-members, but you usually have to pay a premium (a higher price) to use the facilities if you are not a member. The first time you use any gym you have to have an induction session before you are allowed to train on your own. You will usually have to book this in advance.

You also need to bear in mind the location of the facilities and how easily you will be able to get to them. Are you going to have to rely on public transport or getting a lift? If there is going to be a lot of travelling time, how will you fit your training in around your other daily commitments? Remember that you are going to have to keep to the plan for 6 weeks.

Time

You know that your programme is going to last for 6 weeks. You now have to plan how much time you are going to dedicate to it each week over this period. General guidance regarding training suggests that you need to leave some time between training sessions for your body to recover. This is usually one day, especially if a session is quite strenuous. This means that you might want to plan two to three training sessions in any one week.

You also need to decide how long each training sessions is going to last. It needs to be long enough for you to get some benefit from it, but if it is too long you may be too tired to recover sufficiently for the next one. Over-training can be just as bad as under-training, so you need to consider timing issues carefully.

Over to you!

Find out about how much time performers would normally commit to the sort of training programme you are considering undertaking. Make sure you find about the number of sessions in a week and how long each session lasts.

Motivation

You will already have considered your motivation levels in Topic 9.1. If you lack motivation you are going to find this training commitment quite difficult. As you have put this programme together yourself, you will have to rely primarily on self-motivation. This is why it is important that you think carefully about the goals you set – if they are important to you then you are more likely to feel motivated to achieve them.

Cost

This will vary depending on the type of programme you have planned. It is likely that your programme will cost something at some point. As has already been mentioned, if you plan to use facilities such as a gym or swimming pool, you will almost certainly have to pay for this. Using a fitness gym or swimming pool usually involves paying for each session, but you might be able to buy a form of 'season ticket'. If you have to travel to a facility, there may be transport cost involved too. You also need to consider whether you will have to buy any special equipment, clothing or footwear.

Athletes have to be highly motivated to reach elite levels.

Implementing enjoyable factors

This links in with motivation. The more enjoyable your programme is, the more likely you are to stick to it and the more successful it is likely to be. The less enjoyable it is, the less likely you are to complete it. You might like to try out some of the different training methods to find out which you enjoy most. Some people enjoy the social atmosphere of a fitness gym, where they can work out with other people, while other prefer being on their own, say on a distance run. The more 'fun' and enjoyable you can make your programme, the better!

Benefits of your programme

It is important that you feel the benefits of your training programme. This will confirm that your programme is working and will help to keep you motivated, linking in with your personal goals. You will not feel all of the benefits straight away, but if you have considered your short- and medium-term goals carefully then you should be aware of the benefits you likely to achieve in the longer term. The benefits should include feeling a real sense of achievement and making progress, as well as feeling the physical and mental benefits of being active.

Over to you!

Look at the six factors discussed above and put them in rank order from most to least relevant to the programme you are planning. Once you have done this, check whether any of the important factors you have identified are likely to have any negative effects on you personally or on your ability to successfully complete your training programme.

Exercise adherence strategies

Once you have considered the problems you might encounter, you then need to come up with some strategies to achieve success. These might include setting yourself SMART targets, ensuring that you have the support you need from tutors or coaches, and deciding how you will reward yourself for success.

Targets

You should have already set your targets, as they will be central to your overall strategy. These will include your initial goal setting and your aims and objectives. You will already be familiar with SMART targets. In relation to exercise adherence strategies you should consider them as follows:

▸ *Specific* – As you learnt in Topic 9.1, specificity is one of the main principles of training. You need to ensure that your targets are specific and fit in with your aims and objectives.

▸ *Measurable* – This links with the training principle of progression. You need to be able to measure your progress to determine whether you are succeeding. You can use various tests (see Chapter 1, Topic 1.3) to help you with this.

▸ *Achievable* – If you make your programme too difficult, you may find that your motivation levels drop and you are less likely to complete it. This links in with the overload principle of training – you must push yourself, but not too hard.

▸ *Realistic* – This factor links closely with 'achievable'. You must be realistic about what you will be able to achieve over this 6-week period, taking into account your level of fitness at the start of the programme. Again, this links in with the overload principle of training.

▸ *Time-bound* – As this programme is designed to last 6 weeks, it is already time-bound. However, there will also be elements of timing within your programme, related to your short-term aims and the training schedule you have planned.

Figure 9.2 How **SMART** targets relate to **SPORT** principles of training

Specific	**S**pecificity
Measurable	**P**rogression
Achievable	**O**verload
Realistic	**O**verload
Time-bound	**O**verload **R**eversibility

Over to you!

Using Figure 9.2, check that your initial personal fitness training programme meets all of the aspects relating to the principles of training and the SMART strategies. Amend any parts that need changing.

Support and reinforcement

Although you will be planning and implementing the programme yourself, you will need some support as you go along. Your tutor or coach can certainly give you support, including advice with the planning and implementation of your programme. Be sure that you make use of this and do not think that you are totally on your own. Some forms of training can be lonely experiences, but you do have the option of training with other people. You may find it helpful to have a training partner for all or some of your programme. They can offer support, encouragement and **reinforcement**, and may be able to provide feedback regarding your progress.

Rewards for achieving goals

How are you going to reward yourself for making good progress? This may be the first time you have had to take responsibility for deciding something like this on your own. When other people have encouraged you in sporting situations in the past, what sorts of rewards have they offered you? You may be able to use these experiences to set some for yourself. Rewards can take the form of doing something nice, e.g. allowing yourself a treat, going to the cinema to celebrate meeting a target, having a party to celebrate breaking a personal best, or even giving yourself an achievable prize such as a CD. Don't forget that rewards are personal, so each person's may be different. Rewards can also have a cost attached to them so they need to be realistic.

Over to you!

See if you can team up with someone else in your BTEC group to jointly come up with a rewards strategy which you can encourage each other with.

Case study

and power, and aerobic exercise to improve his aerobic endurance. Scott has joined a gym in the centre of town, which is a 30-minute bus ride away. For his aerobic endurance Scott is also intending to join an organised 'boxercise' class which is being run at a local leisure centre. This leisure centre is also a short bus ride away on the outskirts of the town. Scott has planned this closely with his friend Dan, who is going to attend the 'boxercise' class with him but not the fitness gym sessions. Both Dan and Scott are rugby players and are hoping that this programme is going to make them more effective players.

1. Do you think Scott has put together an achievable and realistic programme?

2. What are likely to be the main cost factors Scott is going to have to consider?

3. Can you foresee any problems Scott might face in relation to access to the facilities he plans to use?

4. What time factors will Scott have to consider?

5. List the possible advantages to Scott of Dan attending the 'boxercise' sessions with him.

Scott has planned his personal programme and is about to start the training. He has decided to use weight training to improve his muscular endurance

Assessment activity 9.2 (Unit 11 P2, M2, D1)

With reference to your personal fitness training programme, use the knowledge and understanding you have of your circumstances, the facilities and resources available to you and your own approach to fitness training to:

- Describe personal exercise adherence factors and strategies that are likely to impact on your training performance during the 6-week period when you will be implementing your plan.

Topic check

1 Give three factors you might have to consider in relation to access to facilities you plan to use.

2 Identify the two main time factors you will have to consider.

3 What costs might be involved in taking a fitness training programme?

4 Identify three other exercise adherence factors (excluding access to facilities, time and cost).

5 Who might you turn to for support with your training programme, and why?

6 Which parts of the SMART acronym link to the overload principle of the SPORT acronym?

Being able to implement and review a personal fitness training programme

The next step is implement your plan and follow your 6-week training programme. During this time you must record what you are doing so that you can review the programme once you have completed it.

When you have completed this topic, you should have:

■ implemented your training programme

■ kept a training diary

■ reviewed your training programme

■ identified your strengths and areas for improvement.

Implementing your programme

Implementing your programme means actually carrying it out according to your plan. This will involve several different elements.

▷ *Taking part in planned sessions* – You must take part in all the sessions you have planned. Some of these may be during school/college time, but others will be in your own time and you must make sure that you organise your time appropriately and do not miss any training sessions.

▷ *Perform to the best of your ability* – The only way you are going to get the best out of your planned programme is if you try your hardest in all the sessions you have planned. Failing to do this will result in poor results, which means you are unlikely to achieve the goals you have set yourself.

▷ *Gain agreement for any missed sessions* – It is hoped that you will not miss any sessions, but if you do have to for some reason then you must inform your tutor and get permission to miss the session. You should also try to organise another session to make up for the one you missed. Any missed sessions will come up in your review and may affect your final results.

▷ *The importance of* **commitment** – This has already been discussed, so you will understand its importance in relation to your adherence to the programme. It also links closely to the previous three factors. You will have to be honest regarding the level of commitment you have been able to give to your planned programme.

Key terms

Commitment: a pledge or desire to do something; a will to succeed

Keeping a training diary

You must fill in a training diary as you work through your programme. You must note the date and details of each session and should include the following sections:

▶ *A log of performance and achievement* – You must record details of every session in your diary. You must record what you actually do in relation to what you planned to do, and make a judgement regarding what you think you have achieved. Your log could contain details such as how far you ran and at what speed, how many press-ups you achieved per session, and also how much weight and how many reps and sets you can do for each weight training exercise.

▶ *Programme progression* – This is related to progression as a principle of training. You may not have progressed exactly as planned, but this is not necessarily a problem as long as you record your progress honestly. However, you may have to alter your training plan to take account of this.

▶ *Motivation for training* – This has already been discussed and you should be aware of how important it is. You need to consider it carefully and comment on it honestly in your diary. Only you will know how motivated you were in each of your sessions, and you should be aware that this might have affected your final performance.

Activity

Design a training diary that you can use to monitor your training. You can use the example below to help you with some ideas.

	Date		Motivation H/M/L	Date		Motivation H/M/L
Warm-up						
Mobilisation						
Pulse-raiser						
Stretches						
Cardiovascular training	Level/ Speed	Time		Level/ Speed	Time	
Muscular endurance	Reps	Sets		Reps	Sets	
Resistance training	Wt	Reps		Wt	Reps	
Cool-down						
Pulse lower						
Flexibility training	Reps	Time		Reps	Time	

It is essential that you design your training diary before you start your training programme. Diaries can take a variety of forms and what may be suitable for one person will not be for another.

Reviewing the programme

It is important that you review your training programme and reflect on what you have managed to achieve. Your training diary will help you with this.

During and after performance

You must review your performance on an ongoing basis during the 6-week period of your training programme. Then, at the end you will also have to carry out a final review. Make sure that you are honest in this review as it is important that you are able to identify what went well and anything which did not go quite to plan.

Modifying the programme

You may find that you need to modify the programme as you go along, and this is perfectly acceptable. When you are reviewing your performance you might identify factors you are not happy with. Changing these, or modifying them, is a positive move and shows that you are able to identify where improvements need to be made. Be sure to include the reasons why you made these modifications and link them specifically to the principles of training they relate to.

Strengths and areas for improvement

Your review will enable you to identify your strengths. You should focus particularly on areas of the programme where you feel that your aims and objectives were achieved. You will have set these when you were planning your programme, after initially considering your goals. By setting these in line with your SMART targets you should be able to clearly identify all of the successful areas where you achieved what you set out to do.

As well as strength, you are bound to identify some areas for improvement. Do not be disappointed if you find that there are a number of things which did not go as planned. This is likely to be the first time you have had to plan and implement something as complex as this, so it is likely that you will find quite a lot of things that you would change in any future programme. This is all part of the learning process, and you will be credited for being aware of these rather than being penalised for them.

Case study

Rob has managed to plan and complete his personal fitness training programme. He planned it quite carefully with his tutor and also got help from his football club coach. Rob plays in midfield so he wanted to improve his levels of endurance, but he also wanted to improve his strength as he thought he was too easily pushed off the ball.

To increase his levels of endurance, Rob carried out continuous training which consisted of a long-distance run three times a week. To improve his strength he worked out with weights in a local gym with his older brother; he did this on days he did not go on his run. Rob enjoyed his weights sessions far more than his running sessions and nearly didn't go on two of his planned runs. When Rob reflected on his achievements, he considered that he had made more progress in his strength development than his endurance target.

1. What part do you think Rob's tutor and football coach were able to play in terms of planning and modifying his programme?

2. Do you think Rob's overall choice of programme was a good one and likely to achieve his aims?

3. Do you think Rob's levels of motivation were high throughout his implementation?

4. What might have contributed to Rob enjoying his weight training sessions more than his endurance runs?

5. What factors are likely to have contributed to Rob achieving more in one area than the other?

Assessment activity 9.3 (Unit 11 P3, P4, M3, D2)

You now need to test out and evaluate the personal fitness training programme you have developed. Your task for this assessment activity is to:

- Carry out a 6-week personal fitness training programme, maintaining a training diary.
- Describe and explain the strengths of your training programme, identifying any areas for improvement.

- Justify the suggestions you make related to areas for improvement in your personal fitness training programme.

You should produce a training diary and a written report as evidence for this task.

Topic check

1 What does implementing a programme involve?
2 How often should your training diary be filled in?
3 Identify the four main headings you should include in your training diary.
4 Which two headings should your review process come under?
5 Explain the options you have regarding modifying your programme.

⏸ Assessment summary

The overall grade you achieve for this unit depends on how well you meet the grading criteria set out in Appendix 1 (see page 299). You must complete:

- all of the P criteria to achieve a **pass** grade
- all of the P and the M criteria to achieve a **merit** grade
- all of the P, M and D criteria to achieve a **distinction** grade.

Your tutor will assess the assessment activities that you complete for this unit. The work you produce should provide evidence which demonstrates that you have achieved each of the assessment criteria. The table below identifies what you need to demonstrate to meet each of the pass, merit and distinction criteria for this unit. You should always check and self-assess your work before you submit your assignments for marking.

Remember that you MUST provide evidence for all of the P criteria to pass the unit.

Grading criteria	You need to demonstrate that you can:	Have you got the evidence?
P1	Plan, design and agree, a 6-week personal fitness training programme with a coach	
M1	Contribute own ideas to the design of a 6-week personal fitness training programme	
P2	Describe personal exercise adherence factors and strategies	
M2	Explain personal exercise adherence factors and strategies	
D1	Evaluate personal exercise adherence strategies for overcoming barriers to exercise	
P3	Implement a 6-week personal fitness training programme, maintaining a training diary	
P4	Describe the strengths of the personal fitness training programme, identifying areas for improvement	
M3	Explain the strengths of the personal fitness training programme, making suggestions for improvement	
D2	Justify suggestions related to identified areas for improvement in the personal fitness training programme	

Always ask your tutor to explain any assignment tasks or assessment criteria that you don't understand fully. Being clear about the task before you begin gives you the best chance of succeeding. Good luck with your Unit 11 assessment work!

10 Work experience in the sports industry (Unit 13)

Unit outline

The sports industry is one of the fastest growing in terms of job opportunities. It is closely linked to the leisure industry, and the two are often referred to jointly as 'the sport and leisure industry'. This unit is designed to give you a thorough understanding of the industry and the opportunities and occupations available within it. It will identify the skills you might need in the world of work and will give you opportunities to practise these. You will undertake a full-time work placement for approximately 35 hours in total. At the end of this unit you will review your work placement and give a presentation about it, so you should bear this in mind as you work through the unit, making sure that you record any relevant information.

Learning outcomes

1 Know the range and scope of organisations and occupations within the sports industry.
2 Be able to use relevant documents and skills relating to sport-based work experience.
3 Be able to plan and carry out a project during sport-based work experience.
4 Be able to present and review the project.

The range and scope of organisations within the sports industry

▶ **Getting started**

The sports industry covers a wide range of organisations and occupations. Many of these offer similar opportunities to those in most organisations, such as office, clerical and reception work. However, there is also a wide variety of opportunities relating to specific sports and the facilities which provide them.

When you have completed this topic, you should know:

■ about the different types of organisation in the sports industry

■ about the types and variety of occupations in the industry

■ the responsibilities and skills required for different occupations.

Organisations

The sports industry is made up of several different types of organisation and providers.

The public sector

The public sector includes any organisation that is controlled by the government. It is the biggest employer in the United Kingdom, employing just over 20% of the entire workforce. Anything owned and run by local government is considered to be in the public sector. Examples include:

▶ schools and associated leisure centres

▶ public swimming pools

▶ outdoor playing fields and sports pitches, including athletics tracks

▶ public parks

▶ public golf courses

▶ public beaches.

The majority of major sports facilities are in the public sector. This is mainly because they are expensive to build, set up and maintain, so they are paid for through the tax system and then made available for public use. This means that anyone can use them, often for a reasonable charge.

Private sector

The private sector includes any provider that is privately owned, for example by an individual, a club or an organisation. Examples include:

▶ private golf clubs

▶ private fitness gyms

- private schools
- martial arts clubs
- football clubs
- hotel leisure complexes
- tennis clubs.

In the private sector people pay a membership or annual subscription, and sometimes fees on top of this, in order to use the facilities. The organisations use these funds to provide and run the facilities.

Voluntary

Many golf clubs are in the private sector.

Voluntary organisations are organisations that are reliant on volunteers and charitable funding. They only exist through the goodwill of people committing time and effort. Many voluntary providers use public facilities but do not charge for their services. Many local sports pitches have organised clubs that run teams (e.g. netball, hockey, rugby and football). There are also voluntary organisations such as the Scouts and Girl Guides that provide sporting opportunities.

Joint and dual use

Joint and dual-use facilities are shared with different groups. For example, it is very common for school facilities (swimming pools in particular) to be used by the school during the day, and by the public in the evenings and at weekends. This is known as joint use. Alternatively, the school and the public can share a facility at all times, which is known as dual use. Both of these arrangements have the advantage of making sure that maximum use is made of the facility.

Over to you!

Carry out a survey of your immediate area to find out what provision there is in the public and private sector. Find out how many schools provide dual or joint provision.

Occupations

One of the most impressive things about the sports industry is the number of different occupations within it. Figure 10.1 (page 228) lists some of these and considers the responsibilities each has, and the skills/qualifications required to do the job.

Activity

Find out about other occupations within the sports industry. List any particular responsibilities and skills/qualifications that might be needed to do these jobs.

Figure 10.1 Occupations in the sports industry

Occupation	Responsibilities	Skills/qualifications required
Sports assistant	Any general work in a sports club or leisure centre, e.g. setting up and putting way equipment, organising the facility.	No specific skills but general coaching qualifications would help as some classes/clubs could be run.
Fitness instructor	Running fitness classes or overseeing a fitness gym or weights room.	• Knowledge of fitness and of the correct use of equipment etc. • Fitness Instructor Level 2
Coach	Coaching a particular sport or activity. Possibly running teams as well.	• Usually need to be a skilled performer in that particular sport or activity. • A Level 2 coaching award in the sport in question.
Teacher	Teaching within a school with particular responsibility for physical education. In charge of all of the sporting provisions within a school.	• Usually a good and proficient all-round sportsperson. • A degree is required in order to train and qualify to be a teacher.
Sports development officer	The development of a sport, or a number of sports, in a particular area.	• Knowledge and experience of sport in general or of a sport in particular. • Organisational experience and skills. A degree in Sports Development may be required.
Sports and exercise scientist	Teaching, researching and advising on aspects of sport.	Specialist knowledge with a high level of qualifications – at least degree level.
Physiotherapist	Carrying out physiotherapy on patients or clients, usually in a hospital or a clinic.	Qualified to at least degree level with a specific physiotherapy degree.
Professional performer	Playing for a club or individually as a full-time job.	A very high level of ability and dedication in a particular sport.
Retailer	Selling any form of goods or services connected with the sports industry. This can range from being the owner to the shop assistant selling the goods.	No particular qualifications are needed. The skills could include being a good communicator, having experience and knowledge of the product being sold.

These are just some of the occupations in the sports industry. There are a great many more.

Activity

Discuss the skills required for the jobs that you have found. Are there general skills that all jobs require? Develop a checklist of any general skills that you feel are useful. See how many of these skills you already have and which you need to do more work on.

Assessment activity 10.1 (Unit 13 P1, P2, P3, M1, M2)

The first assessment activity for this unit requires you to prepare for work experience. You should:

- Identify and describe examples of three different types of organisation within the sports industry.

- Describe three different occupations within the sports industry and explain the skills that each require.

- Locate from different sources three advertisements for jobs in the sports industry and use them to identify appropriate work experience opportunities.

You should produce a written report and a job advertisement portfolio as evidence of your work for this assessment.

Topic check

1   Who controls the public sector?
2   Identify four types of public sector provision.
3   What percentage of the workforce is employed in the public sector?
4   How are the public sector provisions paid for?
5   What is the private sector?
6   Give four different examples of private sector provision.
7   How is the private sector financed?
8   Give two examples of voluntary organisations that might provide sporting opportunities.
9   Explain the difference between 'dual use' and 'joint use'.
10 List the responsibilities of and qualifications required for an occupation that particularly interests you in the sports industry.

Documents and skills relating to sport-based work experience

▶ Getting started

In this topic you will find out what skills you have to offer, and how to use these and relevant documentation to obtain work experience. This topic will also help you to prepare for the challenges of finding and carrying out your work placement.

When you have completed this topic, you should know:

- where to look for job vacancies
- what experience you already have and what your work is likely to involve
- what documentation you are likely to need and how to provide this
- how to prepare for an interview
- some skills you can use during your interview.

🔑 Key terms

Body language: the gestures, postures and facial expressions which suggest your physical, mental and emotional state

Dress code: the accepted, or recognised type or style of clothing which is appropriate to be worn

Proof read: thoroughly check a document through for accuracy, spelling etc.

Punctual: on time

Sources of jobs available

There is a wide variety of sources where you can find information about jobs.

▶ *The press* – this can be the local or national press. Newspapers are printed daily and always include sections listing job vacancies. There are also specialist magazines, which might be printed weekly or monthly, which contain an employment/jobs section.

▶ *Publications and periodicals* – these can include books and specialist booklets produced by specific sporting bodies or organisations. Brochures sent out from organisations and sports providers will often indicate where employment possibilities might be available.

▶ *Recruitment agencies* – these are becoming more and more common and popular. Employers like to use them as the company does not have to advertise, and they can often get workers very quickly. Employees like to use them because they can leave their details with the agency and wait to hear from them with offers of work, rather than looking and applying for lots of different jobs themselves.

▶ *Websites* – these are a very good source of information. Websites are being used more and more by organisations, particularly National Governing Bodies, and they often advertise a wide variety of job opportunities. They are regularly updated and they have the great advantage of being a very cheap way of advertising jobs for the employers. For many, this is now their number one option for advertising vacancies.

▶ *The Institute of Leisure and Amenity Management (ILAM)* – this is the professional organisation representing over 7,000 managers in the leisure industry, and it deals with facilities and services in the voluntary, commercial and public sectors.

▶ *SkillsActive* – this is the Sector Skills Council for Active Leisure and Learning. It is directed by employers and deals with sport, recreation, health and fitness, outdoors (e.g. outdoor education and outdoor sport development), playwork (which focuses on young children's care) and even the caravan industry. It was formed in April 2008, and one of its main functions is to link employers with training agencies. This would certainly be an organisation to go to for updated and further information.

> **Over to you!**
>
> Have a look at all of the job sources outlined in the text. See which one has the best range and variety of options relating to the sports industry.

Work experience

You need to be aware of exactly what this involves. The following will help you with this:

▶ Your *placement* is the actual position or job you will be doing – what the job entails, where it is and the responsibilities you will be undertaking. It is important that you are clear about what the employer expects from you and what you are expecting from your placement.

▶ Your placement will be *part-time*, which means that you will not be at work all day, every day. Many employment opportunities are only part-time anyway, either because the work is not enough to require a full-time employee or because more than one person has the overall responsibility for the job. Some people prefer to work part-time as it gives them greater flexibility to organise any other responsibilities they may have.

▶ A *full-time* job usually involves working for the equivalent of eight hours a day, five days a week (or between 35 and 40 hours a week). This is the most common form of regular employment.

Personal information

When you apply for any job you will have to provide some personal information. As part of your assessment for this unit you will be expected to complete an application form and CV containing this personal information.

Application forms

Sports organisations often produce a standard application form for all job or work placement applicants to complete. Application forms typically begin with some basic questions about the applicant (name, address, contact numbers). They then tend to have a few boxes where applicants provide details of their work history and education (schools attended, qualifications achieved).

Most application forms end with a blank box (or even a whole page) where the applicant is asked to write a personal statement describing the reasons they have applied for a job or work placement and how their skills, qualifications or previous experiences make them a suitable candidate.

Bear the following points in mind when completing an application form:

▶ It is always best to photocopy an application form so that you can practise your answers before you complete the version you will send.

▶ Follow the instructions on the form and complete it in the way that you are asked to (e.g. use block capitals where requested and blue or black ink if required).

▶ Answer every question unless it is not applicable (n/a) to you. Where this is the case, put n/a.

▶ Write clearly and legibly.

▶ **Proof read** the form before you send it off, checking your spelling, grammar and punctuation.

▶ Provide information that is directly relevant to the job or work placement – don't write about irrelevant things.

▶ Always tell the truth – don't lie or try to hide the truth about your qualifications or previous experiences.

▶ Provide the names of referees who know you well and who have given you permission to use their names.

▶ Make a photocopy of your completed form in case you get an interview and need to refer to it again.

▶ Send or deliver your unfolded application documents in an unused A4 envelope that is addressed to the person responsible for work placements.

Covering letter

It is good practice to write and send a covering letter with a CV (curriculum vitae) or application form when you are applying for a job or a work placement. Your letter should:

▶ make it clear that you are applying for a work placement

▶ indicate that you have enclosed a number of documents in support of your application

▶ thank the reader for considering your application

▶ say that you look forward to hearing from the reader in due course.

As with the other application documents, you should proof read your covering letter to ensure that there are no spelling, punctuation or grammatical errors.

Curriculum vitae

A person's curriculum vitae (CV) is a concise, chronological record of their work and education history and their achievements. It should also outline key points about them as a person. There are many different ways of setting out a CV. However, it is important to ensure that yours is:

▶ concise and easy to follow

▶ relevant to the job or work placement

▶ word processed and spell checked

▶ truthful.

Your CV is a way of advertising your strengths, ambitions and achievements. It needs to be well organised and well presented to make a good impression on those who read it. It should be short and focused on relevant information, as most employers and work placement recruiters don't have time to read long, rambling CVs and won't be interested in people who don't seem to have the kind of skills, qualities or experience they are looking for. It is essential that your CV is truthful. Lying about qualifications, previous jobs or other matters is unacceptable because it leads to questions about your honesty and trustworthiness. If it is found that you have been dishonest you may be told to leave your work placement.

A CV should include the following:

▶ *Personal details* – name, address, telephone number, mobile telephone number, email, and date of birth.

▶ *Personal profile* – this should be focused and specific to you.

▶ *Skills profile* – try and identify key and personal skills required for the type of work you are applying for. Also try to explain how you have gained these skills through your studies and leisure activities.

▶ *Education and qualifications* – start with your current course and work backwards. Clearly indicate which modules you have taken for modular courses. It might also be useful to highlight specific aspects of modules that demonstrate key strengths, such as leadership or coaching.

▶ *Interests, activities and hobbies* – choose a few and explain your involvement or specific role.

▶ *Referees* – usually two are given, one academic and the other work-related. Your academic referee should be your Head Teacher or Principal. If you don't work, consider asking a team coach, who can comment on your teamwork and leadership potential, to be a referee.

As part of your assessment you are expected to use ICT for both your letter and your CV.

 **Activity**

Using the details above as a guide, produce a CV that highlights your strengths.

Preparation for interview

All employers will expect to interview someone before they offer them a job or a work placement. This is a standard procedure so you must prepare yourself for it.

▶ Develop your telephone skills so that you make a positive impression when you phone to confirm that you will be attending the interview. Alternatively, somebody from the sports organisation might phone to let you know you have an interview. In either case, you should speak clearly but not too quickly, check who you are speaking to and confirm the time and date of your interview in a friendly, confident way. Remember to write down the caller's name, contact number and the interview details if somebody phones you. It always leaves a good impression if you thank the person for calling before you hang up.

▶ Make transport arrangements to get to your interview. This might involve finding out about and planning bus or train journeys. If so, you will need to know how long the journey takes and where to get on and off. If you are travelling by car you will need to work out a route and find out what traffic conditions are like when you will be travelling. If you have never been to the interview location before, it is very helpful to do a practice journey a few days beforehand and to allow yourself plenty of time to get there. You mustn't arrive late, as this will create a bad impression!

▶ Find out about the **dress code** of the organisation. This will enable you to dress appropriately for the interview. People often make initial judgements about an interview candidate's suitability for a job or work placement on the basis of their appearance. A scruffy, unkempt appearance suggests the person is disorganised and doesn't really care what others think about them. People who present themselves well and who have made an effort to dress appropriately suggest they can fit in and think about how others respond to them. A saying to bear in mind is, 'you never have a second chance to make a first impression'.

▶ Find out about the interview procedure. It is helpful to know how many people will be interviewing you, how long the interview will last and whether there are any tasks (such as a presentation) involved in the interview process. Knowing what is going to happen should help you to prepare for the interview and should help you to feel less nervous on the day.

Interview skills

As was pointed out earlier in this topic you have to use skills here just as you would in a sporting situation. Consider all of the following.

Punctuality

The number one, golden rule of interviews is to be **punctual**. That is, arrive on time – don't be late! If you are unavoidably late or simply cannot attend the interview, you should contact the placement setting and let them know as soon as you can.

Using social and personal skills

Social and personal skills relate to the way you behave and treat others. Being considerate, polite and friendly towards other people are positive qualities that will help you to obtain a placement in the sports industry. Being impatient, rude or inconsiderate about other people's needs or feelings is likely to create a negative impression. You should always avoid swearing, being argumentative or rude during interviews. The way you behave and respond to others should convince an interviewer that you have the social and personal skills needed to work in the sport industry.

Demonstrating communication skills

Communication skills are central to work in the sports industry. Verbal and non-verbal skills are needed to develop relationships with others and to interact effectively. Smiling, being relaxed but using appropriate '**body language**', shaking hands at the start and end of the interview, making good eye-contact, speaking clearly and confidently and listening carefully will help to show that you have the kinds of communication skills needed to work in the sport industry.

Listening

The importance of listening during interviews, and in work generally, shouldn't be underestimated. Paying close attention to the interviewer's questions and to what they say about the placement setting will help you answer their questions and prepare to ask some of your own. Listening skills are an important part of any form of work, so it is a very good idea to demonstrate that you have them at your interview.

Asking and answering questions

Interviews are based around a series of questions and answers. Most of the questions are asked by the interviewer. However, towards the end of the interview you will probably be asked whether you have any questions to ask. This is an ideal opportunity to show interest in the placement organisation, the particular sporting environment and the type of work experience that could be gained there. Plan some questions in advance of the interview and use them to find out more about the organisation and what you might be able to experience and learn there.

Over to you!

Where would you like to have a work experience placement? Imagine that you have been invited for interview. Plan five questions that you would like to ask at the end of your interview about the placement and the learning opportunities it provides.

Case study

Mohammed is 16 years old and has recently started his BTEC First in Sport course. His local leisure centre has replied to Mohammed's application for a work experience placement and he has been invited along for an interview. This is the first interview Mohammed has ever attended and he is quite anxious about it.

1. Identify three key points Mohammed needs to be aware of in order to succeed in his interview.

2. What advice would you give Mohammed in terms of dressing appropriately?

3. Is there anything you think Mohammed should prepare and take along with him to this interview?

4. Describe ways in which Mohammed can demonstrate that he has effective communication skills.

Assessment activity 10.2 (Unit 13 P4, P5, P6, M3, D1)

The second assessment activity for this unit requires you to apply for a work experience placement in the sports industry. You should:

- Produce an application for work experience in sport.

- Explain and evaluate within your application your own personal skills and qualities in relation to those required for an occupation and type of work placement in sport.

- Prepare for and undertake an interview for work experience in sport.

You should produce a job application portfolio including letters of application, a CV, a completed application form that includes your personal statement as well as an account of your interview performance as evidence for this assessment.

Topic check

1 Identify the two main types of the press.
2 Give two reasons why recruitment agencies are popular.
3 Why do many employers make use of websites as a priority option?
4 What does ILAM stand for and what is it?
5 Explain what a 'placement' is.
6 What is the difference between part-time and full-time employment?
7 Why should you always photocopy an application form?
8 Why is it important to proof read letters and application forms before sending them off?
9 What does CV stand for and what is it?
10 Explain what a 'dress code' is.

Planning and carrying out a project during work experience

▶ Getting started

Once you have got your work placement you must be clear about its purpose and focus. You will be asked to carry out a work-based project that will be of benefit to the centre and provider. This is designed to give you a deeper and broader knowledge and understanding of the world of work. This topic will help you to fully prepare for this task.

When you have completed this topic, you should:

- have planned what your project will be about
- understand the different themes that you can choose to focus on
- have considered the implications of various regulations
- know which skills you will develop in carrying out your project.

Planning

This is a very important stage, as you will need to choose what you are going to base your project on and then plan the various stages for it.

Aims and objectives

Your aims are what you want to achieve from the project overall, and your objectives are the ways in which you hope to achieve your aim. Your first consideration will be to decide what area you are going to focus on, for example it might be:

▶ coaching

▶ training

▶ acquiring skills

▶ customer care

▶ health and safety

▶ equipment.

Once you have chosen the area you would like to investigate, you can set your aims and objectives accordingly. For example, your aim may be to look at levels of customer care. Your objectives related to this might be to interview people who are responsible for this, to look at the various ways customers are treated and dealt with. Additional objectives could then be set to meet and question customers and obtain feedback from them.

Proposed outcomes and timescales

Remember that your timescale is going to be limited to the 35 hours you will spend on this work experience. You will need to set realistic and achievable targets to ensure

🔑 Key terms

Induction: an introduction or a training period of instruction and learning

Legislation: written laws, also known as statutes and Acts of Parliament

that your aims are met. Your plans need to match the requirements you have to meet in Topic 10.4. To achieve this you need to be clear in your own mind about what the benefits of this project might be.

Arrangements

You will have to consider the arrangements regarding your work placement in general and also in relation to your project more specifically.

▶ *Transport* – you need to plan how you will get to and from your placement. You might not be working the same hours every day. Often there is a requirement to work evening and weekend shifts in the sports industry, and transport arrangements at these times can vary.

▶ *Accommodation* – in some cases it might even be necessary to find some accommodation nearer to the placement. Some specialist areas of the sports industry will provide accommodation for their staff – especially outdoor activity centres.

Many outdoor activity centres will provide accommodation for their staff.

Activity

Research your route to your work placement. Identify the following details:

- which method of transport you will use
- the route you will take
- the time you will leave home and arrive at your placement
- the cost involved
- any problems that may occur.

If you are travelling by bus or train you could include the number of the bus route and the actual route itself.

Requirements

You will need to check these very carefully with the organisation where you are going to do your placement. They should be able to tell you exactly what their requirements will be. Some general requirements that you will probably have to consider include:

▶ *Clothing* – for a sports assistant this will probably be sportswear such as a tracksuit. If you are taking on a receptionist role then you will probably need to wear smart, casual clothing. Many placements use clothing with their logo on it to clearly identify you as a member of staff, while others may have a 'staff uniform', which they might supply you with.

▶ *Equipment* – the placement is likely to provide you with the proper equipment for your role. However, it will be your responsibility to make sure you are familiar with it. Knowing how to put on, adjust, and remove some safety equipment will be essential if you are responsible for using it!

Designing a reflective log

You will be asked to design a log in which you comment on how well each day of your work placement is going and what you have managed to achieve. You will not be on your own at this time, as you will have a supervisor in the work placement setting. Your tutor will also monitor you progress by visiting and keeping in touch with your supervisor. They will be able to give you feedback as you go along. This log is important, as it will form part of your review resources for Topic 10.4.

Themes

These are the general categories you might like to consider investigating during your work placement. They identify specific areas of work and are the categories or departments which placement providers may have in place.

▶ *Marketing* is the department that deals with advertising and making the public aware of what is on offer.

▶ *Recruiting* is the process of selecting and dealing with new staff. It is likely that you will have dealt with recruitment staff when obtaining your own placement.

▶ *Customer service* covers a range of roles from the reception staff to the support staff who clean and maintain the buildings and equipment.

▶ *Staff training* is a priority in many organisations. It helps them to ensure that their staff are fully qualified for their roles and are up to date with anything that may have developed or changed.

▶ *Participation rates* show how many customers are using a facility or service. An organisation needs to know how well it is doing or how successful it is. To achieve this it will keep a regular check on customer numbers and the popularity of what it is offering.

▶ *Health and safety procedures* are always a priority area for any employer, but even more so in the sports industry. Because of the active nature of what is provided, there are many procedures that have to be put in place and monitored.

Over to you!

Try to identify possible areas of interest in the theme that you have chosen. For example, if you decide to look at staff training:

- How is the training organised?
- Can staff do any training they like?
- Is the training usually run within the organisation?
- How much training are staff allowed?

Regulations

All organisations and industries have regulations that set out the legal responsibilities of employers and employees. It is important that you are aware of these before starting your work placement. The **legislation** (Acts of Parliament) relating to these is listed below. They are legally enforceable regulations which have to be in place and which must be complied with.

▶ Health and Safety at Work Act 1974

▶ Management of Health and Safety at Work (Amendment) Regulations 1994

▶ Office Shops and Railways Premises Act 1963

▶ The Health and Safety (Young Persons) Regulations 1997

An internet search will allow you to find out more about these regulations and even to see the documents themselves. You may also find that there is additional legislation and regulations relating to your placement. Your employer will also be aware of these and should be happy to discuss them with you. Most employers carry out an '**induction**' with you when you first start working, during which they will discuss any regulations. This is also a good time to ask about the regulations if you have any questions.

💡 Over to you!

When you have settled on your work placement and your project theme, check which regulations in particular are going to apply to you.

Skills

One of the main reasons for taking this unit is to develop particular skills. The main focus in this topic is planning. You should therefore be planning to develop your personal skills in particular areas, which might include:

▶ *Practical skills* – if you are directly involved in any form of instruction or coaching then you should be able to identify these quite easily.

▶ *Technical skills* – these are skills related to particular techniques, such as assisting with water quality checks for swimming pools and Jacuzzis.

▶ *People-related skills* – you will be interacting with people as a basic requirement in this placement. The skills you need for this are often referred to as 'people skills', which are to do with how well you are able to get on with other people.

▶ *Personal skills* – these are the skills that you have as an individual, related to you as a person. You should be able to identify areas where you plan to develop yourself through this placement process.

Checking water quality

Case study

Leona has always been interested in surfing since she tried it on holiday one year. She has successfully arranged a work experience placement in a surf school on the coast about 50 miles away from her home. The centre is aware that Leona has very limited practical experience but they were very impressed with her application and interview.

Leona is concerned about transport and accommodation issues, and about having the right equipment. She realises she did not ask questions regarding this during her interview. She is not yet sure which theme she is going to base her project on.

1. If you were advising Leona on her planning, what aim would you suggest she sets herself?

2. What objectives might she plan in order to achieve this aim?

3. Which theme would you suggest Leona concentrates upon for her project?

4. What travel and accommodation issues do you think Leona faces and what suggestions would you offer to help her?

5. Can you suggest any solutions to Leona's equipment concerns?

Assessment activity 10.3 (Unit 13 P7, P8, P9, M4, D2)

In the final assessment activity for this unit you are required to:

- Produce a plan for a work experience project, related to a theme and including objectives, timescale and proposed outcomes.
- Undertake the planned project during a work placement.
- Present the project outcomes, explaining the benefits and areas for improvement, and

justifying any recommendations for improvement that you make.

You should produce a written plan, a placement log or diary, witness statements commenting on your performance and a written report or ICT-based presentation about your work placement project as evidence for this assessment.

Topic check

1   Explain the difference between an aim and an objective.

2   What is the timescale for your work placement?

3   Identify any transport issues you might need to consider in an organisation that has shift work.

4   Describe the main responsibility of a marketing department.

5   Why would an organisation be concerned with participation rates?

6   Why are regulations put in place?

7   What is a technical skill?

8   Explain what is meant by 'people skills'.

Presenting and reviewing the project

▶ Getting started

You must now carry out a review of your work placement project and give a presentation. You should have gathered information for this as you progressed though the earlier topics. This topic will look at the process you need to go through, and will identify particular focus points to make sure your review is successful.

When you have completed this topic, you should:

- know the different formats you can use for your presentation
- have reviewed the information you have gathered over the course of this unit
- have considered the benefits of your work placement to you, the centre and the provider of your work experience.

Presentation

You can agree the format of your presentation with your tutor. You have a choice of presentation methods.

▶ You can give an oral presentation, which will involve talking to a group and making use of resources, such as overhead projectors, to make this more successful.

▶ You can put together a written report and submit that.

▶ You can use ICT to present your findings. The most common way of doing this is to put together a PowerPoint presentation.

▶ You can use graphics to illustrate your presentation. There is a variety of ways you can display these (e.g. overhead projector, PowerPoint presentation).

▶ If you were able to collect a lot of data for your project, you will want to include this in your presentation. Using graphics such as bar charts can often help in presenting data clearly.

▶ You might decide to use a combination of presentations, and make a multimedia presentation. As well as the methods listed above include the use of video or audio.

You have the option to use a combination of the above formats. It is up to you to decide which you are most comfortable with and which one you think is going to be the most appealing and successful.

💡 Over to you!

Look at the options available for the possible formats of presentations and decide which one, or ones, you will be using.

Review

The following are the issues you need to consider in this final review. Remember that it is important to plan for these from the beginning of your project. If you fail to do this you will not have everything in place for this topic!

Formative and summative information

Formative information is what you are able to gather as you go along. Summative information is the final conclusion you reach once you have considered all of your formative information.

SWOT analysis

This is a common system of analysis. SWOT stands for:

▶ **S**trengths
▶ **W**eaknesses
▶ **O**pportunities
▶ **T**hreats.

You should try to consider all of these areas when reviewing your project. Being able to identify your strengths and weaknesses is very important. Be very honest when you are doing this. You will not be marked down if you identify a weakness – you are more likely to be credited for being capable of identifying it.

Skills and knowledge

You were asked to consider your skills and knowledge in Topic 10.3. This is your chance to look at how well you have acquired and developed these during the course of your work placement. You should also consider how useful these skills proved to be and whether you think they could be transferred to other situations.

Career development and progression opportunities

This work experience may well be the start of a career for you in the sports industry. Even if it is not, you should be able to use the experience of work itself in the future. This is an aspect you need to consider carefully in line with how you think it has helped you as an individual.

Going through this process might have given you an insight regarding where you would like to be in the future. You will have gained information about the particular sector you worked in and you will have had the opportunity to find out how others progress within the industry. This might be through training or going on a course, or even just through gaining further experience.

Monitoring progress

This is going to be a significant area of your review as it involves you reflecting on everything you did. This will include:

▶ your personal achievements against your aims

▶ achieving your objectives

▶ achieving your targets

▶ the interview process and feedback you gained from that

▶ any work that you have produced

▶ your reflective log, as described in Topic 10.3, which will contain not only your thoughts but feedback from your supervisor, tutor and any other witnesses you can obtain statements from

▶ the actual activities undertaken.

All of the above should be considered as content to be included in the review you put together, as you will then be able to give a clear and concise account of your experience.

Benefits

These should be considered in three distinct categories.

1. *Benefits to yourself* – these should include the knowledge and skills you acquired, techniques developed and progression opportunities you became aware of.

2. *Benefits to the centre* (your school or college) – it is hoped that you will be able to provide the centre with new materials, and that your case study project will provide new information or insights. It could also lead to further work placements for other students in the future.

3. *Benefits to the experience provider* – this might include additional recruitment opportunities and development of the training and induction processes.

Case study

Dulcie is a BTEC First in Sport student. She has completed two units of her BTEC First Diploma so far. One of these was fitness testing and training. Dulcie used the experience she gained here to successfully arrange for work experience in a fitness centre. She had already gained an Assistant YMCA Gym Instructor Award and this is one of the main reasons the centre offered her a place.

Dulcie has a current first aid award and has also volunteered to cover reception duties. After negotiation with the fitness centre, Dulcie has agreed to carry out a customer satisfaction survey during her placement.

1. What particular aims and outcomes do you think Dulcie is likely to have identified with regard to her work placement?

2. What do you think Dulcie is likely to have identified for the four areas of her SWOT analysis?

3. Discuss the benefits to herself you think Dulcie is likely to consider in her review.

4. Explain what benefits to the centre you think Dulcie is likely to identify.

5. What suggestions would you offer to Dulcie for deciding which presentation format to use?

Topic check

1 What is an oral presentation?
2 What might a multimedia presentation include?
3 Explain the difference between formative and summative information.
4 Describe SWOT analysis.
5 Who might benefit from your work placement and the project you carry out while you are there?

Assessment summary

The overall grade you achieve for this unit depends on how well you meet the grading criteria set out in Appendix 1 (see page 300). You must complete:

- all of the P criteria to achieve a **pass** grade
- all of the P and the M criteria to achieve a **merit** grade
- all of the P, M and D criteria to achieve a **distinction** grade.

Your tutor will assess the assessment activities that you complete for this unit. The work you produce should provide evidence which demonstrates that you have achieved each of the assessment criteria. The table below identifies what you need to demonstrate to meet each of the pass, merit and distinction criteria for this unit. You should always check and self-assess your work before you submit your assignments for marking.

Remember that you MUST provide evidence for all of the P criteria to pass the unit.

Grading criteria	You need to demonstrate that you can:	Have you got the evidence?
P1	Describe three different types of organisation within the sports industry, giving examples	
P2	Describe three different occupations within the sports industry and the skills that each require	
M1	Explain the skills required for three different occupations within the sports industry	
P3	Locate three advertisements for jobs from different sources available within the sports industry	
M2	Use advertisements for jobs available in sport to identify appropriate work experience in the sports industry	
P4	Produce an application for work experience in sport	
M3	Explain own personal skills and qualities in relation to those required for an occupation in sport	
D1	Evaluate own personal skills and qualities in relation to those required for an occupation in sport	
P5	Prepare for an interview for work experience in sport	
P6	Undertake an interview for work experience in sport	
P7	Plan a project, related to a theme, for work experience in sport	
P8	Undertake a project in work-based experience in sport	
P9	Present the project, describing the benefits and identifying areas for improvement	
M4	Present the project, explaining the benefits and making recommendations for improvement	
D2	Present the project, evaluating the benefits and justifying recommendations relating to identified areas for improvement	

Always ask your tutor to explain any assignment tasks or assessment criteria that you don't understand fully. Being clear about the task before you begin gives you the best chance of succeeding. Good luck with your Unit 13 assessment work!

11 Effects of exercise on the body systems (Unit 18)

Unit outline

In this unit you will be involved in a series of physical activities and experiments that will help you to understand the short-term effects exercise has on your body. To find out about the long-term effects, you will look at performers in different sports to see how they have developed their body systems to become effective performers with highly efficient energy systems.

The final part of this unit looks at the issue of drug taking in sport: the effects of drugs on performers, and the attitudes of society towards drug taking within sport.

Learning outcomes

1 Be able to investigate the short-term effects of exercise on the body systems.
2 Know the long-term effects of exercise on the body systems.
3 Be able to investigate the fundamentals of the energy systems.
4 Know the impact of drugs on sports performance.

Investigating the short-term effects of exercise on the body

This topic is practically based and will allow you to experience the short-term effects of exercise (e.g. the effects experienced during a training session or a performance). You may find it useful to look back at Chapter 4, which covers anatomy and physiology in more detail, including the three body systems you will be considering in this topic. You do not need to know about these body systems in detail, but you will find it helpful to be aware of what they consist of.

When you have completed this topic, you should know:

- the short-term effects of exercise on the musculoskeletal system
- the short-term effects of exercise on the cardiovascular system
- the short-term effects of exercise on the respiratory system
- some methods to investigate the effects of exercise on these systems.

Musculoskeletal system

This system involves your muscles and bones (skeleton) working together to enable movements to take place (see Chapter 4, Topics 4.1 and 4.2 for more detail). All of your movements, from the smallest nod of your head to the full completion of the high jump, require your musculoskeletal system to operate.

Exercise will affect the musculoskeletal system in many ways. For example, the range of movement in the **joints** is an important aspect of the musculoskeletal system in many sports. Look at the picture of a gymnast performing the 'splits'. You will see that there is a great deal of movement at the shoulders and the hips. Just about everybody could copy the movement of the arms outstretched, but very few could perform the 'splits' with the legs as this gymnast has! It takes a great deal of training and practice to be able to perform this difficult movement.

If you need to increase the range of movement in any of your joints, it is important to do this gradually and steadily. If you rush to do this, and push yourself too hard, you risk injuring yourself, for example by straining a muscle, which can result in micro tears in the muscle fibre. These are caused either by overstretching or overloading a muscle. Imagine the damage you could do if you tried to force the 'splits' position without building up to it gradually.

Cardiovascular system

The cardiovascular system is what regulates the circulation of the blood, the transportation of oxygen and nutrients to the cells of the body and waste products away from these cells (see Chapter 4, Topic 4.3 for more detail). Your cardiovascular system is constantly working, but when you exercise it has to work harder. This is because it has to supply more oxygen to the working muscles as an energy source.

Playing a game of football for 90 minutes requires the cardiovascular system to work much harder than normal. It will have the following short-term effects on the cardiovascular system:

▶ Your heart rate increases. The normal heart rate for an adult is approximately 72 beats per minute. When you exercise this increases greatly.

▶ As well as your heart rate increasing, so does your blood pressure. This is a measurement of the force of the blood against the artery walls as it flows around your body. Because the oxygen you need is being transported in the blood, and exercise increases the demand for oxygen, your blood pressure goes up.

It is quite easy to measure your heart rate. This is a useful skill for you to learn and will help you to investigate the effects of exercise on the body. You can find your pulse:

▶ on the side of your neck (the carotid pulse)

▶ on the inside of the wrist (the radial pulse)

▶ just over the temple at the side of the head (the templar pulse)

▶ in the groin (the femoral pulse).

Over to you!

Using any of the pulse points described, practise taking your pulse rate. Make a note of what it is when you are not active.

Respiratory system

The respiratory system is made up of the organs of the body involved in breathing (taking in oxygen and getting rid of carbon dioxide). This is covered in greater detail in Chapter 4, Topic 4.4.

You should now be aware that exercise increases the demand for oxygen as an energy source. This means that you have to take in more oxygen to cope with that demand. For example, anyone taking part in a marathon is going to be running for well in excess of 2 hours (the world record for this run is 2 hours 3 minutes, set in 2008). In order to keep going for this long, marathon runners constantly need to supply their bodies with oxygen.

Exercise will have the following short-term effects on the cardiovascular system:

▶ Your breathing rate will increase. The average breathing rate is 14–16 breaths per minute, but when you exercise this can increase by up to three times.

▶ Your **tidal volume** will increase. Tidal volume is the amount of air you breathe in and out in a normal breathing cycle. When this increases, you are able to deliver more oxygen and remove carbon dioxide more quickly.

Over to you!

Work out what your resting breathing rate is by counting the number of breaths you normally take in one minute.

Methods of investigation

All participation in physical activity provides you with an opportunity to investigate the short-term effects of exercise on the body. Activities such as football, sprinting, swimming, jogging and using an exercise cycle are very common and are ones you can participate in quite easily as part of your investigation. When you do any of these activities you will affect your musculoskeletal system, your cardiovascular system and your respiratory system. There are some basic and simple physiological tests you can carry out while you are exercising, some of which are listed below.

▶ Monitor your heart rate using a heart rate monitor. These are simple devices, attached to either chest straps or watches, which record and monitor your heart rate while you are exercising. It is a simple way of checking the rise in your heart rate, which you can then note down.

▶ Take and monitor your pulse rate. You should already know how to take your pulse and you can do this to see what levels it reaches while you are exercising.

▶ Take your blood pressure. There are monitors available that give an instant readout of your blood pressure.

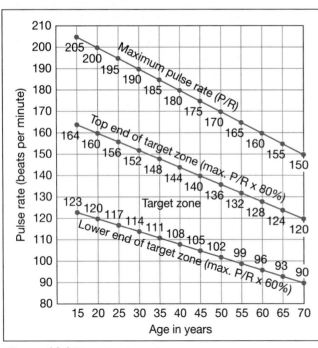

Figure 11.1 Target pulse rates

A heart rate monitor

▶ Do the sit and reach test (see Unit 1, Topic 1.3) to measure your range of movement.

▶ Use a spirometer to measure how much air you breathe in and out. This will give you information regarding your respiratory system.

▶ Record data. You will be required to carry out quite a lot of tests and investigations. For most of these you will need to check your normal levels and then levels when you are exercising. Some measurements may be taken when you have finished exercising. You might want to produce some spreadsheets or tables to help you record this date down. You may also be able use ICT programmes to interpret some of this data and carry out comparisons.

▶ Use ICT downloads such as comparison charts and data presentation information to help with your investigations.

Over to you!

If you have access to any of the methods of investigation described, use each one at least once and record your findings. If possible, use them again in different sports and activities.

Case study

Holly has set herself the task of investigating the short-term effects of exercise on her body systems, and intends to consider the musculoskeletal, cardiovascular and respiratory systems. She regularly plays football and netball as well as being a member of a trampoline club. Holly also trains quite regularly, jogging and visiting a fitness gym as part of her training programme. The gym she attends is quite modern and many of the exercise machines Holly uses have built-in monitors with read-out screens. The school PE department has some heart rate monitors, blood pressure monitors and spirometers which they lend to pupils, and Holly has already booked to use them.

c) the cardiovascular system?

1. Which of Holly's regular sporting activities would be best for her to use when investigating

   a) the musculoskeletal system?

   b) the respiratory system?

2. What sort of monitoring devices do you think Holly has the best opportunity to make use of?

3. Which of the three body systems is likely to be most difficult and challenging for Holly to investigate fully and in depth?

Topic check

1 What makes up the musculoskeletal system?

2 Explain what a joint is and what occurs there.

3 How can muscular strains and micro tears be caused?

4 Describe the function the cardiovascular system performs.

5 What provides energy to working muscles?

6 Identify the two main short-term effects on the cardiovascular system of exercise.

7 What does the respiratory system consist of?

8 Identify the two main short-term effects on the respiratory system of exercise.

9 What does the sit and reach test measure?

10 What does a spirometer measure?

The long-term effects of exercise on the body

▶ Getting started

One of the main reasons for taking regular exercise is to enjoy the long-term benefits that will result over a period of months and even years. It is unlikely that you will experience these over the short period that you will be studying this unit. However, it is important to understand the long-term effects of exercise on the body. This topic will help you to understand what they are and why they are desirable.

When you have completed this topic, you should know:

- the long-term effects of exercise on the musculoskeletal system
- the long-term effects of exercise on the cardiorespiratory system.

🔑 Key terms

Cartilage: tough tissue which covers and protects the ends of bones

Hypertrophy: the enlargement and growth of muscle size

Stroke volume: the amount of blood pumped by the heart during one single beat

Tendons: connective tissue joining muscle to bone

Vital capacity: the total volume of air that you can move in and out of your lungs in one deep breath

Musculoskeletal system

The long-term effects of exercise on the musculoskeletal system can take quite some time to be seen.

▶ **Hypertrophy** is a term for the growth and increase in the size of muscle cells. This is achieved through the principle of overloading (see Chapter 9, Topic 9.1) within strength training to increase muscle size and bulk. The bodybuilder in the photograph is an extreme example of how the size of muscles can be increased over a long period of time. However, an increase in strength is usually seen as a good thing due to the benefits it will bring to many sports performers.

- **Tendons** are the connective tissue that joins a muscle to bone. Long-term training can result in these being strengthened, which reduces the chances of tendon damage and tearing. An untrained performer could put too much stress on the tendons too quickly, which could result in a serious injury.

- Research has shown that weight training can increase bone density. This in turn increases bone strength, which reduces the chances of bone damage and fractures.

- Hyaline **cartilage** is the tough form of tissue that covers and protects the ends of the bone, in particular in the knee. Research has shown that this increases in thickness through exercise, and therefore becomes more effective with less likelihood of damage and injury.

Many sports subject the knees to a lot of wear and tear.

- Synovial fluid is the protective fluid that encases joints such as the knee. Exercise can increase the amount of synovial fluid in a joint, which will help to prevent injuries.

Cardiorespiratory system

This is a combination of the cardiovascular and respiratory systems. Because they are so closely linked, there are some long-term effects which cannot be attributed to one of them in particular. Exercise will have the following long-term effects on the cardiorespiratory system:

- Your resting heart rate will decrease. This is one of the most important and beneficial long-term effects of exercise. If you reduce your resting heart rate by 3 beats per minute, your heart will beat 4,320 fewer times per day! This means that your heart, which is a muscle, will be working more efficiently, with less strain and more chance of remaining healthy for longer. The lowest recorded resting heart rate was for a cross-country skier, with a level of 16! This is 56 beats per minute less than the average.

- Your **stroke volume** will increase. This is the amount of blood which is pumped by the heart during one single beat. Increasing this is a good thing as it means that the flow of blood around the body (with the energy supply of the oxygen contained within it) is far more efficient. The demands of exercise for more energy can then be met more easily.

▶ Your heart will increase in size. This will effectively give you a stronger, healthier heart. Just as stronger leg muscles might enable you to run faster, a stronger heart will enable you to have greater energy levels.

▶ Your **vital capacity** may increase. This is the total volume of air that you can move in and out of your lungs in one deep breath. However, this will only be by a very small amount. If you can increase this then you will have an increased oxygen supply which will allow the muscles to work harder and/or longer.

Over to you!

Carry out a survey of everyone in your teaching group to find out their resting pulse rates. Take the lowest one away from the highest and find out the beats per minute difference between them, and then calculate the daily total.

Case study

Daniel is in Year 11 and he has been asked to give a presentation to the new Year 10 BTEC First Sport group. He has been given the task of explaining to the group what the short-term and long-term effects of exercise are on the body.

Last year Daniel completed a series of experiments and activities related to the short-term effects of exercise. He also managed to train and achieved many of the long-term effects that he has been asked to present. His experience has given him some good ideas for his presentation.

1. How much emphasis do you think Daniel is likely to give to the short-term effects of

exercise, and which ones do you think he will consider to be the most important?

2. Can you think of any particular visual aids Daniel could prepare to help with his talk?

3. Are there any practical activities Daniel could carry out with this group to help to explain some of his presentation?

4. Which of the two systems do you think it is going to be easiest to consider in this talk, and why?

5. Why do you think Daniel was chosen by his tutor to talk to this group?

Assessment activity 11.1 (Unit 18 P1, P2, P3, P4, M1, M2, M3, D1)

You have obtained a job in the fitness suite of a health club. Your manager has asked you to help Jonathan, a new client, to develop his fitness levels to improve his sports performance. Jonathan is 32 years of age and hasn't exercised for a long time. He would like to know what effect a new fitness programme might have on his body.

• You have agreed to prepare some notes about the

short- and long-term effects of exercise on the musculoskeletal, cardiovascular and respiratory systems.

• You should present your work in the form of a written report that describes, explains and analyses the short- and long-term effects of exercise on the body.

Topic check

1   What is hypertrophy?
2   Name the training principle used to help with strength training.
3   What are tendons?
4   Why is an increase in bone density a good thing?
5   Explain the purpose of hyaline cartilage and where it can be found.
6   Why is an increase in synovial fluid good for joints?
7   Identify the two systems that make up the cardiorespiratory system.
8   What is the average resting pulse rate?
9   What is stroke volume?
10 Explain the meaning of vital capacity.

Investigating the fundamentals of the energy systems

The various systems that supply energy to the body can be quite complicated. This topic will help you to understand the basics and some of the terminology related to the energy systems. As before, revising Chapter 4 will help you with some of the anatomy and physiology covered here.

You will have the opportunity to participate in and observe practical investigations of some of these energy systems. These are designed to give you a better understanding of how they work through your own personal experience.

When you have completed this topic, you should:

- know what the different energy systems are
- know what sports use these systems
- understand the energy requirements of physical activity
- know some methods to investigate the energy systems.

🔑 Key terms

Aerobic: where energy is provided using oxygen

Anaerobic: where energy is provided without oxygen

Energy expenditure: the amount of energy used at a specific time

Energy requirements: the levels of energy needed for any specific purpose

Energy systems

There are two types of energy system to consider: **aerobic** and **anaerobic**. The amount of energy required during exercise by the body depends on the intensity and duration of the exercise. Many sports require a combination of both systems at different times or in different phases.

The main energy source our bodies use is ATP (Adenosine triphosphate), which is produced when our bodies break down food.

Anaerobic energy systems

Anaerobic respiration provides energy without using air. This means that it can only be used in short bursts and for short periods. This system can be broken down into two further systems.

▶ The alactic (or phosphocreatine) system is the fastest system to generate ATP as it does not require oxygen. In just about every activity and movement, this is the first energy system we use. As soon as your body senses that you are going to require a maximum effort, this energy system starts up, but it can only last for 5–8 seconds of sustained maximum effort. As a result, this system is your primary energy source for initial short sprints in ball games, long and high jump and other activities that require very quick bursts of energy, such as serving in tennis.

▶ The lactic acid system is the second fastest one. It does not require oxygen either, but it can last for about 60–180 seconds of all-out effort. As a result, this system is your primary energy source for any short-distance running events such as the 100, 200 and 400 metres.

These two systems will work together in many cases. For example, if you initially make a quick movement to get to a ball in hockey, football or rugby, the initial energy source will be the alactic (or phosphocreatine) system. If you then continue running with the ball for more than 5–8 seconds, your lactic acid system will take over. Remember that your body will do this for you automatically, and you will have experienced this happening many hundreds of times without realising it!

If you look at the two photographs you can see that the sprinter has just left the starting blocks and is only about 1 second into her activity. This means that she is currently using the alactic system. The rugby player running with the ball may have started his run using the alactic system but, due to the length of time he has been running, he will have now switched to the lactic system.

Aerobic energy system

This is your long-term energy system, which is used when you continue with an activity for a long period of time. This energy system requires oxygen in order to produce energy. Any long-distance running event (such as a cross-country run) uses this system. If you look back to the photograph of the rugby player, he is going to be playing in an 80-minute game. To be able to keep going for this long he will need to use his aerobic system as well.

Energy requirements of physical activity

When considering **energy requirements** and **expenditure** it is important that you know how this energy is measured. Energy expenditure is measured using calories. A pound of fat stores 3,500 calories (kcal), and to lose a pound a week a person has to eat approximately 500 fewer calories (kcal) per day than they expend. Figures 11.2 and 11.3 give you an indication of the calories used when you walk or run, according to your weight. So, looking at Figure 11.2, if your body mass is 64 kg and you walk at a speed of 4.83 km/hr, then you will burn approximately 4 calories per minute. If you walk at this speed for one hour you will burn 60 × 4 = 240 calories.

Figure 11.2 Calorie consumption per minute for walking

Speed (km/hr)	Body mass (Kg)						
	36	45	54	64	73	82	91
3.22	1.9	2.2	2.6	2.9	3.2	3.5	3.8
4.02	2.3	2.7	3.1	3.5	3.8	4.2	4.5
4.83	2.7	3.1	3.6	4.0	4.4	4.8	5.3
5.63	3.1	3.6	4.2	4.6	5.0	5.4	6.1
6.44	3.5	4.1	4.7	5.2	5.8	6.4	7.0

Source: brianmac.co.uk

Figure 11.3 Calorie consumption per minute for running

Speed (km/hr)	Body mass (Kg)				
	55	65	75	85	95
8	7.1	8.3	9.4	10.7	11.8
9	8.1	9.8	11.0	12.6	14.4
10	9.1	10.8	12.2	13.6	15.3
11	10.2	11.8	13.1	14.7	16.6
12	11.2	12.8	14.1	15.6	17.6
13	12.1	13.8	15.0	17.0	18.9
14	13.3	15.0	16.1	17.9	19.9
15	14.3	15.9	17.0	18.8	20.8
16	15.4	17.0	18.1	19.9	21.9

Source: brianmac.co.uk

Figure 11.4 Calorie consumption for a 68 kg person exercising for 30 minutes

Exercise	Intensity	Calories/½ hour
Aerobics	Moderate	200
Cycling	16 km/hr	220
Swimming	40 metres/min	240
Rowing	Moderate	305

Source: brianmac.co.uk

Over to you!

Find out how much you weigh, then use Figures 11.2 to 11.4 to work out approximately what your daily average energy use from exercise is.

Methods of investigation

You will be required to look at how these energy systems function through either being an observer or a participant. You need to compare and contrast these energy systems to show that you have an understanding of them. By being a participant you will be able to experience the effects at first hand. There are some suggestions below for activities you can use in this investigation, none of which are particularly difficult.

You should consider the following:

▶ the type and duration of movement/activity

▶ any clear physiological effects (e.g. increases in heart or breathing rate)

▶ the possibility of using any form of monitor or measuring device as outlined in Topic 11.1.

The alactic system

You could participate in/observe the following activities in relation to this system.

▶ The vertical jump – this is outlined in Chapter 1, Topic 1.3, so you can use this information to set up this test. It is very easy to set this up without any specific equipment.

▶ A 50-metre sprint – measure 50 m, preferably on a track. Mark out each 10 m section with a cone. Organise your group into sprinters and timekeepers. Ensure that a person stands with a stopwatch at 10, 20, 30, 40 and 50 m. For each sprinter, time the 50 m sprint. Each timer starts their watch on the command 'go' and stops it as the sprinter runs past the distance marker. Collect the scores and then calculate each 10 m section time. The same experiment can be conducted using a video camera to record and play back time more accurately.

The vertical jump test

The lactic system

You could participate in/observe the following activities in relation to this system.

▶ The 400 m run – this simply involves performing/observing a 400 m run around a running track. A similar procedure can be followed to that for the 50 m sprint, by recording each 100 m time.

▶ Ski squats – the picture shows you how these are performed. You should stay braced in this 'sitting' position for a period of time. Every 10 seconds, note the sensations you are experiencing. You may want to rate your pain sensation on a scale from 1 to 10.

Ski squats

The aerobic system

There are some straightforward activities you can perform to investigate this, but they are slightly more difficult to observe. You could try the two methods suggested below, and you could make use of some of the monitoring devices available.

▶ Long-distance running – this must be a sufficiently long distance for the aerobic system to be used, but not excessively long. The use of heart monitors here would be very helpful. This would be most effective by monitoring gradual increases in speed on a treadmill, and examining the effects that the increased speed has on the respiratory and cardiovascular systems. As an alternative you could also look at the multi-stage fitness test and monitor the short-term changes that occur during the progressive run.

▶ Long-distance cycling – this will be easier to perform if you have an exercise cycle (ergometer) with built-in sensors to give you detailed readouts of the heart rate etc.

The investigation could examine a typical training zone cycle. Again using heart rate monitors, record the respiratory and cardiovascular changes that occur during warm-up, training at a moderate intensity and set speed and cool-down.

💡 Over to you!

Carry out the following tasks:

• Perform at least one of the activities in each of the three categories covered.

• Observe another student in at least one activity for each category.

It is a good idea to pair up with a working partner or to work in small groups.

Remember that one of the main aims of this topic is to help you to understand the energy systems. The main way you will gain this understanding is by using the energy systems in a practical situation so that you can explain the requirements to others.

Case study

Laura is a second year BTEC First Sport student who has been chosen by her tutor to give a presentation on the fundamentals of the energy systems to the first year. Laura particularly enjoyed this topic when her group covered it. She took part in all six of the investigation tasks, and paired up with her friend Sadie so that they could observe each other as well as perform.

Laura was quite worried about this topic when she had first looked at it, as it seemed very complex and scientific. However, she was surprised at how clear it all became when she actively took part.

Her tutor has told her that she can use any of the outdoor facilities and a set of heart rate monitors, but she cannot use the indoor facilities as they are being used.

1. Why do you think Laura's tutor chose her to give this presentation?

2. Is there anyone you would suggest Laura asks to help her? If so, what would she ask them to do?

3. How do you think Laura might cover the following in her session?

   • the alactic energy system

   • the lactic energy system

   • the aerobic energy system.

Assessment activity 18.2 (P5, P6, M4)

Jonathan, your client at the health and fitness club, is interested in finding out about different types of physical activity and the way they use energy. He has heard about aerobic and anaerobic exercise but wants to know more. You need to:

• Investigate and describe two types of physical activity that use the aerobic energy system and two that use the anaerobic energy system.

• Explain the energy requirements of four different types of physical activity.

Produce a written report that outlines the links between types of exercise and energy systems as evidence for this assessment activity.

Topic check

1 What does ATP stand for?
2 What is the other name for the alactic energy system?
3 For about how long does the alactic energy system last?
4 For about how long does the lactic energy system last?
5 Name three particular activities that would use the lactic energy system.
6 Explain the main differences between the anaerobic and aerobic energy systems.
7 Name two activities where the aerobic energy system would be used.
8 What is a calorie?

The impact of drugs on sports performance

▶ Getting started

Most drugs are banned, but unfortunately the taking of drugs by sports performers is still quite common. This is a controversial topic, and has been for many years. The pressures and high financial rewards possible mean that some sportspeople may be tempted to use performance-enhancing drugs. It is something which is often featured in the media.

A drug is a substance that alters the chemical balance in a person's body. Drug taking can have very dangerous and damaging results. It is important that you are aware of the impact these drugs can have on the body and energy systems.

When you have completed this topic, you should:

- be aware of some of the types of drugs available
- understand the effects these can have on performance
- understand the negative impact of taking drugs.

🔑 Key terms

Capillaries: very narrow blood vessels connecting the arteries and the veins

Drugs: substances that alter the chemical balance in the body

Performance enhancing: making a performance better or improved

Types of drugs

There are a great number of different **drugs** available. We will only consider the major drug types here, and specifically the ones most commonly linked to sport. Those used in sport are often referred to as '**performance enhancing**', as the cheats who take them do so to try to improve their performance.

Anabolic steroids

This is probably the most 'famous' category of drugs and the leading type of performance enhancing drug found during drug testing. Anabolic steroids are officially known as anabolic androgenic steroids (usually just steroids for short), and they are available as both natural and synthetic compounds. They are very similar to the male hormone testosterone, which has two main effects:

- ▶ promoting the development of male characteristics
- ▶ stimulating the build-up of muscle tissue.

There are more than 100 different types of anabolic steroid available. The most common are nandrolone, testosterone, stanozolol and boldenone. They are usually taken in tablet form, but some of the steroids are taken as injections directly into the muscles.

Steroids were originally developed because they helped to cure anaemic conditions (caused by a lack of iron in the body), they eased wasting conditions and bone diseases, and were also useful in the treatment of breast cancer. As with many of the other categories of drug, steroids do have some good uses too, and many were developed as medical treatments.

Erythropoietin (EPO)

This drug comes under the general category of 'hormones and related substances'. Commonly shortened to EPO, it occurs naturally in the kidneys and regulates the production of red blood cells. It has a similar effect to what is known as 'blood doping'. This is where the blood is more efficient at carrying and supplying oxygen by increasing the oxygen-carrying red blood cells.

Growth hormone (HGH)

HGH stands for human growth hormone. It is a protein-based hormone that stimulates both growth and cell reproduction in humans and other animals. It is used clinically to treat growth disorders in children and hormone deficiencies in adults. It first started being used in sport in the 1970s, but it proved to be a very difficult drug to detect. It was not really until 2004 that an effective blood test was developed to check for it.

Amphetamines

These come under the general heading of 'stimulants'. There are many categories of these and they are often contained in small doses in treatments for colds, hay fever and asthma. They are designed to stimulate the body, especially in people who may be tired or who lack alertness. Performers have to be very careful when taking prescribed medications, as these may have traces of this drug in them which could show up when they are tested.

Diuretics

These are also commonly known as 'masking agents'. They are often taken to prevent the detection of other substances which have been taken. They reduce excess body fluids (can effectively keep you lighter) and, taken under proper medical supervision, they can control high blood pressure.

Beta blockers

These are quite commonly prescribed drugs which calm and control the heart rate, so they are vital for some people with dangerous heart conditions. They may actually decrease the level of performance for some performers, as it would reduce their levels of alertness.

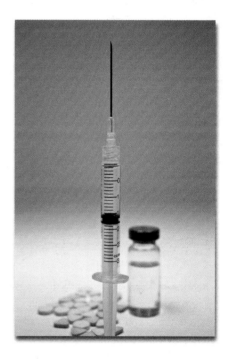

Over to you!

Carry out a web search for a recent illegal use of steroids by a sports performer and see what the particular substance was called.

Over to you!

Either on your own or with a group see how many activities you can identify which have particular weight divisions within them and where the taking of diuretics might be happening.

Cannabis

This comes under the general category of 'social drugs'. Some of the performance enhancing drugs are not illegal as such, but considered to be illegal if used by sports performers to help them. For example, no sports performer has ever been prosecuted or sentenced and imprisoned for taking steroids, but cannabis is what is known as a controlled drug and is therefore illegal under any circumstances.

Activity

Research recent sports stars that have been in trouble for taking cannabis. Find out what disciplinary action was taken against them. Discuss whether you feel cannabis should be dealt with by the sports governing body or the law courts.

Effects on performers

Clearly, performers would not take these drugs if they did not think they were going to have a positive effect on their performance. As the drugs lead to effects that performers would be unlikely to achieve without them, taking such drugs is considered to be cheating by the sporting authorities.

▶ Steroids – these are often known as 'training drugs' as they enable people to train harder and for longer. Other perceived benefits include increasing muscle strength and increasing competitiveness. They have been commonly used by sprinters and weightlifters in particular, due to possible improvements in speed and strength.

▶ EPO – because this can increase the levels of red blood cells, it is considered to increase stamina levels, so it is used by endurance athletes such as marathon runners.

▶ Growth hormone – this can increase muscle mass and decrease body fat and has been taken along with steroids to gain similar advantages.

China's Wang Jing celebrates after winning the women's 100 meters final at the 2009 National Games. However, she has since been stripped of her title after failing a doping test.

▶ Amphetamines – because a stimulant increases alertness and reduces fatigue, these are seen as something that can help a performer to keep going in their activity or event.

▶ Diuretics – because these can help to reduce weight, they are commonly taken by performers who compete in certain weight categories (e.g. boxers) or who need to lose weight quickly. In some activities, such as horse racing and gymnastics, it is an advantage to be small and lightweight. The other main reason to take a diuretic is to cover up another drug, such as a steroid, which is being taken.

▶ Beta blockers – these slow down the heart rate, which can help a performer to relax more. This would be a big advantage in events such as shooting or archery. Sometimes they have been taken just to calm the nerves before competing.

▶ *Cannabis* – this is considered to have a similar effect to beta blockers, to act as a calming influence.

Negative impact of drugs

The negative impact of drugs very clearly outweighs what some performers see as the positive effects. This is why they are banned and illegal in competitive sport. The main negative effect is that they can give some performers an unfair advantage. The other big concern relates to the physical dangers and damage that can be caused by these drugs.

▶ *Steroids* – there is a very long list of negative effects of taking steroids. They can cause liver disorders and heart disease, jaundice, liver tumours, cancer, sexual and physique problems, reduced sperm production, sterility, impotence, disrupted menstrual cycles, baldness, acne, growth of facial hair, deepening of the voice, miscarriage of babies and extreme behavioural disorders such as extreme aggression. When you see a list as long as this you wonder how the supposed positive effects can even be considered!

▶ *EPO* – this can increase the risk of heart attacks or a stroke, as the hormones can thicken the blood, which makes it more difficult for the blood to flow through the small **capillaries**.

▶ *Growth hormone* – the most serious effect is on the nervous system, in particular a disease known as Creutzfeldt Jacobs's disease, which can be fatal.

▶ *Amphetamines* – taking these can be fatal. There are several examples where they have led to performers having a serious lack of judgement and, because they do not feel tired or fatigued, carrying on beyond their normal limits and pushing themselves too hard. Other side effects include high blood pressure and headaches, strokes and increased and irregular heartbeats, anxiety and body tremors, insensitivity to serious injuries and addiction.

▶ *Diuretics* – these can cause dehydration, muscle cramps, headaches and nausea.

▶ *Beta blockers* – slowing the heart rate down too much can be very dangerous, not only to the circulatory system but also by reducing concentration levels.

▶ *Cannabis* – this can be an addictive drug and one that can lead to taking more dangerous substances, such as cocaine or heroin. It is also considered to cause psychiatric disorders in many people.

There are also some general negative impacts related to drug taking in sport.

▶ *The ethical aspect* – taking banned substances is quite simply cheating. No other form of cheating is allowed in sport, which is why it is considered to be wrong and unfair in all organised sports. This is why all sports insist that performers are tested regularly and dealt with and banned if they are found guilty. Some performers have even been banned for failing to take a test!

▶ *The image of sport* – people who take part in sport and who watch sport expect the performers to be 'clean' and to deserve their victories and success.

▶ *Society's values* – drug taking is often an issue outside of sport, and all members of society expect sport to set a good example with regard to being healthy and respectable.

Activity

Find out what the most recent, high-profile example of drug taking is by a famous sports performer. Find out how this affected both their sports performance and their health.

Case study

Jason and Natasha have been chosen by their tutor to lead a group discussion. Jason has been given the task of trying to convince the group that drug taking in a particular instance is good thing. He has been told to choose a particular activity or event and make a case for how taking a particular drug would improve the performance.

Natasha has been given the task of making the case for the continuing ban on drug taking in sport. She has been told not to use specific examples but to come up with some general reasons why this should be the case.

1. If you were advising Jason, which particular drug would you suggest he concentrates on?

2. Which particular sport or event would you suggest he focuses on?

3. What is Jason likely to focus on as the most advantageous reason for the performer choosing to take drugs?

4. Which particular medical aspects would you suggest Natasha concentrates on in her preparation?

5. Which general negative impact would you suggest Natasha concentrates on?

Assessment activity 11.3 (Unit 18 P7, P8, M5)

Your manager at the health and fitness club has asked you to give a presentation to a group of new members, focusing on the effects of drugs and the impact that drugs have on sports performance. You should:

- Describe four different types of drugs used to enhance sports performance, and their effects.

- Describe and explain the negative impact of drugs.

You should produce a presentation, using PowerPoint or another ICT programme, carry out your presentation in front of a group of learners and obtain witness statements about your performance as evidence for this assessment activity.

Topic check

1 Give the full, technical name for steroids.
2 Identify the two main effects of taking steroids.
3 What positive medical effects can steroids have?
4 What does EPO stand for?
5 Explain the main effect for a sports performer of taking amphetamines.
6 What are diuretics also commonly known as?
7 What are steroids often also known as?
8 Identify the types of performer who might choose to take EPO.
9 Give three negative effects of taking diuretics.
10 What is the main ethical reason against taking drugs?

▌▌ Assessment summary

The overall grade you achieve for this unit depends on how well you meet the grading criteria set out in Appendix 1 (see page 301). You must complete:

- all of the P criteria to achieve a **pass** grade
- all of the P and the M criteria to achieve a **merit** grade
- all of the P, M and D criteria to achieve a **distinction** grade.

Your tutor will assess the assessment activities that you complete for this unit. The work you produce should provide evidence which demonstrates that you have achieved each of the assessment criteria. The table below identifies what you need to demonstrate to meet each of the pass, merit and distinction criteria for this unit. You should always check and self-assess your work before you submit your assignments for marking.

Remember that you MUST provide evidence for all of the P criteria to pass the unit.

Grading criteria	You need to demonstrate that you can:	Have you got the evidence?
P1	Describe the short-term effects of exercise on the musculoskeletal, cardiovascular and respiratory systems	
M1	Explain the short-term effects of exercise on the musculoskeletal, cardiovascular and respiratory systems	
P2	Investigate the short-term effects of exercise on the musculoskeletal, cardiovascular and respiratory systems, with tutor support	
M2	Independently investigate the short-term effects of exercise on the musculoskeletal, cardiovascular and respiratory systems	
P3	Describe the long-term effects of exercise on the musculoskeletal system	
M3	Explain the long-term effects of exercise on the musculoskeletal, cardiovascular and respiratory systems	
D1	Analyse the short- and long-term effects of exercise on the musculoskeletal, cardiovascular and respiratory systems	
P4	Describe the long-term effects of exercise on the cardiorespiratory system	
P5	Describe two types of physical activity that use the aerobic energy system and two that use the anaerobic energy system	
M4	Explain the energy requirements of four different types of physical activity	
P6	Investigate different physical activities that use the aerobic and anaerobic energy systems, with tutor support	
P7	Describe four different types of drugs used to enhance sports performance and their effects	
P8	Describe the negative impact of drugs	
M5	Explain the negative impact of drugs	

Always ask your tutor to explain any assignment tasks or assessment criteria that you don't understand fully. Being clear about the task before you begin gives you the best chance of succeeding. Good luck with your Unit 18 assessment work!

Unit outline

This unit is primarily practical in nature. The event you will be planning will be too large to plan and run on your own, so this unit gives you the opportunity to work in small groups and teams. This unit links closely with Unit 7 (Chapter 6), but the types of event you are likely to organise will be different, and the team approach will make it quite a different experience. However, the team approach means that everyone involved must contribute equally, so the event will be broken down and individuals given responsibility for different areas. You will be expected to spend between 8 and 12 weeks planning the event. You will also have to review the planning process and the event itself once it is over, so you must record information throughout the unit so that you have information to base your review on.

Learning outcomes

1 **Be able to plan a sports event.**
2 **Be able to contribute to the organisation of a sports event.**
3 **Be able to contribute to the running of a sports event.**
4 **Be able to review the success of a sports event.**

Planning a sports event

A 'sports event' can be a number of different things. Whatever type of event you decide to organise, the planning process will be very important. Some aspects of your planning will relate specifically to your event, but many of them will apply to all types of events. There are a lot of roles and responsibilities involved in organising an event. You need to identify what these are and allocate people within your group or team to be responsible for them.

When you have completed this topic, you should:

- understand the planning process for a sports event
- be aware of the types of event you might organise.

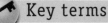

Key terms

Agenda: a list, or outline of things to be discussed and matters to be acted upon

Disclaimer: document saying that the organisers of an event will not be held responsible for any accident or injury that happens during the event

Income: payment or money received

Venue: the place where an activity or event happens

The planning process

You should be allocated between 8 and 12 weeks for this, so you will have plenty of time to put a full plan together. You need to look at all of the different aspects and areas that are identified below, as you will need to consider all of them.

The nature of the event

Each type of event has its own particular requirements and you will need to identify these.

- ▶ *Type of event* – there is a big difference between a formal dinner event and a sports competition. You have a very large range of options to choose from, so this is going to be your first main decision.

- ▶ *Size* – it is supposed to be a small-scale event, so do not be too ambitious. Make sure it is a manageable size in a manageable area.

- ▶ *Aims and objectives* – as with any other planning you will need to identify what the aim of your event is (e.g. a charity fundraiser). Then you will need to identify how you are going to put the whole event together.

- ▶ *Location* – the decision where your event is to take place is also important. You need somewhere people can get to easily, so transport links will have to be considered.

Over to you!

The first choice you will have to make is the type of event you are going to plan. Make this an early priority as other factors are dependent on this choice. Think about it now and draw up a shortlist.

Timings

There are lots of time factors to consider, including:

▶ *The time of year* – weather conditions could be a factor here.

▶ *The day of the week* – is it to be a weekday or a weekend? This might affect who can attend.

▶ *The time of the day* – daytime or evening? A sports dinner would probably need to be an evening event.

▶ *Start and finish times* – you need to decide how long the event will last overall. Can you set a definite finish time? Many sports events are very difficult to set time limits on. A football match may last 90 minutes, but how long will each tennis match take? An uneven cricket match can finish very quickly.

Team roles, responsibilities and meetings

You need to make sure that everyone within your team knows exactly what they are doing. It is best to agree this and then write it down. This way everyone can be sure what they are expected to do and will know who to go to for anything else.

You will need to have well-organised team meetings at regular intervals. Make sure you consider the following:

▶ how often and when these are to take place

▶ who is to run and control them

▶ setting an **agenda** so that you know the focus of the meeting

▶ keeping a record (usually known as 'minutes') of what is discussed

▶ clarifying what has been agreed and what action is to be taken.

Other considerations

▶ *Identifying resources* – this will include all of the things you will need in order to run your event successfully. As soon as you choose the type of event you are going to organise, you need to start to identify the resources needed for it. For example, a 5- or 7-a-side football tournament will probably require corner flags, goals, nets, at least one ball per game, whistles, stop watches, and yellow and red cards.

What resources would you need for a five-a-side football tournament?

▶ *Staffing* – as you will be working in a team, you might be able to provide most of the staff among yourselves. However, it is unlikely that you will be able to do it all. For example, you might need some specialist staff such as cooks/caterers for a sports dinner. You could also engage the help of qualified referees for a football tournament.

⚙ Activity

Using the activity you have chosen, decide how you are going to divide your group. You will also need to give each person a role to fulfil in running the activity. This could include marketing, checking application forms, designing and managing a league, refereeing, scoring etc.

▶ *Budget and costings* – think about how much money you will to have to spend to run the event. You need to balance this against any **income** you are hoping to get. You may have to pay for the **venue**, and there will probably be other costs involved too. For example, you might need to hire equipment, pay for staff or even pay for insurance. There may also be advertising costs and costs for trophies and cups.

▶ *Constraints* – these are anything you can identify which might restrict you in any way, such as your age. You might find that bookings have to made through an adult and that a deposit has to be paid.

▶ *Contingency planning* – this means having plans in place to deal with any problems that might crop up, such as bad weather if the event is outdoors.

▶ *Risk assessment* – whatever event you decide to run you must carry out a risk assessment. Look back at Chapter 5, Topic 5.4 for details of how to do this. Even if it is not a 'physical' event, there are likely to be certain risks involved. Carrying out a risk assessment minimises the chances of problems, accidents and injuries.

▶ *Disclaimers/informed consent* – this involves getting permission for people to take part in your event, should this be necessary. Younger people may need authorisation from their parents to attend. If there is some element of physical activity then you will need both the consent and the **disclaimer**. This makes it clear that the person taking part is aware of what the activity involves.

▶ *First aid procedures* – these have to be in place. You need to make sure that you have qualified first aiders present who have valid qualifications. Organisations such as the Red Cross and St Johns Ambulance have volunteers who might be willing to help. It is worth contacting them to find out. You could also find out what the first aid procedures are at school or college. Make sure that you follow them and that members of staff are available to help.

▶ *Promotional activities* – you want your event to be a success, so you will have to promote it! This might include some form of advertising or a promotional handout or leaflet. Leaflets could have application forms and consent forms on them.

▶ *Methods for evaluating the event* – part of your assessment will be based on your evaluation of how well the event went. So, you must be prepared to consider how you are going to judge this. You are likely to come up with a variety of methods of evaluating, such as customer survey questionnaires, participant questionnaires or recorded interviews, but it is important that you plan for it!

Personal diary

Although you are going to be a member of a team, you will have a particular role and area of responsibility. You will be assessed on this, so you need to provide evidence for it from your diary. This should include the following:

▶ a log of notes

▶ a record of the team meetings

▶ a record of the meeting outcomes

▶ the actions that were taken as a result of decisions taken at meetings.

Remember that all of these should be related to your particular area of involvement. In Topic 12.4 you will be asked to carry out a review of the event, and the information in your diary will be essential for this.

Over to you!

Identify someone in the local community who has been involved in the planning of a sports event. See if they would be prepared to come along and talk to your group about how they planned it.

Types of sports events

Some of these have been mentioned earlier to help with examples for planning. However, there are plenty of other options.

Sports competitions

There are many different competition possibilities. Remember that this is a one-off event, so long-term leagues will not be an option. You need to consider the competition formats that will be suitable for this time of event:

▶ one-day leagues – everyone plays everyone else

▶ knockouts – only the winners go through

▶ round robin – a form of mini-league where several groups play in separate leagues

▶ combination – you can use a combination of the choices above at different stages in the competition, e.g. starting with a league and then progressing to a knockout final stage.

Any form of sport event is acceptable, such as wheelchair basketball.

If you are going to stage a competition it is probably worth planning to have at least one meeting to discuss the format this will take. Then you can discuss the advantages and disadvantages of each system before making a decision.

Other types of activity

▶ *Sports activity day* – this could be one particular sport or a variety of different sports all on the same day. Look at Chapter 6, Topic 6.2 for further guidance on this.

▶ *Summer training camp* – although it is called a 'camp', it does not involve an overnight stay. You will need to focus on a particular activity for this. Different sports are likely to require different formats, so you will need to research which is best for your activity.

▶ *An educational event* – this does not have to be a practical event, you could cover some sort of theory aspect as well. Examination revision sessions are becoming more and more popular and you may be able to put one of these together. An event based on getting some form of award or qualification might come into this category as well, and there are many Level 1 coaching and officiating courses you could organise.

▶ *Sports charity dinner/fundraiser* – these are becoming increasingly popular and can have many different formats. They will involve quite complex costing issues, as you will have to pay out for a venue, food etc. and charge people to attend, with the object of making a profit.

▶ *Community-based events* – these will be based in your own community and would reflect what the community wanted and could support. This sort of event will probably also be dependent on what facilities are available in the community.

▶ *Outdoor event* – these are often very popular but can be reliant on good weather. A warm, sunny day can result in a very successful and well-attended event, but bad weather can result in an event being postponed or even cancelled.

▶ *Indoor events* – these are usually a safer option because they avoid any possible bad weather problems that might ruin your event. You will also have a large choice of different types of indoor facilities, from swimming pools to sports halls.

Over to you!

Your tutor will divide you into groups. In your group, discuss the type of event you are interested in. Present a case for people to choose your activity, using the information that you have produced in the previous tasks. The group will be required to decide which event idea is the most successful and provide reasons for this decision.

Case study

Sean and five of his friends have decided to organise a sports dinner. One of Sean's friends is Rory, whose mother owns and runs a local restaurant. Another member of the team is Katherine, and her mum is the cook in charge of the school canteen.

Some of the team want to make it a formal dinner with a smart dress code, while others want a more casual buffet-style meal. The group is also undecided about whether there should be any form of entertainment, such as having a guest speaker, or finishing the evening off with a disco/dance session.

The other big discussion point among the group is the venue. They have been told that they can hire the school hall and canteen, but there is also a nearby community hall they can use which is cheaper.

1. What is the first major decision the group has to make?

2. Do you think five people will be enough to organise this type of event?

3. What specific roles and responsibilities would you give to each of the five members of the team?

4. It appears that the team may have the choice of two caterers. What are the main advantages and disadvantages of each of the two mums?

5. What are the main budget/costing issues the team will have to deal with?

Assessment activity 12.1 (Unit 20 P1, M1)

This assessment activity requires you to work as a member of a team or small group to plan a sports event of your choice. You will need to:

• Work as part of a team or group to identify and choose, from a number of options, a sports event that you will help to plan and run.

• Produce a plan for your chosen sports event, outlining and explaining the planning process to meet given participant or customer requirements.

Your evidence for this assessment activity should include an individual plan and a group presentation of it, together with witness statements commenting on your performance.

Topic check

1 Over how many weeks are you expected to plan this event and what scale of event is it supposed to be?

2 What are the four main factors to consider in relation to the nature of an event?

3 Explain what is meant by a 'target audience'.

4 Identify four timing factors you need to consider.

5 What is a 'constraint'?

6 Identify the five most important factors relating to meetings.

7 Describe what a risk assessment is and its purpose.

8 What four forms of evidence should you include in your personal diary?

Contributing to the organisation of a sports event

▶ Getting started

You are going to be asked to contribute to the organisation of your sports event as part of a team. In Topic 12.1 you looked at the planning process for the event and decided which particular aspect you will be responsible for. This topic will guide you through some of the things you may have to consider in your role, as well as some organisational issues that you may need to take into account.

When you have completed this topic, you should:

■ understand the requirements of the people the event is being organised for

■ know the type of organisational issues you and your team will have to consider.

🔑 Key terms

Needs analysis: a way of identifying requirements

Revenue: form of income (money that comes in)

Teamwork: a combined effort, working together as a team

Participant or customer requirements

Depending on the type of event you have chosen, you will be organising it for either customers (e.g. a fundraising dinner) or participants (e.g. an athletics meeting). There is likely to be some sort of charge or fee involved, and if people are paying they will want value for money. You, as an organiser, may also be a customer yourself if you have to pay for someone else's services (e.g. coaches or cooks).

You and your team are likely to have to consider the following factors in relation to your customers or participants.

Event type

As discussed in Topic 12.1, different types of event will have different requirements. You should aim to consider both of the following in terms of both participant and customer:

▶ *Needs* – these must be clearly identified. For a fairly long event (e.g. an all-day event) there will need to be refreshments. For an outdoor event you will need to provide shelter from direct sun and heat on a hot sunny day and somewhere warm and dry on a cold winter day. You should try to carry out what is called a **'needs analysis'**. This means reviewing your tasks and overall objectives to decide what needs to be done. This should be part of your planning team meetings.

💡 Over to you!

Ask yourself and your team the five questions related to roles and responsibilities (see page 273) to make sure that everything is covered.

▶ *Satisfaction* – if you are able to correctly identify all of the needs, you should be able to provide satisfaction. Remember to obtain feedback from customers and participants to use in your review of the event. These should tell you whether or not customers and participants were satisfied.

Aims and objectives

You will already have considered your aims and objectives in general terms in your planning. Now you need to focus on the following areas:

▶ *Fundraising* – if you are not going to be charging customers, you might not be getting any **revenue**. The alternative is some form of fundraising, such as raffles, donations, or even sponsored activities.

▶ *Providing information* – there is likely to be a great deal of information relating to your event. It can range from letters sent out before the event to providing signs on the day for car parking, toilets, refreshment areas etc. Your event will be far better organised if you provide full and clear information.

▶ *Education* – one of your main aims could be to include some educational aspect in your event. This means there should be some gain or benefit for your participants or customers from taking part in the event.

▶ *Raising awareness* – if you are organising a fundraising event you will be specifically aiming to raise awareness of the sport or other cause for which you are raising funds.

▶ *Health* – your focus may be on a particular aspect of health or maintaining a healthy lifestyle.

▶ *Fitness* – your focus may be on a particular aspect of fitness which might be appealing to many customers and participants.

▶ *Wellbeing* – this is related to making your customers and participants feel good (the 'feel good' factor).

Organisation

The actual organisation of your event is likely to be the most challenging aspect of the project. It is closely linked to all the planning you carried out in Topic 12.1. You need to consider and carefully organise the following.

Resources

This will cover a great many things, including:

▶ *The venue* – this is probably your biggest and most important resource. Without it your event cannot take place. Each venue will be different, and you will have to organise the use of yours very carefully.

▶ *Finance* – collecting money and paying it out requires a great deal of organisation. You may have to deal with cheques and cash, and you will have to give receipts for any money you receive. All of the money will have to be accounted for, and you might have to arrange for a bank account to be opened or used.

> **Over to you!**
>
> As a team, carry out a needs analysis for your event. Then divide your group, with each member of your team focusing on developing a needs analysis for the aspect which they are in charge of.

> **Activity**
>
> Within your group, discuss fundraising opportunities and decide which is the most appropriate. You may also have to plan the fundraising activity. So, within your group, draw up an outline of the fundraising activity that you have chosen. You will need to plan dates, times and costs of your activity to make sure that it is profitable.

▶ *Transport* – your team and the participants in your event will all have to get there, and this may require you to organise some form of transport. You will have to consider the number, type and size of vehicles, which might range from a normal family car to 52-seater coach. Transport can be expensive, so this will be closely linked to finance.

▶ *Staffing* – it is likely that your event team will provide most but not all of the staff. Specialist staff such as coaches, caterers and presenters all have to be organised and booked in advance.

▶ *Catering* – you might get someone in to do this, but you may still have to buy the food and drink for them to prepare. You may have to transport it, prepare it, serve it and clear up afterwards. There are many organisational challenges in this area alone!

You may need to organise officials for your event.

▶ *Entertainment* – this may be central to your event. If you are having some sort of entertainment you are likely to need an electricity supply, somewhere for performers to set up and perform, and possibly even a rehearsal.

Participation

You and the other members of your team need to consider your participation in the organisation of the event.

▶ *Roles* – What exactly is everybody going to do? Does everybody know what their role is? Are there any roles which overlap?

▶ *Responsibilities* – Within their specific role, does everyone understand what they are responsible for? Is everything which is going to happen clearly someone's responsibility?

▶ **Teamwork** – think of this as you would any other team activity, such as a game of football. If you do not work together you will not be successful. And, just as in a football game, you will all have a position to play.

▶ *Meetings* – these must be held regularly. They will be part of your overall assessment.

▶ *Communication* – effective clear communication at all times is vital for the successful organisation of your event.

Health and safety

You will have planned the health and safety aspects of your event, but you must be sure to organise practicalities such as pitch inspections and safeguarding spectators. This will be an ongoing issue throughout the event.

Contingencies

Remember that these are the 'what if?' possibilities. You have to presume that they may need to be used, so you must be sure that they are organised. Some example areas follow:

▶ *Weather* – this could force you to move your event from outside to inside, in which case someone will have to make that decision and organise the changes.

▶ *Accidents* – these can happen and must be planned for, from the most minor through to the most serious.

▶ *Change in numbers* – you may have too few participants turning up for team events, or more customers or spectators than you had expected, both of which can cause you problems.

▶ *Staff shortages* – it is important that everyone turns up on the day, but you must have reserves in place to cover for anyone who does not make it.

▶ *Non-arrival of equipment* – this could be a disaster! No portable goal posts for a five-a-side football tournament would cause real problems.

Case study

Olivia and five of her friends have formed a team to plan and run a cheerleading competition. All six of them are in a successful cheerleading club in their area, which is why they have chosen this event. They are considering organising the competition into tiny, mini, youth, junior and senior categories, as they know this is the format used in other competitions.

Olivia has been offered two venues. One has outside facilities only and the other has the option of a large indoor hall as well. The price difference between the two is considerable, with the outdoor-only option being much cheaper.

Olivia and her friends have planned the event for the first week in September when they return to school after the summer break. As part of the day they intend to provide a cheerleading demonstration themselves, showing their winning routine as a 'curtain raiser'.

1. Identify six specific organisational responsibilities for this particular event, one for each member of the team.

2. Which of the six responsibility areas do you think is the most important for this particular event?

3. What advice would you give the team regarding the number of categories they are considering including in the competition?

4. What advice would you give the team regarding the final venue choice?

5. Do you have any thoughts about the time of year the event is being held? Is this likely to cause any organisational problems?

Topic check

1 What is a 'needs analysis'?

2 Why is it important to ensure customer satisfaction?

3 If money is not to be raised by charging to attend, how else could it be raised?

4 Identify the connection between fundraising and raising awareness.

5 What is the 'feel good' factor?

6 Identify the main resource you are likely to need.

7 In terms of participation, what are three things you need to consider relating to roles?

8 In terms of participation, what are two things you need to consider relating to responsibilities?

9 Why is it important to have regular meetings?

10 Describe what is meant by contingencies and give two examples.

Contributing to the running of a sports event

▶ **Getting started**

This topic concentrates on your contribution to the running of the event. It covers three distinct areas which will enable you to focus on the three phases of your event. These will apply no matter what type of event you have planned or what your role is.

When you have completed this topic, you will be able to contribute to:

- setting up the event
- running the event
- clearing up and sorting out at the end of the event.

Key terms

Fit for purpose: clearly achieving the desired aim, objective or requirement

Laminated: covered with a waterproof see-through covering

Legible: clear and easy to read

Setting up

The first factor you must consider here is the time element. Some of the setting up may be able to be done on the day, but there may be other arrangements that need to be put in place in advance.

Signs

You will have prepared these beforehand as part of your planning. You should consider the following:

▶ How many signs are needed, and how many people are needed to set them up?

▶ Where are the signs to be located? A venue/site plan map will help you here.

▶ What are they to be placed on? Are they to be attached to posts and placed in the ground? Do you need to fix them on internal walls or windows? If so, are you allowed to use sticky tack for this?

▶ Are the signs **fit for purpose**? Are they **laminated** for outside use in case it rains? Are they clear and **legible**?

Over to you!

How many signs are you going to need for your event? Can you answer all of the questions raised in connection with signs?

Sports equipment and other equipment

Your event may require very little sports equipment or quite a lot. Looking after it and making it available in the correct place at the correct time is important. You will need to link this back to the initial equipment planning you did in Topic 12.1. Remember that this is all related to the setting-up phase of your event, so it must all be placed where it is first going to be used.

Your planning will have identified whether you need any other equipment. Outdoor seating can be a major consideration as this can take a long time to set up and must be done in plenty of time.

Entertainment and refreshments

As was identified in Topic 12.2, entertainment could be quite complex to set up. If you are providing entertainment you will already know what is required for this. It can take some time to set up, and even if it is not scheduled to take place until later in your day it might need to be set up early.

If you have organised an outdoor event, setting up the refreshment area could be quite a large task. One factor to take into consideration with food and drink is that there is always a lot of waste. Bins and bin bags need to be set out for people to put their used packaging and waste food, cups etc. into.

Will refreshments be provided at the event?

During event

There will still be plenty of work to do during the event, including the following:

▶ *Responding to unexpected occurrences* – you will have contingency plans in place, but this refers to things which you have not planned for. The whole team must be prepared to respond to anything that crops up.

▶ *Food and drink service* – this should be carefully monitored. During a long event this is going to be busy all day, and may be very busy at certain times such as at lunch time.

▶ *Meeting customer requests* – it would be wise to have a specific area where customers know they can go with any requests or enquiries. You might need to have a rota in place for this to be manned at all times.

▶ *Instructing* – you will need to have a base from which instructions are given out. Ideally you will have an announcer using a PA (public address) system through which they can give instructions quickly and easily.

▶ *Officiating* – for any sporting event/competition your officials are going to be important personnel. Making sure they are in the right place at the right time and that they can hand results in will be ongoing tasks.

▶ *Monitoring* – this will involve monitoring everything that is going on. By checking that everything is running smoothly you should be well placed to react if there are any problems.

▶ *Supervising* – each area should have an allocated supervisor who will be responsible for that area while the event is underway.

Setting down

The end of the event will not be the end of the day for you! Just as there were many things to set up before the event, so there will be many things to set down or pack away at the end of the event.

▶ *Sports equipment* – this all has to be counted up, checked, collected in and put away or stored.

▶ *Waste disposal* – all of the rubbish from the event has to be collected up and disposed of. You should recycle as much of this waste as you can.

▶ *Signs* – all of the signs you put up will have to be taken down. If you made a map/plan of where these were put up it will make the task of taking them down far easier.

Over to you!

Draw up a map or plan of your venue and mark down the position of every sign you plan to put up. Using this will help you to collect them all back up again.

Case study

Olivia and her team have planned their cheerleading competition event and the day has arrived. They decided only to have three categories for the competition, youth, junior and senior. They also decided to book the venue with both the outside and indoor facility, so that the competitors could practise outside and the competition could take place in the indoor hall. For refreshments the team have asked their mothers to run a drinks and food service station which they will set up in the reception area. Olivia and her friends have been very pleased with the response to their competition as they have eight teams entered for each of the categories. However, they did not originally plan for a total of 24 teams in their event and are a little concerned about how their team of six will cope on the day.

1. What issues will the team have to consider in relation to setting up?

2. Suggest one specific aspect of the event that each of the six members of the team should take responsibility for.

3. With 24 teams attending, what is going to be the main factor for the organisers to consider?

4. Are there any setting-up tasks that the team could delegate to other people?

5. Which factors are likely to be most challenging for the team during the event?

Topic check

1 What is the first factor you need to consider in the setting-up phase?
2 Describe three different factors relating to the issue of signs for an event.
3 What arrangements should be put in place to deal with customer requests?
4 During the event, which factor must all of the team be prepared to deal with?
5 Why would it be useful to have some sort of public address system to use on the day?

Reviewing the success of a sports event

▶ Getting started

Once the event is over, it is important to carry out a review to see how successful the different phases were, and your role in these. It is hoped that you will have had some systems in place to gather information and feedback during the course of the unit, and this topic will help you with this. You should consider your options well in advance of the event.

When you have completed this topic, you should:

■ have considered the various methods available for collecting feedback
■ understand how to review the information you have gathered
■ know how to measure the success of the event.

🔑 Key terms

Assessor: an independent judge or adviser
Breaking even: making neither a loss nor a profit, but covering any costs
Feedback: information passed on to you by others regarding what you have done
Success criteria: a set of factors that need to be achieved in order to measure success
Unbiased: honest and fair, not taking sides

Methods for collecting feedback

Remember that there is going to be a lot going on when your event is underway. However, it is crucial for your overall assessment that you can accurately review how well it went, and you will have to produce some evidence to illustrate this. So, you need to have plans in place to make sure that you are able to collect this evidence.

Documentation

There is a variety of documents that will help you to gather the evidence you need.

▶ *Questionnaires* – these are documents with specific questions for participants or customers. It is up to you to decide what these questions are. Try to be specific and relate them clearly to particular aspects of your event. For example, 'Were there enough signs put up and were they all clear?' Using a grading guide for answers also helps, for example a scale from 1 to 5 where 1 = excellent, 2 = good, 3 = satisfactory, 4 = unsatisfactory, 5 = poor. Make these questionnaires quick and easy to answer but detailed enough to give you all the information you need.

💡 Over to you!

Design a questionnaire that you could use to review your event. After the event has finished, either hand out or post your questionnaire to the people who attended, to gain the views of the participants and organisations that were involved.

▶ *Observation sheets* – these must also be specific to your event. You must identify the particular aspects of the event that you would like people to observe. You might find that you need to produce different versions of these sheets for different areas, phases or individuals within the team. You also need to decide who is going to complete them – if it is a big event you are unlikely to be able to get everyone to fill one in.

▶ *Witness statements* – these will be completed by specific people involved in your event. If you 'employed' someone to work with you on the day, you might like to get them to comment on how well they were dealt with and organised and how well they thought the event went. The witness should be left to give their views freely, rather than being asked specific questions, but you might like to put some general headings on a prepared sheet to help them with this.

▶ *Customer comment cards* – if customers will be attending your event, you should aim to get basic **feedback** from all of them by using comment cards. Part of your assessment will focus on your ability to design and use these cards as a source of feedback and information gathering.

Review

Once you have collected feedback on the event you can review the comments that you received from different sources.

The team can provide feedback for each other.

▶ *Yourself* – you will have had specific roles and responsibilities in the planning, organising and running stages of your event. You should be able to look back at these, and at your personal diary, and give your opinion.

▶ *The team* – the rest of your team are in a very good position to provide feedback, as they will have been involved in all of the stages of the event too. They will have inside knowledge and, like you, will have kept personal diaries. You will also be able to provide feedback for them.

▶ *An assessor* – your tutor will be asked to complete an observation sheet to confirm whether or not the criteria for this unit have been met.

▶ *Participants* – these are an important source of information. They are the group who will not necessarily know you before the event, so they are likely to give you an honest, fair and **unbiased** opinion. As they are the people at whom your event was aimed, for whom you planned, organised and ran it, their views are invaluable.

▶ *Customers* – not all events will have customers, but if yours does it is very important that you obtain their feedback, as they will have been the target group at whom the event was aimed. This makes them the most important group to get independent feedback from.

Over to you!

Make sure that you have a system in place to obtain feedback from all of the people identified in this review section.

Success

The success of your event can be considered against what is known as '**success criteria**', which is a set of factors that tell you how well you did. You should consider the success of the event against the following factors in particular.

▶ *The aims and objectives* – you will have set these in Topics 12.1 and 12.2. If you achieved your aims and objectives then you can consider that the event was a success. However, you may find that it is not as simple as this – you might not have achieved all of your aims and objectives but still have had a degree of success. Try not to be too negative about this but comment on the overall success of the event.

▶ *The budget* – you should be able to be very specific here. You will know if you made a profit or a loss and you will have been required to keep a record of all of the finances. Even **breaking even** in relation to your budget would be considered to be a success.

▶ *Deviation from plans* – this refers to the success of your contingency plans and how you responded to unexpected occurrences when running the event. Having to deviate from your plans does not mean failure; it is how you cope with unexpected circumstances that matters. If you were able to put something right or improve something this would be considered a success.

▶ *Strengths and areas for improvement* – it is hoped that you will have 'played to your strengths' and had a successful event. For your event you should be able to clearly identify areas that you were successful in and areas that required some improvement.

Activity

Analyse your event and, using the table below as a guide, complete a strengths and areas for improvement profile for your event.

	Strengths	Explanation	Areas for improvement	Explanation
1				
2				
3				

▶ *Recommendations for future events* – you may have chosen this unit option because this is an area you would like to be involved in as a possible career. Even if this is not the case, part of your assessment is to consider how lessons learnt from completing this unit will inform (help you with) any future planning.

Case study

Sean and his team are in the process of reviewing their sports dinner event. The team decided to make the dinner a formal dress event with a guest after-dinner speaker, who they booked through a contact at a local sports club. Sean's and Rory's mothers were asked to prepare all of the food, and the team employed four waitresses to help serve it.

The chosen venue was the community hall and the team had to employ the caretaker for the afternoon and evening to oversee the running of the event on the day.

The team had high expectations that their event would make quite a big profit, but in the end they just about broke even after paying out all of the wages. They had planned to pay themselves, but there was not enough money left over and the two

mums had to work for free. In spite of this, the only real disappointment for the team was that not all of the customers took notice of the dress code and arrived too casually dressed, but the team decided to let them stay.

1. Will the team be able to use all of the methods of documentation recommended for collecting feedback?

2. Can you match a particular person to each of the sources for feedback?

3. How successful do you think this event was overall?

4. How successful was the event against the budget criteria?

5. What was the main 'deviation from plans' that the team had to deal with?

Assessment activity 12.2 (Unit 20 P2, P3, P4, P5, M2, D1)

As a member of a team or group, you now have to work with others to deliver the sports event you have chosen or planned together. You will need to:

- Contribute to the organisation of the event.
- Contribute to the running of the event.
- Design and use methods for collecting feedback on the success of your chosen event.

- Assess the feedback received about your event, identifying strengths and areas for improvement and making and justifying recommendations for future events.

Your evidence for this assessment should include a portfolio demonstrating your involvement in the event, including witness statements and your own account, and an individual presentation reviewing the extent to which the event was a success.

Topic check

1 What is a questionnaire?
2 Identify the two most important factors needed to make a questionnaire effective.
3 What are success criteria?
4 Who is likely to be asked to fill in an observation sheet?
5 Who are likely to be your most important independent feedback sources?
6 Why are these independent sources so important?
7 How many customers should be asked to fill in a customer comment card?
8 If you deviated from your plans, would this indicate a lack of success?
9 To succeed against budget criteria, do you have to make a profit?
10 Who is going to be your assessor?

Assessment summary

The overall grade you achieve for this unit depends on how well you meet the grading criteria set out in Appendix 1 (see page 302). You must complete:

■ all of the P criteria to achieve a **pass** grade
■ all of the P and the M criteria to achieve a **merit** grade
■ all of the P, M and D criteria to achieve a **distinction** grade.

Your tutor will assess the assessment activities that you complete for this unit. The work you produce should provide evidence which demonstrates that you have achieved each of the assessment criteria. The table below identifies what you need to demonstrate to meet each of the pass, merit and distinction criteria for this unit. You should always check and self-assess your work before you submit your assignments for marking.

Remember that you MUST provide evidence for all of the P criteria to pass the unit.

Grading criteria	You need to demonstrate that you can:	Have you got the evidence?
P1	Produce a plan for a chosen sports event, outlining the planning process to meet given participant or customer requirements	
M1	Produce a plan for a chosen sports event, explaining the planning process to meet given participant or customer requirements	
P2	Contribute to the organisation of a chosen sports event	
P3	Contribute to the running of a chosen sports event	
P4	Design and use methods for collecting feedback on the success of a sports event	
P5	Assess feedback received, identifying strengths and areas for improvement	
M2	Assess feedback received, evaluating strengths and areas for improvement, providing recommendations for future events	
D1	Assess feedback received, evaluating strengths and areas for improvement, justifying recommendations for future events	

Always ask your tutor to explain any assignment tasks or assessment criteria that you don't understand fully. Being clear about the task before you begin gives you the best chance of succeeding. Good luck with your Unit 20 assessment work!

Appendix 1 Assessment and grading criteria

Grading guide Unit 1

To achieve a **pass**, you must show that you can:	To achieve a **merit**, in addition to the pass criteria, you must show that you can:	To achieve a **distinction** grade, in addition to the pass and merit criteria, you must show that you can:
P1 Describe the fitness requirements for achieving excellence in a selected sport	**M1** Explain the fitness requirements for achieving excellence in a selected sport	
P2 Describe three different fitness training methods used to achieve excellence in a selected sport		
P3 Describe four different lifestyle factors that can affect sports training and performance		
P4 Carry out four different fitness tests for different components of fitness, recording the results accurately		
P5 Interpret your test results and personal level of fitness	**M2** Explain your test results and personal level of fitness, identifying strengths and areas for improvement	**D1** Evaluate your test results and personal level of fitness, considering the level required to achieve excellence in a selected sport
P6 Describe the effects of psychological factors on sports training and performance	**M3** Explain the effects of psychological factors on sports training and performance	**D2** Analyse the effects of psychological factors on sports training and performance

Grading guide Unit 2

To achieve a **pass**, you must show that you can:	To achieve a **merit**, in addition to the pass criteria, you must show that you can:	To achieve a **distinction** grade, in addition to the pass and merit criteria, you must show that you can:
P1 Demonstrate use of practical skills, techniques and tactics appropriate for one team sport		
P2 Demonstrate use of practical skills, techniques and tactics appropriate for one individual sport	**M1** Describe use of tactics appropriate for one team and one individual sport	**D1** Justify use of tactics appropriate for one team and one individual sport, identifying areas for improvement
P3 Describe the rules, regulations and scoring systems for one team sport		
P4 Describe the rules, regulations and scoring systems for one individual sport	**M2** Assess, using appropriate examples, the rules, regulations and scoring systems for one team and one individual sport	
P5 Describe the main roles and responsibilities of officials in one team sport		
P6 Describe the main roles and responsibilities of officials in one individual sport		
P7 Produce, with tutor support, an observation checklist that could be used to review the sports performance of an individual or a team	**M3** Independently produce an observation checklist that could be used to review the sports performance of an individual or a team	
P8 Use the observation checklist to review the sports performance of an individual or a team, identifying strengths and areas for improvement	**M4** Explain the strengths and areas for improvement of an individual or a team, in one individual sport or one team sport, justifying recommendations for improvement	
P9 Use the observation checklist to review own sports performance in an individual sport or team sport, identifying strengths and areas for improvement	**M5** Explain own strengths and areas for improvement in an individual sport or team sport, providing recommendations for improvement	**D2** Analyse own strengths and areas for improvement in an individual sport or team sport, justifying recommendations for improvement

Grading guide Unit 3

To achieve a **pass**, you must show you can:	To achieve a **merit**, in addition to the pass criteria, you must show that you can:	To achieve a **distinction** grade, in addition to the pass and merit criteria, you must show that you can:
P1 Describe the organisation and provision of two outdoor and adventurous activities	**M1** Compare the organisation and provision of two outdoor and adventurous activities	
P2 Describe the health and safety considerations associated with participation in two outdoor and adventurous activities	**M2** Explain health and safety considerations associated with participation in two outdoor and adventurous activities, identifying precautions and actions that can be taken, or used, in relation to them	**D1** Explain precautions and actions that can be taken, or used, in relation to health and safety considerations associated with participation in two outdoor and adventurous activities
P3 Produce a risk assessment for a selected outdoor and adventurous activity		
P4 Describe environmental impacts associated with participation in two outdoor and adventurous activities	**M3** Explain the environmental impacts associated with participation in two outdoor and adventurous activities, identifying precautions and actions that can be taken, or used, to reduce them	**D2** Explain precautions and actions that can be taken, or used, to reduce the environmental impacts associated with participation in two outdoor and adventurous activities
P5 Demonstrate techniques and skills appropriate to two outdoor and adventurous activities	**M4** Review and justify choice of techniques demonstrated in outdoor and adventurous activities	
P6 Review the performance of another individual participating in two outdoor and adventurous activities, identifying strengths and areas for improvement		
P7 Carry out a review of own performance in outdoor and adventurous activities, identifying strengths and areas for improvement	**M5** Explain identified strengths and areas for improvement in own performance in outdoor and adventurous activities, making recommendations for further development of identified areas for improvement	**D3** Justify recommendations relating to identified areas for improvement in own performance in outdoor and adventurous activities

Grading guide Unit 4

To achieve a **pass**, you must show that you can:	To achieve a **merit**, in addition to the pass criteria, you must show that you can:	To achieve a **distinction** grade, in addition to the pass and merit criteria, you must show that you can:
P1 Describe the structure and function of the skeletal system		
P2 Describe the different types of joint and the movements allowed at each	**M1** Explain the movements occurring at two synovial joints during four different types of physical activity	
P3 Identify the major muscles of the body		
P4 Describe the different types of muscle and muscle movements	**M2** Give examples of three different types of muscular contraction relating to three different types of physical activity	**D1** Analyse the musculoskeletal actions occurring at four synovial joints during four different types of physical activity
P5 Describe the structure and function of the cardiovascular system		
P6 Describe the structure and function of the respiratory system	**M3** Explain how the cardiovascular and respiratory systems work together to supply the body with oxygen	**D2** Evaluate how the cardiovascular system and respiratory system work together to supply the body with oxygen and remove carbon dioxide

Grading guide Unit 5

To achieve a **pass**, you must show that you can:	To achieve a **merit**, in addition to the pass criteria, you must show that you can:	To achieve a **distinction** grade, in addition to the pass and merit criteria, you must show that you can:
P1 Describe four different types of injuries associated with sports participation and their underlying causes	**M1** Explain why certain injuries and illnesses are associated with sports participation	
P2 Describe two types and signs of illnesses related to sports participation		
P3 Demonstrate how to deal with casualties suffering from three different injuries and/or illnesses, with tutor support	**M2** Independently deal with casualties suffering from three different injuries and/or illnesses	
P4 Describe six risks and hazards associated with sports participation	**M3** Explain risks and hazards associated with sports participation	**D1** Give a detailed account of why participants are at risk of injury whilst taking part in sport
P5 Describe four rules, regulations and legislation relating to health, safety and injury in sports participation	**M4** Explain four, rules, regulations and legislation relating to health, safety and injury in sports participation	
P6 Carry out and produce a risk assessment relevant to a selected sport	**M5** Describe contingency plans that can be used in a risk assessment	**D2** Justify the use of specialist equipment to minimise the risk of injury

Grading guide Unit 7

To achieve a **pass**, you must show that you can:	To achieve a **merit**, in addition to the pass criteria, you must show that you can:	To achieve a **distinction** grade, in addition to the pass and merit criteria, you must show that you can:
P1 Describe the skills, qualities and responsibilities associated with successful sports leadership, using two examples of successful sports leaders	**M1** Explain the skills, qualities and responsibilities associated with successful sports leadership, comparing and contrasting two successful sports leaders	**D1** Evaluate the skills and qualities of two contrasting leaders in sport, commenting on their effectiveness
P2 Plan and lead a sports activity, with tutor support	**M2** Independently plan and lead a sports activity	
P3 Review the planning and leading of a sports activity, identifying strengths and areas for improvement	**M3** Explain strengths and areas for improvement and development in the planning and leading of a sports activity	
P4 Contribute to the planning and leading of a sports event		
P5 Review own performance while assisting with the planning and leading of a sports event, identifying strengths and areas for improvement	**M4** Explain strengths and areas for improvement in assisting with the planning and leading of a sports event, making suggestions relating to improvement	**D2** Evaluate own performance in the planning and leading of a sports activity and event, commenting on strengths and areas for improvement and further development as a sports leader

Grading guide Unit 8

To achieve a **pass**, you must show that you can:	To achieve a **merit**, in addition to the pass criteria, you must show that you can:	To achieve a **distinction** grade, in addition to the pass and merit criteria, you must show that you can:
P1 Describe the technical and tactical demands of a chosen sport	**M1** Explain the technical and tactical demands of a chosen sport	
P2 Assess the technical skills and tactical awareness of an elite performer, identifying strengths and areas for improvement	**M2** Assess the technical skills and tactical awareness of an elite performer, explaining strengths and areas for improvement	
P3 Assess own technical skills and tactical awareness in a chosen sport, identifying strengths and areas for improvement	**M3** Assess own technical skills and tactical awareness in a chosen sport, explaining own strengths and areas for improvement	**D1** Compare and contrast own technical skills and tactical awareness with those of an elite performer and the demands of a chosen sport
P4 Produce a six-week training programme, with tutor support, to develop own technical skills and tactical awareness	**M4** Independently produce a six-week training programme to develop own technical skills and tactical awareness, describing strengths and areas for improvement	**D2** Evaluate the training programme, justifying suggestions made regarding improvement
P5 Carry out a six-week training programme to develop own technical skills and tactical awareness		
P6 Review own development, identifying goals for further technical and tactical development, with tutor support	**M5** Independently describe own development, explaining goals for technical and tactical development	**D3** Analyse own goals for technical and tactical development, suggesting how these goals could be achieved

Grading guide Unit 10

To achieve a **pass**, you must show that you can:	To achieve a **merit**, in addition to the pass criteria, you must show that you can:	To achieve a **distinction** grade, in addition to the pass and merit criteria, you must show that you can:
P1 Describe the nutritional requirements of a selected sport	**M1** Explain the nutritional requirements of a selected sport	**D1** Evaluate the nutritional requirements of a selected sport describing suitable meal plans
P2 Collect and collate information on own diet for two weeks		
P3 Describe the strengths of own diet and identify areas for improvement	**M2** Explain the strengths of their own diet and make recommendations as to how it could be improved	**D2** Justify recommendations made regarding improving their own diet
P4 Create a personal nutritional strategy, designed and agreed with an adviser	**M3** Contribute own ideas to the design of a personal nutritional strategy	
P5 Implement a personal nutritional strategy		
P6 Describe the strengths of the personal nutritional strategy and identify areas for improvement	**M4** Explain the strengths of the personal nutritional strategy and make recommendations as to how it could be improved	

Grading guide Unit 11

To achieve a **pass**, you must show that you can:	To achieve a **merit**, in addition to the pass criteria, you must show that you can:	To achieve a **distinction** grade, in addition to the pass and merit criteria, you must show that you can:
P1 Plan, design and agree, a 6-week personal fitness training programme with a coach	**M1** Contribute own ideas to the design of a 6-week personal fitness training programme	
P2 Describe personal exercise adherence factors and strategies	**M2** Explain personal exercise adherence factors and strategies	**D1** Evaluate personal exercise adherence strategies for overcoming barriers to exercise
P3 Implement a 6-week personal fitness training programme, maintaining a training diary		
P4 Describe the strengths of the personal fitness training programme, identifying areas for improvement	**M3** Explain the strengths of the personal fitness training programme, making suggestions for improvement	**D2** Justify suggestions related to identified areas for improvement in the personal fitness training programme

Grading guide Unit 13

To achieve a **pass**, you must show that you can:	To achieve a **merit**, in addition to the pass criteria, you must show that you can:	To achieve a **distinction** grade, in addition to the pass and merit criteria, you must show that you can:
P1 Describe three different types of organisation within the sports industry, giving examples		
P2 Describe three different occupations within the sports industry and the skills that each require	**M1** Explain the skills required for three different occupations within the sports industry	
P3 Locate three advertisements for jobs from different sources available within the sports industry	**M2** Use advertisements for jobs available in sport to identify appropriate work experience in the sports industry	
P4 Produce an application for work experience in sport	**M3** Explain own personal skills and qualities in relation to those required for an occupation in sport	**D1** Evaluate own personal skills and qualities in relation to those required for an occupation in sport
P5 Prepare for an interview for work experience in sport		
P6 Undertake an interview for work experience in sport		
P7 Plan a project, related to a theme, for work experience in sport		
P8 Undertake a project in work-based experience in sport		
P9 Present the project, describing the benefits and identifying areas for improvement	**M4** Present the project, explaining the benefits and making recommendations for improvement	**D2** Present the project, evaluating the benefits and justifying recommendations relating to identified areas for improvement

Grading guide Unit 18

To achieve a **pass**, you must show that you can:	To achieve a **merit**, in addition to the pass criteria, you must show that you can:	To achieve a **distinction** grade, in addition to the pass and merit criteria, you must show that you can:
P1 Describe the short-term effects of exercise on the musculoskeletal, cardiovascular and respiratory systems	**M1** Explain the short-term effects of exercise on the musculoskeletal, cardiovascular and respiratory systems	
P2 Investigate the short-term effects of exercise on the musculoskeletal, cardiovascular and respiratory systems, with tutor support	**M2** Independently investigate the short-term effects of exercise on the musculoskeletal, cardiovascular and respiratory systems	
P3 Describe the long-term effects of exercise on the musculoskeletal system	**M3** Explain the long-term effects of exercise on the musculoskeletal, cardiovascular and respiratory systems	**D1** Analyse the short- and long-term effects of exercise on the musculoskeletal, cardiovascular and respiratory systems
P4 Describe the long-term effects of exercise on the cardiorespiratory system		
P5 Describe two types of physical activity that use the aerobic energy system and two that use the anaerobic energy system	**M4** Explain the energy requirements of four different types of physical activity	
P6 Investigate different physical activities that use the aerobic and anaerobic energy systems, with tutor support		
P7 Describe four different types of drugs used to enhance sports performance and their effects		
P8 Describe the negative impact of drugs	**M5** Explain the negative impact of drugs	

Grading guide Unit 20

To achieve a **pass**, you must show that you can:	To achieve a **merit**, in addition to the pass criteria, you must show that you can:	To achieve a **distinction** grade, in addition to the pass and merit criteria, you must show that you can:
P1 Produce a plan for a chosen sports event, outlining the planning process to meet given participant or customer requirements	**M1** Produce a plan for a chosen sports event, explaining the planning process to meet given participant or customer requirements	
P2 Contribute to the organisation of a chosen sports event		
P3 Contribute to the running of a chosen sports event		
P4 Design and use methods for collecting feedback on the success of a sports event		
P5 Assess feedback received, identifying strengths and areas for improvement	**M2** Assess feedback received, evaluating strengths and areas for improvement, providing recommendations for future events	**D1** Assess feedback received, analysing strengths and areas for improvement, justifying recommendations for future events

Appendix 2 Normative data tables

Figure 1 Sit and reach test national norms for 16 to 19 year olds (cm)

Classification	Male	Female
Excellent	> 35	> 38
Above average	28–34	30–37
Average	18–27	18–29
Below average	10–17	10–17
Poor	< 10	< 10

Source: brianmac.co.uk (visit the website for data for adult athletes 20+)

Figure 2 National norms for 16 to 19 year olds using the grip dynamometer

Gender	Excellent	Good	Average	Fair	Poor
Male	> 56	51–56	45–50	39–44	< 39
Female	> 36	31–36	25–30	19–24	< 19

Source: brianmac.co.uk (visit the website for data for adult athletes 20+)

Figure 3 Multi-stage fitness (bleep) test scores table

Gender and age (yrs)	Excellent	Good	Average	Fair	Poor
Males 14–16	12/7	11/2	8/9	7/1	<6/6
Females 14–16	10/9	9/1	6/7	5/1	<4/7
Males 17–20	12/12	11/6	9/2	7/6	<7/3
Females 17–20	10/11	9/3	6/8	5/2	<4/9
Males 21–30	12/12	11/7	9/3	7/8	<7/5
Females 21–30	10/8	9/2	6/6	5/1	<4/9
Males 31–40	11/7	10/4	6/10	6/7	<6/4
Females 31–40	10/4	8/7	6/3	4/6	<4/5
Males 41–50	10/4	9/4	6/9	5/9	<5/2
Females 41–50	9/9	7/2	5/7	4/2	<4/1

Each score implies the test level and the number of shuttles completed successfully
(e.g. 4/6 = level four and six shuttles completed)

Source: www.peworld.org

Figure 4 Three-minute step test (men) – heart rate

Age	18–25	26–35	36–45	46–55	56–65	65+
Excellent	< 79	< 81	< 83	< 87	< 86	< 88
Good	79–89	81–89	83–96	87–97	86–97	88–96
Above average	90–99	90–99	97–103	98–105	98–103	97–103
Average	100–105	100–107	104–112	106–116	104–112	104–113
Below average	106–116	108–117	113–119	117–122	113–120	114–120
Poor	117–128	118–128	120–130	123–132	121–129	121–130
Very poor	> 128	> 128	> 130	> 132	> 129	> 130

Figure 5 Three-minute step test (women) – heart rate

Age	18–25	26–35	36–45	46–55	56–65	65+
Excellent	< 85	< 88	< 90	< 94	< 95	< 90
Good	85–98	88–99	90–102	94–104	95–104	90–102
Above average	99–108	100–111	103–110	105–115	105–112	103–115
Average	109–117	112–119	111–118	116–120	113–118	116–122
Below average	118–126	120–126	119–128	121–129	119–128	123–128
Poor	127–140	127–138	129–140	130–135	129–139	129–134
Very poor	> 140	> 138	> 140	> 135	> 139	> 134

Figure 6a Vertical jump test national norms for 16 to 19 year olds

Gender	Excellent	Above average	Average	Below average	Poor
Male	> 65 cm	50–65 cm	40–49 cm	30–39 cm	< 30 cm
Female	> 58 cm	47–58 cm	36–46 cm	26–35 cm	< 26 cm

Figure 6b Vertical jump test norms for adult athletes (20+)

Gender	Excellent	Above average	Average	Below average	Poor
Male	> 65 cm	60 cm	55 cm	50 cm	< 46 cm
Female	> 55 cm	50 cm	45 cm	40 cm	< 36 cm

Source: www.brianmac.co.uk

Figure 7 One-minute press-ups

Gender	Excellent	Good	Average	Poor
Male	> 40	30–39	18–29	< 17
Female	> 30	20–29	13–19	< 12

Figure 8 One-minute sit-ups

Gender	Excellent	Good	Above average	Average	Below average	Poor	Very poor
Male	> 49	44–49	35–41	35–38	31–34	25–30	< 25
Female	> 43	37–43	33–36	29–32	25–28	18–24	< 18

Figure 9 Skinfold measurement totals

		Excellent	Good	Average	Below average	Poor
Normal	Male	60–80	81–90	91–110	111–150	150+
	Female	70–90	91–100	101–120	121–150	150+
Elite athlete	Male	40–60	61–80	81–100	101–130	130+
	Female	50–70	71–85	86–110	111–130	130+

Figure 10 What does my BMI score mean?

Height (inches)	60	61	62	63	64	65	66	67	68	69	70	71	72	73	74	75	76
Weight (lbs)																	
130	25	25	24	23	22	22	21	20	20	19	19	18	18	17	17	16	16
135	26	26	25	24	23	22	22	21	21	20	19	19	18	18	17	17	16
140	27	26	26	25	24	23	23	22	21	21	20	20	19	18	18	17	17
145	28	27	27	26	25	24	23	23	22	21	21	20	20	19	19	18	18
150	29	28	27	27	26	25	24	23	23	22	22	21	20	20	19	19	18
155	30	29	28	27	27	26	25	24	24	23	22	22	21	20	20	19	19
160	31	30	29	28	27	27	26	25	24	24	23	22	22	21	21	20	19
165	32	31	30	29	28	27	27	26	25	24	24	23	22	22	21	21	20
170	33	32	31	30	29	28	27	27	26	25	24	24	23	22	22	21	21
175	34	33	32	31	30	29	28	27	27	26	25	24	24	23	22	22	21
180	35	34	33	32	31	30	29	28	27	27	26	25	24	24	23	22	22
185	36	35	34	33	32	31	30	29	28	27	27	26	25	24	24	23	23
190	37	36	35	34	33	32	31	30	29	28	27	26	26	25	24	24	23
195	38	37	36	35	33	32	31	31	30	29	28	27	26	25	25	24	24
200	39	38	37	35	34	33	32	31	30	30	29	28	27	26	26	25	24
205	40	39	37	36	35	34	33	32	31	30	29	29	28	27	26	26	25
210	41	40	38	37	36	35	34	33	32	31	30	29	28	28	27	26	26

- Underweight = < 18.5
- Normal weight = 18.5 to 24.9
- Overweight = 25 to 29.9
- Obese = > 30

Index

dislocation 111
diuretics 265, 266, 267
dress code 234
drugs 10, 264–9
dual-use facilities 227
duty of care 139
dynamic balance 4
dynamic risk assessment 70
dynamic strength 3
dynamic stretching 210
dynamometer 19, 303

eating during exercise 124
eatwell plate 185
eccentric contraction 95
educational events 276
electronic communication 135
elite performance 169
emails 135
employment in the sports industry 61,
    227–8
energy requirements and expenditure 260
energy system 258–9
enjoyment 216
entertainment 280, 283
enthusiasm 137
environment
    activity session planning 144
    impact of outdoor activities on the
        environment 71–2
    injuries related to 108
    weather conditions 126, 163, 164
equality 139
equipment
    injuries caused by faulty equipment 119
    for officials 45
    organising for a sports event 135–6,
        154, 155, 283
    outdoor and adventurous activities 75
    regulations 39
    risks and hazards 125
    work experience 239
erosion 72
erythropoietin (EPO) 265, 266, 267
ethics 139
etiquette 44, 47, 139
eustress 8
expected outcomes 144
expiration 101

explosive strength 3
extension 90
extrinsic motivation 24

fair play 47
Fartlek training 212
fats 183
feedback
    activity session 147, 148
    evidence of sports participation 35, 77
    leading a sports event 158
    sports performance 52, 80–1
    success of a sports event 286–7
feeling the benefits of training 216
first aid 116–18, 154, 155, 274
fitness, components of 2–5
fitness tests 16–23
fitness training methods 6–7, 210–13
FITT acronym 209
flexibility tests 18
flexibility training 210
flexion 90
food diary 188–9, 198–9
food preparation 186, 193
formative information 245
40 metre sprint 20
fractures 111
free weights 211
full-time job 231

gaseous exchange 102
gender 13
glycogen 183
goal setting 176–8, 204–6
goniometer 18
grading guide 291–302
gravity 110
grazes 111
grip dynamometer 19, 303
growth hormone 265, 266, 267

Hawkeye 48
hazards 70, 122–6
health and safety 40, 46–7, 52, 68–71,
    139, 154, 280
Health and Safety Executive (HSE) 69
healthy diet 12, 185–6
heart 96, 256
heart attack 113
heart muscles 93

heart rate 20, 251, 252, 255
hot weather 126
human growth hormone 265, 266,
    267
humour 138
hypertrophy 254
hypoglycaemia 114

illegal drugs 10
illnesses 113–14, 119, 120
individual sports 34–5
informed consent 16, 17, 274
injuries
    causes 106–10
    dealing with 116–19
    types 110–12, 119, 120
inspiration 101
Institute of Leisure and Amenity
    Management (ILAM) 231
insurance 139
intensity of training 109
interaction 76
intercostal muscles 101
interval training 212
interviews 234–6
intrinsic motivation 24
involuntary muscles 93
iodine 185
iron 185
isometric contraction 95

jewellery 124
job vacancies 230–1
jobs in the sports industry 61, 227–8
joint facilities 227
joints 88–9

knee joint 88
knowledge 51

lactic acid system 259, 261
leadership 134–41, 145–6, 155
leadership awards 60
leadership style 137, 138
lean body mass 21
legislation 126–7, 241
levers 109
lifestyle 8–15, 206
listening 235
loading 106–7